Personality and psychotherapy

Personality and psychotherapy

Theory, practice and research

Duncan Cramer

Open University Press
Milton Keynes · Philadelphia

Open University Press
Celtic Court
22 Ballmoor
Buckingham
MK18 1XW

and
1900 Frost Road, Suite 101
Bristol, PA 19007, USA

First Published 1992

British Library Cataloguing in Publication Data

Cramer, Duncan
  Personality and psychotherapy: Theory, practice
and research.
  I. Title
  158

  ISBN 0–335–09434–1
  ISBN 0–335–09433–3 pbk

Library of Congress Cataloging-in-Publication Data

Cramer, Duncan, 1948–
  Personality and psychotherapy: theory, practice, and research/
Duncan Cramer.
    p.   cm.
  Includes bibliographical references and indexes.
  ISBN 0–335–09434–1 – ISBN 0–335–09433–3 (pbk).
  1. Personality. 2. Psychotherapy. I. Title.
BF698.C712 1991
616.89–dc20   91–21910
                                                        CIP

Typeset by Graphicraft Typesetters Ltd, Hong Kong
Printed in Great Britain by Biddles Ltd, Guildford and King's Lynn

To family and friends

Contents

Preface

Few books on the field of personality make an explicit attempt to systematically cover the two issues which have long intrigued and puzzled those who have tried to develop a satisfactory and comprehensive account of this area. These two concerns are the related questions of what brings about serious forms of psychological disorder and distress (such as anxiety and depression) and how best these problems can be treated. Since the psychological principles which have been put forward to explain the development of these distressing disorders are often similar to those which underlie and account for the treatment of these problems, the validity of these theoretical propositions can be investigated in the realistic and exacting setting of practical attempts to help alleviate and resolve these disorders. While the difficulties of adequately testing these principles in this way should not be underestimated, they pose a fascinating and important problem which urgently requires a concerted and determined effort at solving.

Just as many texts on personality have failed to pay sufficient attention to the painstaking and complicated research concerned with trying to assess the value of psychological principles when applied to treating behavioural problems, so numerous books outlining the theories and techniques of psychotherapy and counselling have also neglected to discuss and to comment on this important work on treatment, as well as other studies which have tried to elucidate the underlying nature of psychological distress. To further understand and enhance the process and effectiveness of psychological treatments, it is necessary (and also our responsibility) to test the adequacy of the ideas which guide our thinking. While the results of such research at present do not appear to offer us any simple solutions to what are undoubtedly complex issues, there does not seem to be any more promising way around these obstacles.

This modest book has two major aims. The first is to draw attention to the way in which the interests of the fields of personality and psychotherapy are closely related and to suggest that it is fruitful to study them together. The second aim is to illustrate some of the various means by which the principles that constitute theories of personality and psychotherapy have been tested and to present the main findings of some of that research. This work will have been successful if it entices a few of its readers to explore some of these issues in more detail and to take up the demanding and fulfilling challenges which have been sketched out.

1

Introduction

The concept of personality

The term 'personality' is primarily used by psychologists in two rather diverse senses. It is most obviously employed to refer to psychological differences which distinguish individuals from one another. So, for example, we may describe someone as aggressive if we believed they behaved in a more aggressive manner than most people we know, or have known. If we thought everyone acted in an equally aggressive way, then we could not differentiate them in terms of their aggressiveness. Consequently, the concept of personality has been introduced to describe and draw attention to the fact that the behaviour of people differs in various ways. Since the number of ways in which the behaviour of individuals can vary is potentially enormous, if not infinite, we need to be selective about what particular differences we discuss because of the limited time we have available.

Psychologists, in their endeavour to understand personality, have also had to restrict what they have studied. Three different approaches to this problem can be discerned. One group of researchers has concentrated on a single characteristic which distinguishes people, such as their aggression, need for achievement or anxiety. This work will not be explicitly discussed since most of the kinds of explanations put forward for the development of these traits are covered in the third approach. Another group, associated with the development and application of the statistical techniques of factor analysis, has tried to determine the chief ways or dimensions in which people vary. A major example of this approach is Eysenck's biobehavioural theory described in Chapter 5. A third group has put forward general explanations of human behaviour which can be used to account for the tremendous variety of ways in which people differ. This third group comes closest to reflecting the second principal meaning of personality, which is concerned with describing what it means to be a person. In other words, this approach offers some principles which try to explain why individuals behave the way they do or, in popular parlance, 'what makes people tick'. Most of the theories in this book fall into this last category.

A major concern of many personality theories is trying to explain why people experience serious psychological problems, such as being very anxious or depressed. The kinds of psychological problems that individuals can suffer from are myriad. The nature and prevalence of some of these disorders are described in Chapter 2. One way, then, in which people differ from one another is in terms of whether they have these problems. Psychological distress is itself an important personality characteristic, which causes many people who are troubled by it to seek psychological help. Since the understanding of psychological distress is a common focus for many personality theories, the adequacy of these explanations can be more readily compared and evaluated when they are concerned with the same issue. Consequently, variations in psychological distress will be the main personality characteristic, or individual difference, discussed in this book. As many of these theories provide general explanations of human behaviour, the same underlying principles can be used to account for other personality characteristics. Indeed, you can test your own grasp of these theories by trying to explain aspects of personality not specifically covered in this text.

Some readers may find discussing psychological problems rather morbid. Apart from its obvious practical value, there are two reasons why this need not be so. Firstly, as will be elaborated later, many personality theorists view the absence of serious psychological distress as indicating psychological well-being. Consequently, these theories are not just concerned with explaining why certain people develop psychological problems. They are, at the same time, interested in describing why other people do not show these problems. In other words, these theories also state what it means to be psychologically healthy and how this comes about. These theories are as much explanations of the absence of these problems as their presence. Secondly, understanding why people behave in ways which are unrewarding and distressing is puzzling and problematic, and poses a challenge for psychological explanations of human behaviour. As a result, offering a convincing account of the development of psychological disorders provides a taxing test for the adequacy of personality theories.

Psychotherapy

Not only are many personality theories concerned with trying to explain psychological distress, they are also interested in suggesting psychological ways in which this distress may be alleviated and overcome. These forms of psychological treatment are frequently referred to as psychotherapy, and are also used in counselling when thought appropriate. Since the principles put forward to explain the development of psychological distress by a particular personality theory are often similar to those underlying its treatment, the effectiveness of the treatment can be partly used to evaluate the validity of these principles, provided this is carefully done.

For instance, client- or person-centred theory proposes that psychological distress reflects a lack of self awareness and self acceptance. This lack of self acceptance arises as a result of only feeling accepted by other people who are important to us when we become what they want us to be rather than what we are ourselves. To help someone to learn to accept themselves and to be themselves, it is necessary to accept them for who they are and not for who we want them to be (i.e. to accept them without conditions or unconditionally). So, the principle underlying the person-centred theory of the development of psychological distress is lack of unconditional acceptance, while the principle behind the person-centred approach to therapy is the provision of unconditional acceptance. As we shall see, it is somewhat easier to test the validity of this principle in psychotherapy than in the development of psychological disorder. However, if we find that unconditional acceptance accounts for the effectiveness of psychotherapy, this does not mean that it will alleviate all psychological distress since not everyone either seeks or receives psychotherapy. Consequently, we need to be cautious about the extent to which we can generalize findings based on psychotherapy patients to other people in general.

Many of these theories, then, are theories of both personality and psychotherapy. The application of these psychological principles to the treatment of psychological problems illustrates the practical potential of these theories, which may otherwise seem rather abstract and academic. Furthermore, it provides another opportunity for understanding the nature of their principles. Since prevention is better than cure, the validity of these principles should also be evaluated in terms of their ability to prevent these disorders from arising. However, implementing such intervention programmes is more difficult than providing psychotherapy. Firstly, since the number of people who may develop psychological problems is relatively small, either a large group of people would have to take part or a smaller number of those most at risk would need to be selected. Secondly, participants would have to be followed up over a fairly long period to ensure that they did not subsequently develop problems.

Table 1.1 Theoretical orientations of American Clinical Psychologists (percentages)

Orientation	1960[1]	1973[2]	1980?[3]	1981[4]	1981[5]	1985[6]	1986[7]
Eclectic	36	55	41	30	30	40	29
Psychodynamic	35	16	11	30	27	12	21
Behavioural	8	10	7	14	6	6	16
Cognitive	–	2	12	6	8	11	13
Person-centred	4	1	9	3	2	8	6
Other	17	16	20	17	27	23	15
Sample size		855	415	479	410	682	579

[1]Kelly, 1961; [2]Garfield & Kurtz, 1976; [3]Smith, 1982 (undated, counselling psychologists included); [4]Norcross & Prochaska, 1982; [5]Prochaska & Norcross, 1983a; [6]Watkins et al., 1986 (counselling psychologists); [7]Norcross et al., 1989.

Some idea of the practical relevance and relative influence of these theories in guiding the kind of psychological treatment offered can be gleaned from surveys carried out amongst practitioners of psychotherapy, who include psychiatrists, clinical psychologists and social workers as well as therapists and counsellors. Most surveys have been conducted on clinical psychologists in the American Psychological Association, who have been periodically questioned over the years from as early as 1960 (Kelly, 1961). The percentage of clinical (and, in two cases, counselling) psychologists who endorsed a particular theoretical orientation in these surveys are shown in Table 1.1.

One difficulty with comparing the results of these surveys over time is that in several of them, the terms for some of the theoretical orientations have differed. None the less, in general the categories were similar. It is clear from these studies that the majority of clinical psychologists do not hold one particular theoretical view and prefer to describe themselves as eclectic, endorsing two or more views. What it meant to be eclectic was explored in some of the surveys. Garfield and Kurtz (1977), for instance, followed up 154 clinical psychologists who had previously described themselves as 'eclectic' to find out which theoretical approach they were most likely to favour. The two most popular orientations were the behavioural and psychodynamic ones. Some of the implications of holding an eclectic perspective on personality will be considered in the final chapter.

While the death-knell for the psychodynamic approach has been rung by some of its adversaries, there is little sign that its influence has waned over the last few years. It remains the single most popular approach among American clinical psychologists. The next two most common perspectives are the behavioural and cognitive approaches. The person-centred approach is less frequently endorsed. But, when psychologists were asked by D. Smith (1982) to list the three most currently influential psychotherapists, Carl Rogers, the originator of person-centred theory, received the highest number of votes. The next three most influential therapists were Albert Ellis (cognitive therapy), Sigmund Freud (psychoanalysis) and Joseph Wolpe (behaviour therapy). If participants were answering this question in terms of who they saw as having been most influential on psychotherapists in general (as is implied) rather than who had been most influential on them, then there appears to be a discrepancy between their own theoretical position and those they see as being most influential. In other words, the influence of Rogers and Ellis is less than would have been surmised from the number of clinicians who endorsed a person-centred or cognitive perspective.

There is also evidence from the few surveys in which these questions were asked that therapists are generally satisfied with their theoretical orientation and, more importantly, that these theoretical views influence their therapeutic practice. About 80 per cent of therapists reported being either quite or very satisfied with their theoretical orientation, with only about 13 per cent expressing any sense of dissatisfaction (Norcross & Prochaska, 1982; Prochaska & Norcross, 1983a). In addition, more than 94 per cent of them said their theoretical orientation influenced their therapeutic practice either frequently or always.

Evaluating theories

The fact that a large number of theories have been put forward to account for personality indicates that there is little agreement on explaining human behaviour. How do we decide which theory provides the most accurate account of personality? Various criteria have been suggested for judging the utility of a theory. These include the following considerations.

1 *Testability*. Theories consist of a number of concepts and propositions or assumptions concerning their subject. If none of these propositions is, in principle, disprovable, then the theory cannot be tested since it cannot be shown to be false (Popper, 1963). For example, it has been claimed that the proposition, from operant conditioning theory, that 'behaviour which is reinforced is more likely to be repeated' cannot be examined since what is defined as being reinforcing is an event which causes behaviour to be repeated! In other words, if the behaviour is not repeated, then the event could not have been reinforcing. Tautologies like this are true by definition and so cannot be evaluated empirically. However, this proposition is not necessarily untestable if a reinforcing event is defined as an event which causes more than one kind of behaviour to be repeated. In other words, if the reinforcing

event can be specified independently of the behaviour to which it is subsequently applied, then this proposition can be evaluated.

Many so-called untestable propositions can, in fact, be tested if an attempt is made to operationalize their concepts. To operationalize a concept means to be able to measure it, or to change it. For example, to measure anxiety, we could simply ask people whether or not they felt anxious, or how anxious they felt. If the theory we were investigating stated that anxiety could not be assessed by simply asking people how anxious they felt, then we need to be able to measure it in some other way. If this cannot be done, then that aspect of the theory cannot be evaluated. Some theoretical propositions have had to await the development of new techniques to measure their concepts before they could be tested. One of the advantages of operationalizing concepts is that it should force us to specify more clearly what we mean when we use certain concepts. Theories which can be tested are more useful than those which cannot be evaluated in this manner. The way in which theoretical propositions can be empirically examined is extensively illustrated in later chapters.

2 *Empirical support.* We can have more confidence in the value of theories whose propositions have been tested and confirmed than those whose propositions have been tested and disconfirmed. The empirical support for a proposition needs to be carefully evaluated in terms of how it was investigated, an issue which is explored more fully in the chapters in which they are described.

3 *New findings.* Theories which lead to the discovery of new findings are more useful than those which simply account for what we already know. Whether or not any personality theories have yet met this rather stringent criterion is rather difficult to judge. Eysenck (1976a) has claimed that classical conditioning theory led to the development of a new form of psychological treatment for obsessive–compulsive disorders called 'flooding' and in this way has demonstrated its worth.

4 *Comprehensiveness.* The more comprehensive the theory is, the more phenomena it tries to explain. A comprehensive personality theory is one which accounts for a variety of different aspects of behaviour, and in doing so, shows the way in which these characteristics can be related.

5 *Economy.* A theory which consists of fewer propositions to explain the same phenomena is more elegant than one which has more propositions and consequently is often easier to use.

6 *Logical consistency.* Finally, theories with fewer contradictions are easier to apply and test than those with more inconsistencies.

In trying to grasp what a useful theory is, it may be helpful to compare it with a map of an area such as a town. Both theories and maps represent reality but obviously do not reflect its full and changing complexity. In other words, theories and maps simplify reality, but in doing so they highlight certain important features. We may find a map handy if we are not very familiar with the layout of a town or if we wanted to describe it to someone new to the area. Similarly, we may find a personality theory valuable if it helps us understand ourself and other people better. In fact, each of us most probably has our own implicit or lay theory of how people operate psychologically, just as we have some mental picture of what the town may be like, even if it is not a very accurate one. Indeed, Kelly's personal construct theory of personality, described in Chapter 7, proposes that we all hold such theories. However, as we may seldom discuss these theories, we may not be very aware of them. If you do not find the theories covered in this book particularly plausible, you may like to articulate your own views and see how they compare with the ones described.

The propositions and concepts of a theory are similar to the ways in which the features of a town, such as schools, parks and hospitals, are displayed on a map. If we do not know how these places are represented on the map, then we will not be able to test our understanding of the map. In other words, the means by which a school or hospital is denoted needs to be specified, just as the way in which the propositions and concepts of a theory are required to be operationalized before they can be tested. The more features of the town which can be accurately identified from the map, the better that map is. An accurate map will provide us with much new information about places we did not know of and the more ground it covers the more useful it will be. Simpler maps with consistent information will be easier to read.

To be able to compare fairly the relative merits of different maps, it is necessary that they describe the same area. In the same way, to judge the relative value of different theories of personality, it is important to ensure that they are concerned with describing similar phenomena. Since the focus of most of the major theories of personality seems to be the explanation of the development and treatment of psychological distress, these theories can be most equitably evaluated in terms of how adequately they explain these two phenomena.

Empirical research

The theories outlined in this book have generated and continue to generate an enormous amount of empirical research. Because of its potential importance in helping to evaluate ideas by either providing or not providing evidence for them, research which is most directly relevant to the main assumptions of these theories will be selected for discussion wherever possible. In view of the mass of research which has been conducted and the limitations of space, it is only possible to choose a small number of these studies and to describe them briefly. Since many of the theories covered in this book are concerned with putting forward psychological principles for treating serious psychological problems, the most appropriate group for assessing the value of these principles are patients seeking treatment for these problems. Consequently, wherever relevant research has been carried out on psychotherapy patients, these *clinical* studies will be selected in preference to so-called *analogue* studies on non-patients. Where the appropriate kind of clinical research is not available, analogue studies will be reviewed in its place. Preference will be given to studies in which participants have been recruited from the community rather than from psychology courses since community volunteers are more likely to be more seriously disturbed (Bernstein & Nietzel, 1974; Little *et al.*, 1977).

Summary

The concept of personality is usually generally understood as referring both to differences in behaviour between individuals and to the principles put forward to explain these differences. So far, there is little agreement on what these principles are and a number of different theories of personality have been proposed. The adequacy of theories can be evaluated in terms of various criteria such as the range of phenomena to which they apply, their ability to generate new discoveries, their empirical support, and the testability, number and consistency of their propositions. Most of the major theories of personality have either been principally concerned with or extensively applied to explaining the development and treatment of psychological distress. Consequently, the adequacy of these theories can be compared in their application to these two issues. Furthermore, since the principles put forward by a theory to explain the development of psychological disorders are generally similar to those used to treat these disorders, the validity of these principles can be evaluated in the realistic context of helping people to overcome these problems. In other words, the practical value of these theories can be assessed in terms of how effective their treatments are and how well they explain the effectiveness of these treatments.

2

Nature and prevalence of psychological distress

Presenting problems of psychotherapy patients

What kinds of psychological problems do people suffer from and how common are these? One way of finding out is to ask patients who seek psychological help what their problems are. Kadushin (1969) categorized the problems people initially presented when attending one of three kinds of psychotherapy clinic in New York city. The three types were psychoanalytic, pastoral and hospital clinics. By far the largest number of participants came from the psychoanalytic clinics and these patients were of a higher socio-economic status than those from the other two types of clinics. Patients typically presented more than one problem, with psychoanalytic patients listing about four and the others about three problems each.

The three most common problems for each group are shown in Table 2.1. These were: lack of self-esteem, social isolation and anxiety for the psychoanalytic patients; marital difficulties, lack of self-esteem and anxiety for the pastoral patients; and bodily complaints, anxiety and problems with work for the hospital patients. In a smaller scale study on psychotherapy at a medical school, the three most common presenting complaints were general anxiety, lack of self-esteem and physical symptoms (Strupp *et al.*, 1964).

Psychiatric classification systems

Psychiatrists have long been interested in developing systems for clas-

Table 2.1 Problems presented to three types of psychotherapy clinics in New York (percentages)

Problem	Psychoanalytic	Pastoral	Hospital
Low self-esteem	49	33	12
Social isolation	42	14	13
General anxiety	33	21	24
Marital difficulties	15	34	12
Bodily complaints	23	15	51
Work difficulties	28	15	21
Number of problems	4.0	2.7	2.8
Number of patients	1111	195	134

sifying psychological problems and provide another view on the plethora of psychological problems that people have. The two most widely used systems are the Diagnostic and Statistical Manual of Mental Disorders, produced by the American Psychiatric Association and generally referred to by the abbreviation DSM, and the 'Mental Disorder' chapter of the International Classification of Diseases developed by the World Health Organization and usually known as ICD. Both systems have been regularly revised. The present edition of the *DSM* is the revised form of the third version, known as DSM-III-R and published in 1987. DSM-IV is scheduled for around 1994. The current version of the ICD is the ninth revision, which was printed in 1978 and is referred to as ICD-9. ICD-10 is due out in about 1992 and is intended to be the final revision.

Ideally, a psychiatric diagnostic system should tell us something about the cause (aetiology) of a disorder, its course or prognosis, and its appropriate treatment. However, since there is much disagreement about these issues at present, these diagnostic systems are purely descriptive and aim simply to provide a common language for referring to, and recording information on, psychological problems. To serve this function, it is essential that they should be used in the same way. Consequently, it is important to establish the extent to which different clinicians agree on the diagnosis of the same patient's problems. Studies which have investigated the reliability of psychiatric diagnosis will be examined once these two systems have been briefly outlined.

Psychological problems in *DSM-III-R* are listed in two major groups called axes. The first axis consists of clinical syndromes (e.g. anxiety, depression and schizophrenia) and other problems which are treated but which are not thought to reflect psychological disturbance (e.g. antisocial behaviour, marital problems and bereavement). While the second axis contains the developmental disorders which usually first appear in (but are not restricted to) infancy, childhood and adolescence (e.g. mental retardation, autism and enuresis or bed-wetting) as well as the personality disorders (e.g. paranoid, antisocial and narcissistic). Examples of the major categories within each axis and of more specific disorders are illustrated in Table 2.2.

Since the 1988 draft version of the 'Mental, Behavioural and Developmental Disorder' chapter of *ICD-10* (Sartorius *et al.*, 1988) appears to be much more like *DSM-III-R* than the *ICD-9* revision, its categories (together with examples of more specific disorders) are presented for comparison in Table 2.3. These two widely used systems are becoming increasingly similar. One long-standing distinction which has been lost in these revisions (first in *DSM-III* and then in *ICD-10*) is that the broad categories of the psychotic and neurotic disorders are not as apparent, although the terms 'psychotic' and 'neurotic' are still used to describe some individual symptoms and disorders.

The expression *psychotic* is not a precisely defined word and generally refers to behaviour which reflects a gross distortion of reality, such as experiencing serious hallucinations (e.g. hearing voices insulting you or holding a running commentary on your behaviour) and delusions (e.g. believing that your thoughts are being directly controlled by others) without being aware of their nature. It also includes catatonic behaviour such as remaining in an apparently uncomfortable position for prolonged periods. Psychotic disorders cover schizophrenia, delusional disorders and mood disorders with psychotic features.

The term *neurotic* is generally used to refer to less serious symptoms than psychotic ones, and which are typically recognized as being inappropriate. They include such symptoms as anxiety, depression, obsessions, compulsions and phobias.

Examples of specific psychological disorders

Because of the immense range of psychological disorders, only a few problems can be selected to show how efforts have been made to define them more specifically. The descriptions have been taken from *DSM-III-R* as they are more detailed than those of the forthcoming *ICD-10* which is not yet readily available.

Alcohol dependence

This problem is diagnosed when at least three of the following nine characteristics are present for at least a month: (1) greater use than intended; (2) persistent desire or unsuccessful attempts to cut down or control use; (3) much time spent trying to obtain it or recovering from its effects; (4) frequently intoxicated when expected to carry out major obligations or when its use would be dangerous; (5) use reduces important

Table 2.2 Examples of major categories and specific disorders in *DSM-III-R*

Axis I

Clinical syndromes
- Organic mental disorders (e.g. senile dementia, alcohol intoxication, nicotine withdrawal)
- Psychoactive substance use disorders (e.g. alcohol, cannabis, cocaine, inhalant, nicotine dependence and abuse)
- Schizophrenia (e.g. catatonic, disorganized, paranoid)
- Delusional disorders (e.g. grandiose, jealous, persecutory types)
- Mood disorders (e.g. bipolar, major, dysthymic or neurotic depression)
- Anxiety disorders (e.g. panic disorder, agoraphobia, social phobia, simple phobia, obsessive–compulsive disorder, post-traumatic stress disorder, generalized anxiety)
- Somatoform disorders (e.g. hysterical neurosis-conversion type, hypochondriacal neurosis)
- Dissociative disorders (e.g. multiple personality, psychogenic fugue, depersonalization neurosis)
- Sexual disorders (e.g. fetishism, paedophilia, sexual masochism, inhibited orgasm, premature ejaculation)
- Sleep disorders (e.g. insomnia, hypersomnia, nightmares, sleepwalking)
- Factitious disorders (e.g. Munchausen syndrome)
- Impulse disorders not classified elsewhere (e.g. kleptomania, pathological gambling, pyromania)
- Adjustment disorders (e.g. mood, conduct, work)
- Psychological factors affecting physical condition (e.g. obesity, migraine headache, painful menstruation)

Conditions not attributable to a mental disorder but a focus of attention or treatment
Examples are academic underachievement, antisocial behaviour, uncertainty about career choice, interpersonal problems with colleagues or partner

Axis II

Disorders usually first seen in infancy, childhood, or adolescence
- Mental retardation
- Pervasive developmental disorders (e.g. autism)
- Specific developmental disorders (e.g. arithmetic, reading, writing, speech articulation, motor coordination)
- Disruptive behaviour disorders (e.g. attention-deficit hyperactivity)
- Eating disorders (e.g. anorexia nervosa, bulimia nervosa, pica)
- Elimination disorders (e.g. encopresis, enuresis)
- Speech disorders not elsewhere classified (e.g. stuttering)

Personality disorders
Examples are paranoid, schizoid, antisocial, narcissistic, dependent, obsessive compulsive

Table 2.3 Examples of major categories and specific psychological disorders in *ICD-10*

- Organic, including symptomatic, disorders (e.g. dementia)
- Mental and behaviour disorders due to psychoactive substance use (e.g. alcohol, cannabis, cocaine, tobacco)
- Schizophrenia, schizotypal states and delusional disorders
  - Schizophrenia (e.g. catatonic, hebephrenic, paranoid)
  - Persistent delusional disorders
- Mood (affective) disorders
  - Bipolar affective disorder
  - Recurrent depressive disorder
- Neurotic, stress-related and somatoform disorders
  - Phobic disorder (e.g. agoraphobia, social phobia, specific phobia)
  - Other anxiety disorders (e.g. panic disorder, generalized anxiety disorder)
  - Obsessive–compulsive disorder
  - Reaction to severe stress and adjustment disorders (e.g. post-traumatic stress disorder, emotional and/or conduct disorder)
  - Dissociative and conversion disorder (e.g. psychogenic fugue)
  - Somatoform disorders (e.g. hypochondriasis, psychogenic pain)
  - Other neurotic disorders (e.g. depersonalization–derealization syndrome)
- Behavioural syndromes and mental disorders associated with physiological dysfunction and hormonal changes
  - Eating disorders (e.g. anorexia nervosa, bulimia nervosa, over-eating)
  - Psychogenic sleep disorders (e.g. insomnia, hypersomnia, sleepwalking, nightmares)
  - Sexual dysfunction (e.g. orgasmic dysfunction, premature ejaculation)
- Abnormalities of adult personality and behaviour
  - Specific personality disorder (e.g. paranoid, schizoid, dyssocial, obsessive–compulsive, dependent)
  - Habit and impulse disorders (e.g. pathological gambling, pyromania, kleptomania)
  - Disorders of sexual preference (e.g. fetishism, paedophilia, sado-masochism)
- Mental retardation
- Developmental disorders
  - Specific developmental disorders of speech and language (e.g. simple speech articulation disorder)
  - Specific developmental disorders of scholastic skills (e.g. reading, spelling, arithmetical)
  - Pervasive developmental disorders (e.g. childhood autism)
- Behavioural and emotional disorders with onset usually occurring in childhood or adolescence
  - Hyperkinetic disorder
  - Conduct disorder
  - Other behavioural and emotional disorders with onset usually occurring during childhood (e.g. enuresis, encopresis, pica, stuttering)

---

activities; (6) continued use despite knowing that it causes or aggravates other problems; (7) marked tolerance for its intake or effects; (8) withdrawal symptoms (e.g. tremor of the hands, nausea, anxiety); and (9) often taken to relieve or avoid withdrawal symptoms.

Schizophrenia

Among the main criteria for identifying schizophrenia are the presence of such symptoms as prolonged hallucinations, implausible delusions, incoherent and marked disconnection of thought, and inappropriate movements or emotions for at least a week, together with a reduced interest in work, personal relationships, and looking after oneself.

Major depression

The two principal features of this disorder are either depressed mood, or loss of interest or pleasure most of the time, together with at least four of the following seven symptoms for at least two weeks: (1) unexpected change in appetite or weight; (2) sleeping too much or too little; (3) physically agitated or apathetic; (4) tiredness or lack of energy; (5) feeling worthless or unnecessarily guilty; (6) indecisiveness or reduced ability to think or concentrate; and (7) thoughts of death.

Neurotic depression

Neurotic depression, on the other hand, may be diagnosed if a major depressive episode has not been shown during the first two years of the problem and the person has generally felt depressed over this period, as well as having at least two of the following six symptoms: (1) poor appetite or overeating; (2) insomnia or hypersomnia; (3) low energy or fatigue; (4) low self-esteem; (5) poor concentration or difficulty making decisions; and (6) feelings of hopelessness.

Agoraphobia

Agoraphobia is a fear of being in situations in which it might be difficult or embarrassing to escape or in which help might not be available if various symptoms occur such as dizziness, falling, loss of bladder or bowel control, and chest pains. Because of this fear, the person restricts their movement outside the home or needs someone to go with them. Clinically, it is more commonly associated with panic attacks.

Simple phobia

A simple phobia is an intense fear of a particular object or situation, other than the fear of a panic attack or being socially humiliated or embarrassed. This fear disrupts the person's normal activities and causes them marked distress.

Obsessive–compulsive disorder

Obsessions are persistent thoughts or impulses, such as thinking of killing one's child or of being infected, while compulsions are repetitive actions aimed at thwarting the object of the obsession. These behaviours usually occupy an hour or more a day, cause distress, and interfere with other everyday activities.

Obsessive–compulsive personality disorder

A person with an obsessive–compulsive personality disorder has a widespread tendency to be inflexible and a perfectionist, as shown by having at least five of the following nine characteristics: (1) overly strict and often unattainable standards which frequently prevents tasks from being completed; (2) over-preoccupation with details so that the activity is not carried out; (3) unreasonable insistence that own way is followed or that others will not do things correctly; (4) strong work orientation to the exclusion of pleasure and personal relationships; (5) indecisiveness; (6) excessively moralistic; (7) restricted show of affection; (8) lack of generosity of time, money, or presents unless personal gain is anticipated; and (9) inability to discard worn-out or worthless objects, even those without sentimental value.

Conversion disorder

This appears to be a physical disorder, such as paralysis, false pregnancy or loss of sensation, which has no obvious physiological cause and seems to be an unintentional expression of a psychological need or conflict.

Fetishism

The essential characteristic of this disorder is the person is distressed by, or has acted on, recurring and intense sexual urges and sexually arousing fantasies for at least six months involving non-living objects (e.g. women's clothing) not used for cross-dressing nor specifically designed for genital stimulation (e.g. vibrator).

Multiple personality

Not to be confused with schizophrenia, this disorder refers to the existence within a person of two or more distinct and relatively enduring personalities.

Anorexia nervosa

This disorder is characterized by the following four features: (1) refusal to maintain body weight over a minimal normal weight, typically 15 per cent below that expected; (2) intense fear of gaining weight or becoming fat, even though underweight; (3) feeling of fatness even when obviously underweight; and (4) in women, absence of at least three consecutive periods when normally expected.

Reliability of psychiatric diagnosis

How reliable is psychiatric diagnosis? In other words, how much agreement is there between clinicians on when to apply these psychiatric labels? Obviously, any answer to this question may depend on such factors as which diagnostic system is being used, how familiar the clinicians are with that scheme, how broad the categories are, and which disorder is being diagnosed. Since one of the aims of *DSM-III* and its revision *DSM-III-R* was to improve its reliability by making more explicit the criteria by which the psychiatric terms were to be assigned, it will be instructive to examine how consistently this scheme can be employed.

Although *DSM-III* was introduced in 1980, there have been surprisingly few published studies which have investigated its reliability. The major study seems to have been one of the original field trials of the draft version of the new system, in which clinicians from all over the United States and who had already used it on 15 patients took part (Spitzer *et al.*, 1979). Clinicians interviewed the same patient either together, or separately but as close together in time as possible. One problem with separate interviews is that the information provided to the clinician by the patient may be different so that agreement between clinicians would be expected to be less in this situation. None the less, this kind of diagnosis is a more stringent test of the classificatory system since it is more likely to occur and is potentially more problematic.

When measuring the degree of agreement between two people, it is important to make allowances for the fact that two individuals will occasionally agree just by chance. For example, if you throw two dice a number of times, the same faces will sometimes come up even though this coincidence does not denote any agreement about some outside event. The index or statistic which corrects for chance agreement is kappa (Shrout *et al.*, 1987) and was used to assess the reliability of the diagnoses. A value of 1.00 indicates perfect agreement, while that of near zero suggests chance agreement, with figures of 0.70 and above being generally considered as an acceptable level of consensus. It should be noted that this statistic is difficult to interpret if too many or too few of the same diagnoses are made.

Table 2.4 Reliability of *DSM-III* diagnosis for major disorders

Major disorders	Frequency (%)	Interview Together	Separate
Affective (mood)	44.6	0.77	0.59
Substance use (psychoactive)	22.0	0.90	0.74
Organic mental	12.9	0.74	0.83
Schizophrenic (schizophrenia)	12.9	0.82	0.82
Adjustment	11.2	0.74	0.60
Anxiety	10.5	0.74	0.43
Axis I major		0.78	0.66
Axis II personality	60.6	0.61	0.54
Number of patients	281	150	131

The kappa values for the together and separate interviews are given in Table 2.4 for the more common diagnoses. As expected, the reliability is generally lower for the separate than for the joint interviews, apart for the organic mental disorders and schizophrenia where it is equal or higher. The extent of agreement is acceptable for all diagnostic categories in the joint procedure except for the personality disorders taken together. For the separate interviews, diagnostic reliability is less than acceptable for the major affective, anxiety, adjustment and personality disorders. Needless to say that in a study of this kind it was not possible to determine the extent to which collusion between clinicians may have occurred. None the less, these initial results are encouraging and further studies are required to determine how replicable they are.

Because of its recent introduction, it may still be too early to expect many studies to have investigated the reliability of *DSM-III-R*. Reports on the reliability of *DSM-III* have been so few, however, that it is unrealistic to hope that the situation will be different for its interim revision. One investigation which has appeared has restricted itself to the diagnosis of the anxiety disorders whose *DSM-III* reliability as we have just seen was less than desirable (Mannuzza *et al.*, 1989). Since the patients taking part were those attending anxiety clinics, greater agreement might be expected than if a more varied range of patients had been seen. Clinicians taking part had received up to 60 hours of training in three diagnostic systems (a draft version of *DSM-III-R*, *DSM-III* and *Research Diagnostic Criteria*). Patients were interviewed separately (up to 60 days apart) for lifetime (i.e. past and present) problems of anxiety.

The level of agreement expressed in kappa for the *DSM-III-R* diagnosis of five anxiety disorders is shown in Table 2.5. Agreement was good for agoraphobia but generally poor for simple phobias and generalized anxiety

Table 2.5 Reliability of *DSM-III-R* diagnosis of lifetime anxiety

Diagnosis	Number of patients	Kappa
Agoraphobia	43	0.81
Social phobia	51	0.68
Panic disorder	36	0.67
Generalized anxiety	11	0.39
Simple phobia	29	0.31

disorders. Interestingly, reasons for disagreements for the three diagnostic systems taken together were analysed. About half of them were due to patients giving different, diagnostically relevant information to the interviewers. For example, patients would tell one interviewer they avoided many situations, while mentioning only a few situations to the other interviewer. About a quarter of the disagreements were the result of mistakes made by the interviewer, mainly by failing to obtain further details. For example, one interviewer diagnosed an additional simple fear of aeroplanes, while the other clarified that it was a fear, not of aeroplanes, but of people in them and so it was related to their social phobia. Finally, less than a fifth of the disagreements were due to ambiguities in the diagnostic criteria, one of which was the difficulty of defining when a problem caused marked distress or interfered with normal activities.

Prevalence of psychological disorders

How many people suffer from psychological disorders? One attempt to answer this question is to find out what proportion of people consulting a doctor or mental health professional are diagnosed as having a psychological problem. However, since not everyone who experiences serious psychological distress seeks professional help, the question of how many people suffer from psychological disorders can only be properly answered by carrying out a survey of people who statistically represent the population of interest. This is usually done by approaching people aged 18 years or over who live in households in a particular area and so excludes the homeless, the institutionalized (e.g. in hospitals and prisons), and those who cannot be contacted or who are unwilling to take part. As the proportion of people who do not participate in such community surveys can be as high as 32 per cent (Regier *et al.*, 1988), their figures may be misleading. These surveys have also shown that a substantial proportion (over 30 per cent) of people diagnosed as having

Table 2.6 Estimated percentage and median onset age of lifetime prevalence of *DSM-III* disorders in the United States

Diagnosed disorder	Frequency (%)	Age
Alcohol abuse/dependence	13.3	21
Phobia	12.5	13
Drug abuse/dependence	5.9	18
Major depression	5.8	25
Depressive neurosis	3.3	
Obsessive–compulsive	2.5	23
Personality disorder	2.5	
Panic	1.6	24

a recent psychological disorder had not visited a doctor or a mental health specialist (Shapiro *et al.*, 1984), so that surveys of patients do not include a significant number of people suffering from psychological problems.

When determining what proportion of people have psychological disorders, it is necessary to specify what time period is being covered since some of the individuals being questioned may not be experiencing a problem at the time of the interview but may have had one previously. However, the memory of such problems may be less reliable the further back one goes. In addition, people who have died as a consequence of their problems or who develop problems later on will not be included. One of the largest surveys conducted on the prevalence of psychological disorders is that of the National Institute of Mental Health Epidemiologic Catchment Area Program in the United States which covered 18 571 adults in five areas (Regier *et al.*, 1988). On the basis of this study, the overall proportion of adults in the United States to have previously experienced various psychological problems (defined largely in terms of *DSM-III*) was estimated to be 32 per cent. The percentages for the more specific and common diagnostic categories are shown in Table 2.6. Also presented in this table are estimates from the same study, but including both institutionalized and non-institutionalized adults (Burke *et al.*, 1990), of the age at which half the people first experiencing these disorders (apart for depressive neurosis and personality disorders) were reported to have occurred.

Although the largest community surveys on the prevalence of specific forms of psychological disorders have taken place in the United States, various other studies have been conducted elsewhere. One measure which has been developed to assess psychological problems in different countries as defined by the *ICD* is the Present State Examination (Wing *et al.*, 1977).

Table 2.7 One-month prevalence rates for affective and anxiety disorders in different countries

Country	n	Disorders	
		Affective (%)	Anxiety (%)
Australia[1]			
Canberra	157	5.0	3.5
Britain			
London[2]	237	9.7	1.3
London[3]	310	7.9	2.9
Edinburgh[4]	576	5.9	2.8
Greece[5]			
Athens	489	2.0	8.2
Uganda[6]			
Two villages	191	3.7	20.4
United States[7]			
New Haven	5034	5.6	6.1
Baltimore	3481	4.3	12.5
St Louis	3004	5.8	5.1
Durham	3921	3.5	12.2
Los Angeles	3131	5.7	5.9

[1]Henderson et al., 1981; [2]Wing et al., 1978 (women only); [3]Bebbington et al., 1981; [4]Dean et al., 1983 (only women); [5]Mavreas et al., 1986; [6]Orley & Wing, 1979; [7]Regier et al., 1988.

While this instrument has been used to survey psychological distress in various countries such as Australia, Britain, Greece and Uganda, comparisons are difficult to make across studies due to differences between them. However, because of similarities in the way affective and anxiety disorders were defined, it is most appropriate to examine the one-month prevalence rates for these problems, which are presented in Table 2.7. The rates are given separately for the five American sites to show the variability which might exist within a country. The prevalence of affective disorders ranged from 3.5 per cent in Durham to 7.9 in London, while for anxiety disorders it varied from 2.9 in London to 20.4 in Uganda. Orley and Wing (1979) suggest that the high rates of affective disorder observed in Uganda, particularly among women, may be due to their lack of treatment, greater physical illnesses, or more adverse experiences.

As previously mentioned, the studies so far described have not attempted to estimate the lifetime risk or probability of first developing a psychological disorder by a particular age. One investigation in a small, mainly rural area in Sweden calculated that by the age of 80, about 28 per cent of men and 49 per cent of women would have experienced

Table 2.8 Annual incidence and lifetime risk aged 15–54 of schizophrenia in seven countries in persons

Location	Annual incidence (per 10 000)	Lifetime risk (%)
Aarhus, Denmark	1.8	0.56
Honolulu, Hawaii	1.6	0.53
Nagasaki, Japan	2.1	0.74
Dublin, Ireland	2.2	0.84
Nottingham, England	2.4	0.84
Moscow, Russia	2.8	1.13
Chandigarh, India		
Urban	3.5	1.15
Rural	4.2	1.74

depression of a kind similar to major depression as defined by *DSM-III* (Rorsman *et al.*, 1990).

An international study examined the extent to which the less frequent disorder of schizophrenia was found in ten countries, as diagnosed by commonly adopted criteria (Sartorius *et al.*, 1986). As shown in Table 2.8, in seven of the countries the annual incidence of people initially contacting any kind of helping agency, including traditional and religious healers, and diagnosed as having the disorder was estimated as well as the lifetime risk of developing schizophrenia. The annual incidence per 10 000 of the population aged between 15 and 54 varied from 1.6 in Hawaii to 4.2 in rural India. Consequently, it can be seen from the relatively few studies which have carefully investigated the prevalence of psychological disorders in some of the less industrialized countries in the world that psychological disorders are not restricted to industrialized nations and appear worldwide.

Some people who seek professional help for psychological reasons are not diagnosed as having psychological disorders. About 3 per cent of individuals without a diagnosed psychological disorder sought help for psychological problems compared with about 17 per cent with one (Shapiro *et al.*, 1984). Since the number of people without a diagnosed psychological disorder is high, the proportion of people without such diagnoses who went for psychological help is substantial and was estimated to account for about a third of all such visits. In other words, the implication of these results is that many people seeking psychological help do not have serious psychological disorders.

Summary

People show a wide variety of psychological problems. Systems for classifying these problems, such as the *Diagnostic and Statistical Manual (DSM)* of the American Psychiatric Association, have already been revised a number of times in an effort to improve the extent to which these disorders are diagnosed in the same way. There is some evidence that *DSM-III* can be more reliably applied than its predecessors, but in view of its widespread use, the number of studies which have assessed its reliability is surprisingly small and too few to place much confidence on these findings. Community surveys which have tried to determine how common psychological disorders are which are serious enough to require professional attention have suggested that about 30 per cent of the people interviewed suffer from such problems. The most common of these problems include alcohol and drug abuse or dependence, phobias and depression. Many people with psychological disorders do not receive professional psychological help while a considerable proportion of those who seek psychological treatment are not necessarily considered to be seriously disturbed and do not require long-term assistance.

3

Behavioural approach. I: Classical and operant conditioning

The behavioural approach to personality and psychotherapy is based on the assumption that much of human behaviour is learned. The tremendous variety of psychological characteristics which people display, including their psychological problems, is largely a function of what they have learned during their lifetime. Consequently, learning theorists are not interested in trying to classify psychological disorders because they believe that the forms which such disorders can take is likely to be very varied. What is important, however, is to clearly specify the behaviour or response which we are interested in changing and to try to discover the conditions or stimuli which determine it. In order to alter behaviour, we have to modify the conditions which bring it about. The central problem of these theories is to find out how learning occurs.

Although a large number of different theories of learning have been proposed (Hilgard & Bower, 1981), the two major theories that have been applied to the explanation and treatment of psychological disorders are classical conditioning and operant conditioning. These theories initially explored the way in which learning occurs in animals because the conditions under which it took place could be more carefully controlled and because it was felt that learning in animals would be simpler and therefore easier to understand than that in humans. Although Skinner first introduced the term 'behaviour therapy' in a technical report to describe the application of operant conditioning principles to the treatment of psychiatric inpatients (Lindsley *et al.*, 1953), Eysenck (1959a, 1960) subsequently used it to refer to techniques based primarily on classical conditioning. Consequently, psychological treatments founded

largely on the principles of classical conditioning are sometimes generally referred to as *behaviour therapy*, while those derived from operant
conditioning principles are known as *behaviour modification*. However, this
distinction is not always maintained and the two terms are often used
interchangeably (Ullmann & Krasner, 1965), with behaviour therapy being
the more popular name. The use of the term is sometimes broadened to
include any treatment based on the application of other well established
and accepted psychological principles.

Classical conditioning theory

One of the first learning theories to be used to explain psychological
disturbance was developed by the Russian physiologist, Pavlov (1927,
1962). Pavlov was initially interested in how the digestive glands in the
mouth worked and which he was studying in dogs. He originally thought
that whenever food was placed in the mouth, the glands would
automatically secrete their digestive fluids. This was a natural reaction
which was unlearned and which he called an *unconditioned* (or more
properly, an *unconditional*) *reflex*. However, he noticed that the glands
would start to secrete saliva before the food was put into the dog's
mouth once the dog had become familiar with the situation. In fact,
dogs would begin to salivate as soon as they noticed events which were
usually associated with feeding. This simple observation implied that
even so-called natural reflexes could be modified by learning.

What Pavlov then did was to investigate the conditions under which
this learning took place and to put forward what has become known as
classical conditioning theory. Perhaps one of the better ways to understand
the concepts of this theory is to give an example of what Pavlov did
when studying the conditions which brought about natural or
unconditioned reflexes and what he discovered as a result. Suppose, for
example, that you wanted to train or condition a dog to salivate to the
sound of a buzzer. Now dogs do not usually salivate to such a sound.
Consequently, the sound of the buzzer is known as a *neutral stimulus*
since it does not produce salivation. Dogs normally respond to such
novel stimuli by paying attention to them, or by showing what is called
an *orientation response* in which they prick up their ears.

$$\text{NS} \qquad \rightarrow \qquad \text{OR}$$
$$\text{(neutral stimulus)} \qquad \text{(orientation response)}$$

If the buzzer is sounded a number of times, the dog becomes used or
habituated to it and no longer pays attention to it.

$$\text{Repeated NS} \rightarrow \text{Habituation (or loss of OR)}$$

Before the dog can be conditioned to salivate to the buzzer, habituation to the buzzer must have occurred. When this has happened, a healthy but hungry dog will salivate a good deal when given some food. The food in this case is called the *unconditioned stimulus (UCS)* because it automatically causes the dog to salivate. The production of saliva is referred to as the *unconditioned response (UCR)* as it always occurs when food is presented.

$$UCS \quad \rightarrow \quad UCR$$
$$\text{(food)} \qquad \text{(saliva)}$$

To teach the dog to salivate to the buzzer, it has to be fed very soon after the buzzer has sounded.

$$NS \quad + \quad UCS \quad \rightarrow \quad UCR$$
$$\text{(buzzer)} \qquad \text{(food)} \qquad \text{(saliva)}$$

After doing this a few times, the dog will begin to salivate when it hears the buzzer. When this starts to occur, the previously neutral stimulus is now called the *conditioned stimulus (CS)* while the salivation becomes the *conditioned response (CR)*.

$$CS \quad \rightarrow \quad CR$$
$$\text{(buzzer)} \qquad \text{(saliva)}$$

The presentation of the UCS (food) with the CS (buzzer) is referred to as *reinforcement* and is necessary for the CR (saliva) to be maintained. If the CS (buzzer) is given without the UCS (food), the CR (salivation) will eventually disappear or become *extinguished*.

When the CR (salivation) has been extinguished, it may reappear if some time later the CS (buzzer) on its own is presented. This phenomenon is known as *spontaneous recovery*. In order to explain its occurrence, Pavlov thought that extinction was an active process in which the conditioned response was inhibited.

Pavlov also noted that once a stimulus had been conditioned to a response, then other similar stimuli would produce a response which was almost the same but which was less strong than the original conditioned response. For instance, if a buzzer with a frequency higher than the initial one was rung, then the dog would also salivate to it, but not as much as it had done to the first buzzer. The more similar the new stimulus is to the initial one it was associated with, the stronger the conditioned response will be. This phenomenon is known as *stimulus generalization*.

Dogs could also be taught to *discriminate* between similar stimuli. For example, the dog could be trained to salivate to the sound of one buzzer but not to that of another. It was while Pavlov was teaching dogs to make difficult discriminations between very similar stimuli that he noticed his dogs began to behave in ways which he thought were analogous to a nervous breakdown in humans. Consequently, he referred to this behaviour as an *experimental neurosis*. The dogs tried to desperately escape from the situation they were in and would be unable to make the same discriminations afterwards as they had shown before.

There were five main ways in which he could bring about experimental neuroses in his dogs.

1 *Difficult discriminations.* Firstly, they could be produced by forcing dogs to make difficult discriminations as previously outlined. In one experiment Pavlov was interested in finding out how well dogs could distinguish one shape from another, such as an ellipse and a circle. To investigate this problem, he fed the dog when a circle was presented but not when an ellipse was displayed. After a while, the dog started to salivate to the circle but not to the ellipse. Once this discrimination was learned, the ellipses which were shown became progressively more circular until the dog could no longer distinguish the two shapes. After spending about three weeks trying to train the dog to make this discrimination, the dog refused to cooperate and tried to remove itself from the experimental set-up. It also could no longer make the original distinction between the ellipse and the circle and had to be retaught to do this.

2 *Generalization of an intense, unpleasant stimulus.* Secondly, experimental neuroses could be brought about by trying to generalize a response to a strong, unpleasant stimulus from one part of the body to others. In one situation, a dog was taught to salivate whenever it received a mild electric shock. Gradually, the strength of the shock was increased so that even when the shock was fairly strong the dog would salivate and even wag its tail to the shock. Once, however, the shock was applied to another part of the dog's body, it would become extremely restless and excited.

3 *Long CS-UCS interval.* A third way of inducing these neuroses was to gradually increase the interval between the presentation of the CS and the UCS.

4 *Rapid alteration of two conditioned stimuli.* A fourth method was to quickly present in succession two conditioned stimuli, one conditioned to evoke a particular response and the other conditioned so it would not be shown.

5 *Fatigue, illness and castration.* Finally, tiredness, illness and castration caused the dog's cooperative behaviour to stop when being conditioned.

Pavlov suggested that these methods resulted in the breakdown of the dog's behaviour by upsetting the balance between the physiological processes of excitation and inhibition in the brain, although the way in which this was described to occur was not very clear. He went on to try out various remedies to treat his dogs which had become disturbed and advocated the use of rest, bromide, or a mixture of bromide and caffeine.

Although Pavlov's work on experimental neurosis stimulated other people to study it further, the way in which this behaviour is related to human neuroses is not apparent. It would seem that the dogs learned to associate the experimental situation with difficult or unpleasant tasks and that this did not affect their behaviour more generally.

Finally, two other points Pavlov made about classical conditioning must be mentioned. Firstly, he thought that conditioning in animals involved what he called the *primary signalling system*, which reflected reality in terms of sensory perceptions and impressions such as sights and sounds. Unlike other animals, however, humans had in addition a *secondary signalling system*, which represented the world in terms of words and symbols. Although Pavlov believed the same principles governed the way in which both systems worked, he thought that most human conditioning took place through suggestion in the secondary signalling system.

The second point he noted is that the personality of his dogs differed and that these differences affected the ease with which they could be conditioned. Two extreme types stood out in particular. One was similar to what the 5th century BC, Greek physician Hippocrates called the 'sanguine temperament'. These dogs were generally very active and attentive, but when they were presented with the same stimulus in the quiet experimental chamber, they soon fell asleep. The only way to condition them was to give them a variety of stimuli in fairly quick succession. The second type of dog had a melancholic temperament and was characterized by being cautious and afraid. However, once these dogs became used to the experimental situation, they conditioned so well that one of them was called Brains.

Classical conditioning of fears

One of the first psychologists to demonstrate classical conditioning in humans was the American psychologist Watson who coined the term 'behaviourist' (Watson, 1913). Although Pavlov's work had not yet been translated into English, Watson had heard about it and wanted to show that emotional responses such as love, fear and rage could be learned or conditioned in a similar way. Accordingly, Watson and Rayner (1920) undertook to see if they could make a seemingly fearless 11-month-old baby boy called 'Albert' afraid of something of which he was not previously frightened. After trying out a wide variety of different objects which young children are normally frightened of such as a rat, rabbit, mask and burning newspaper, they eventually discovered that Albert was afraid of a loud noise made by hitting a steel bar with a hammer. So they decided to see if they could make Albert frightened of a rat by hitting the bar whenever they put the rat in front of him. In terms of Pavlov's classical conditioning procedure, the rat was the neutral stimulus, the loud noise the unconditioned stimulus, and fear the unconditioned response.

$$NS \rightarrow OR$$
$$\text{(rat)} \qquad \text{(approach)}$$

$$UCS \rightarrow UCR$$
$$\text{(loud noise)} \qquad \text{(fear)}$$

Every time Albert attempted to approach the rat, they banged the bar. After doing this seven or more times, Albert became frightened and started to cry whenever he saw the rat. In other words, he had been conditioned to be frightened of the rat.

$$CS + UCS \rightarrow CR$$
$$\text{(rat)} \quad \text{(loud noise)} \qquad \text{(fear)}$$

This fear was shown to similar objects such as a rabbit, dog or fur coat, but not to dissimilar ones such as building blocks. It also persisted for at least a month. As a result of this demonstration, Watson and Rayner suggested that many clinical phobias may be acquired in the same way as Albert's fear of furry objects, except that these fears would most probably only remain in people who were 'constitutionally inferior'. Before commenting on the adequacy of Watson's ideas on the development of phobias, the application of classical conditioning to the treatment of various psychological problems will be first discussed.

Classical conditioning applied to therapy

Watson and Rayner had intended to remove Albert's fear but he was taken away from the area before they could do so. A few years later, however, Jones (1924) with the advice of Watson tried a variety of methods for overcoming the fears of young children, two of which seemed particularly effective. One method, called *direct conditioning*, involved associating the frightening situation with a pleasant one. This was successfully used with a three-year-old boy called Peter who was afraid of rabbits. To overcome this fear, Peter was given a sweet to eat while the rabbit was brought as close as possible to him without interfering with his eating. This procedure was carried out once or twice a day for two months, when his fear of rabbits had disappeared. The second method was *social imitation* in which the child who was frightened of some object such as a rabbit was put together with children fearlessly playing with a rabbit.

Some years later, Mowrer and Mowrer (1938) applied the principles of classical conditioning to treating enuresis (bed-wetting). According to them, children urinate in bed when asleep because they have failed to learn to associate the sensations of a full bladder with the reaction of waking up. If children could be woken up as soon as they had wet the bed, then gradually they would learn to waken when their bladder was full. So they prepared a special pad containing an electrical contact which would close when the sheet was wet. The closed contact would set off a bell, thereby waking up the child.

In terms of classical conditioning, the sensation of the full bladder is the neutral stimulus to be conditioned, the sound of the bell is the unconditioned stimulus, and the reaction of waking up is the unconditioned response which becomes conditioned.

$$NS \quad + \quad UCS \quad \rightarrow \quad CR$$
$$\text{(full bladder)} \quad \text{(bell)} \quad \text{(waking up)}$$

This method, called the *bell-and-pad procedure* or the *urine alarm*, has been found in a number of studies to have been successful with 75 per cent of children treated, although 41 per cent of those who were followed up relapsed to wetting their bed (Doleys, 1977).

At about the same time *aversion therapy*, also based on classical conditioning, was developed to treat alcoholism (Lemere *et al.*, 1942). This method consisted of associating the sight, smell and taste of the patient's favourite alcoholic drink with the feeling of wanting to vomit induced by a drug. In terms of classical conditioning, the sensation of alcohol was the neutral stimulus, the feeling of nausea was the aversive unconditioned stimulus which led to the conditioned response of distaste and avoidance.

$$NS \quad + \quad UCS \quad \rightarrow \quad CR$$
$$\text{(alcohol)} \quad \text{(nausea)} \quad \text{(distaste)}$$

Patients were given four to six sessions of this therapy within 3–7 days, after which they received one or two booster sessions at any time they desired a drink or routinely at 6 and 12 months after the original treatment. The effectiveness of this therapy was followed up over 13 years on 4097 patients, of whom 40 per cent had relapsed after one year and 77 per cent after ten or more years (Lemere & Voegtlin, 1950).

Aversion therapy has also been used to treat chronic persistent vomiting in a nine-month-old boy, who by then weighed 12 lb and was being fed through the nose (Lang & Melamed, 1969). In this case, electric shock was the aversive stimulus which was applied as soon as he began to vomit and which was continued until he stopped. After about 12 sessions his vomiting ceased and he had gained 4 lb in weight.

A couple of studies have compared the effectiveness of single-trial traumatic aversion therapy for alcoholism, in which the unconditioned stimulus was paralysis of the respiratory muscles for one minute, with procedures anticipated to be therapeutically inert or ineffective (Clancy *et al.*, 1966; Madill *et al.*, 1966). In one study, patients with alcoholism were randomly assigned to one of three treatments (Madill *et al.*, 1966). In one condition, patients were given an intravenous injection of a drug which although painless caused breathing to stop for about one minute by paralysing the respiratory muscles. When paralysis began, a bottle containing their favourite alcoholic drink was held to their lips until they started to breathe again when it was taken away. In a second condition, patients were injected with the paralysing drug but they were not presented with the alcohol. In the third condition, they did not receive the injection but were given the bottle of alcohol. If the effectiveness of aversion conditioning is due to the association of paralysis with alcohol, then the first condition should be more effective than the other two conditions. However, although the level of abstinence was greater after all three treatments, there was no significant difference between the three conditions in terms of whether or not they reported remaining abstinent during the three months after treatment, despite the fact that the patients who received the drug were more afraid in terms of self-ratings and two out of the three physiological measures used to assess anxiety.

Only a summary was provided of the second study (Clancy *et al.*, 1966), which compared four treatments. Aversion therapy was similar to that used in the previous study except that a smaller dose of the drug (10 vs 20 mg) was administered and the drug was given immediately after the patient had tasted an alcoholic drink. The three other treatments were control conditions. One was similar to aversion therapy except that patients were injected with saline solution instead of the drug. The second control condition was the usual hospital treatment of individual, group and drug therapy, while the third control group consisted of patients who had been seen at the hospital but who had refused treatment. Although abstinence was significantly greater for aversion therapy than for the usual hospital treatment and for those refusing treatment, there was no difference between aversion therapy and its saline control. The failure to find a difference between these two treatments may have been due to fear rather than paralysis *per se* being the unconditioned stimulus. However, this interpretation cannot be checked since no evidence was provided in this brief report that patients in these two conditions were equally fearful. It is clear from the results of the first study, however, that a treatment in which patients were less afraid was as effective in increasing abstinence as those in which they were more fearful. A further problem with interpreting the results of this second study is that it is not stated that patients were randomly assigned to the three therapy conditions. Consequently, it is not certain whether the patients in these three conditions were equivalent in terms of other characteristics. Further evidence on the relative effectiveness of aversion therapy will be offered in the next chapter.

Table 3.1 Lifetime prevalence of phobias in women and men (percentages)

Phobia	Women (n = 10 954)	Men (n = 7 618)
Spiders, bugs, mice, snakes	6.63	2.44
Heights	4.57	3.16
Being on public transport	3.80	1.33
Being in water	3.58	1.28
Storms	2.95	0.83
Being in a crowd	2.79	1.45
Going out of house alone	1.88	0.39
Speaking to strangers or meeting new people	0.84	0.66

Critique of the classical conditioning model of phobias

The development of aversion therapy has provided a practical opportunity for examining whether the use of shock as an unconditioned stimulus leads to fear of the neutral stimulus as implied by Watson's classical conditioning model of phobias. Although adults may be less likely to show their fear than children, there are few reports of phobias developing in patients as a result of aversion therapy. For example, patients treated with electrical aversion therapy for sexual problems or alcoholism typically report feelings of indifference or revulsion rather than anxiety (Marks & Gelder, 1967; Hallam et al., 1972) and patients receiving electrical aversion therapy for alcoholism even showed no physiological signs of anxiety (Hallam et al., 1972). If fear is not the conditioned response, what is?

There are three other observations which a simple classical conditioning model of phobias does not adequately handle. Firstly, the range of phobias reported is restricted. For example, community surveys have found that the most common phobias are of small animals, such as spiders and mice, and height (Bourdon et al., 1988). The lifetime prevalence of selected phobias are shown separately for women and men in Table 3.1. If phobias simply developed as a result of the association of neutral stimuli with aversive experiences, then a wide range of different phobias would be expected to be shown.

Secondly, the establishment of a conditioned response requires the repeated association of the neutral stimulus with the unconditioned stimulus. Consequently, phobias should develop towards objects which are more commonly associated with unpleasant experiences.

Thirdly, unlike phobias conditioned responses normally quickly extinguish when not reinforced or when human subjects are simply asked not to show them (Bridger & Mandel, 1965; Wilson, 1968). For example, in one study a physiological measure of anxiety called the galvanic skin response was conditioned to a blue but not a yellow light using a mild electric shock on 50 per cent of the occasions the blue light was presented (Wilson, 1968). When subjects were told that the shock would only be given after the yellow light, the galvanic skin response was extinguished to the blue light and conditioned to the yellow one more or less immediately in those subjects who believed the experimenter and even though no shocks were subsequently administered.

In an attempt to deal with these problems from a classical conditioning perspective, Seligman (1971) proposed the *preparedness* theory of phobias. He suggested that humans biologically predisposed to be afraid of potentially dangerous natural situations, such as predators, unfamiliar surroundings and the dark, were more likely to survive and have children than those who were not. Because of their possible adaptive value, phobic responses were quick to condition and slow to extinguish to these kinds of stimuli. Consequently, phobias of natural events were more common than those of similarly hazardous human artefacts such as knives, ladders, electric sockets and cars.

This idea was tested by rating the pretechnological adaptiveness of the phobias and obsessions of 69 and 82 patients, respectively, and relating it to theoretically relevant aspects of these disorders and their treatment, such as how early and quickly they had developed and how effectively they had been treated (DeSilva et al., 1977). According to the theory, phobias and obsessions which emerged early and quickly and which were difficult to treat should have been rated as being potentially more adaptive. However, contrary to these expectations, no relationship was found between these factors and rated adaptiveness. Although efforts have been made to investigate the preparedness theory in the laboratory, the relevance of these studies to phobic behaviour is unclear since more direct measures of fear such as self-reports and avoidance responses were not taken (Cook et al., 1986).

In a further endeavour to deal with some of the problems of the classical conditioning model of phobias, Eysenck (1976b, 1979) has proposed an *incubation* of fear hypothesis, which suggests that under certain conditions the conditioned stimulus (e.g. the rat in Watson's study) when presented alone will lead to an increase (i.e. incubation) rather than a decrease (i.e. extinction) in the conditioned response of fear. The four conditions which are thought to make enhancement more likely are: (1) conditioned responses which have drive or motivating properties; (2) strong unconditioned stimuli; (3) short exposure to the conditioned stimulus; and (4) individuals who are neurotic introverts. As Eysenck (1979) himself admits, there is little evidence as yet for this hypothesis since most studies show extinction and not enhancement.

One of the earliest, and perhaps still most influential, attempt to handle the difficulty that the classical conditioning theory has in explaining why phobias did not extinguish more readily is Mowrer's (1947) two-factor theory of avoidance learning. However, since this theory involves both classical and operant conditioning theory, discussion of it will have to wait until after the operant conditioning theory of learning has been outlined.

Operant conditioning theory

The second major theory of learning to be applied to the explanation and treatment of psychological disorders is Skinner's (1938) operant conditioning theory. Skinner distinguished two kinds of behaviour called *respondent* and *operant* responses. A respondent response is a natural reflex (e.g. salivation or pupil dilation) which is automatically produced by a particular stimulus (e.g. food or light) but which can be modified through classical conditioning.

Operant responses, on the other hand, do not seem to be under the control of any particular stimulus and make up most of our behaviour such as walking, swimming, reading and writing. These responses are affected by events which follow them. If the events are favourable or positively reinforcing, then that behaviour is more likely to occur on similar occasions in the future. If the events are unpleasant or negative, then that behaviour is less likely to occur in similar future situations. For example, if you receive a high mark for writing an essay you will be more likely to write essays than if you are given a low mark. This observation was called the *law of effect* by Thorndike (1898) and is the basis of operant conditioning theory.

Operant behaviour is usually enacted in response to a particular situation but, unlike respondent behaviour, it is not invariably brought about by that situation. For instance, it is usual to write notes when listening to a lecturer, but it is not customary to make notes while listening to a friend. Behaviour, such as note-taking, is known as a *discriminated operant* since it is only carried out in certain settings called *discriminative stimuli*.

$$S^D \quad \rightarrow \quad R \quad \rightarrow \quad S^R$$

discriminative stimulus (lecture)	operant response (note-taking)	reinforcing stimulus (approval)

Skinner was primarily interested in the effects of reinforcement on operant behaviour. A *reinforcer*, or *reinforcing stimulus*, is defined as any event which follows an operant response and which increases the chance it will recur. For example, if you nod your head in approval every time someone says something you agree with and you notice that person then says more and more things you agree with, your head nodding would be called a reinforcer.

Various general classes of reinforcers have been distinguished. *Innate* (or *primary*) *reinforcers* are differentiated from *conditioned* (or *secondary*) *reinforcers*. An innate reinforcer is any stimulus which is naturally pleasant (e.g. water when thirsty) or unpleasant (e.g. pain), while a conditioned reinforcer is a stimulus which has become associated with an innate reinforcer (e.g. the buzzer for Pavlov's dogs). Most of human behaviour is controlled by conditioned reinforcers. Conditioned reinforcers which have become associated with more than one innate reinforcer are known as *generalized reinforcers*. A good example of a generalized reinforcer is money which can be used to satisfy many of our needs. Other important generalized reinforcers include attention, approval and affection from others. We may sometimes give these reinforcers inadvertently to bring about behaviour we do not want. For instance, paying attention to someone being sulky or angry may be more likely to make them behave that way.

Positive reinforcers are distinguished from *negative reinforcers*, although this distinction may be less easy to remember. Since a reinforcer is defined as any stimulus which follows and which raises the probability of operant behaviour occurring, both positive and negative reinforcers increase the chances of an operant response being made. However, they do so in different ways. A positive reinforcer is a stimulus which is presented after an operant response has been shown and which is pleasant, whereas a negative reinforcer is a stimulus which is taken away following an operant response and which is unpleasant. For example, if you wanted someone to spend more time studying, every time they started to study you could either show them approval (positive reinforcement) or stop criticizing them (negative reinforcement). The effect of both kinds of reinforcers would be the same (i.e. more time spent studying). Negative reinforcement, therefore, is not to be confused with *punishment*, which is an unpleasant stimulus presented after an operant response has taken place (e.g. criticizing them when they have already begun to study). The general effect of punishment is to decrease the probability of an operant occurring. Skinner (1953) believed that since this effect is only temporary, it is not a very effective way for changing behaviour. However, later research suggested that punishment may be an effective way of modifying behaviour under certain circumstances (Azrin & Holz, 1966).

Finally, *continuous reinforcement* is distinguished from *partial* (or *intermittent*) *reinforcement*. Continuous reinforcement is when a reinforcer is presented every time a particular operant occurs, which is unusual. Normally, reinforcement happens occasionally or intermittently. Skinner was particularly interested in the effects of different kinds or *schedules* of partial reinforcement on operant behaviour (Ferster & Skinner, 1957). One of his major contributions was to show that different schedules of reinforcement produce characteristic patterns of responding and extinction. In general, more frequent responses and slower extinction occurs with partial than with continuous reinforcement. Consequently, it is both more effective and economical to use partial rather than continuous reinforcement.

There are four main simple schedules, which vary in two principal ways. Firstly, they can be either *interval schedules*, where a reinforcer is presented after a certain amount of time has elapsed, or *ratio schedules*, where reinforcement is offered according to the number of operant responses which have been made. And secondly, they can be either *fixed schedules*, where reinforcers are given after a fixed amount of time has passed (*fixed-interval schedule*) or a fixed number of responses have been made (*fixed-ratio schedule*), or *variable schedules*, where reinforcement is administered after a variable amount of time has elapsed (*variable-interval schedule*) or a variable number of responses have been produced (*variable-ratio schedule*). Each of these four reinforcement schedules produce consistent and characteristic rates of responding. Generally, learning to respond on a ratio schedule takes longer than on an interval one, but once learned, more responses are made on a ratio than on an interval schedule.

So far, the discussion has assumed that the response to be conditioned occurs naturally. Responses which are not usually made can be taught by a procedure called *shaping* (or the *method of successive approximation*), where actions which are similar to (or approximate) the desired behaviour are successively reinforced. For example, if you wanted to teach a pigeon to walk around with its head stretched high, you would reinforce it each time it raised its head a little higher than previously until you had achieved the desired result. Using this technique, two psychologists built up a very successful business training animals to perform various acts for shows and advertisements on television (Breland & Breland, 1966). One of their star performers was called 'Priscilla, the Fastidious Pig'. In her act Priscilla would switch on the TV set, eat breakfast at table, pick up her dirty clothes and put them into a basket, vacuum clean the floor, go shopping, and take part in a quiz show where she would answer questions by pressing buttons which would flash either 'Yes' or 'No'. Now Priscilla was not a particularly clever pig. Because pigs grow so quickly, a new Priscilla had to be trained every few months.

The importance of reinforcement for causing behaviour to occur more frequently is perhaps most clearly illustrated by seeing what happens when reinforcement is given randomly, a procedure known as *non-contingent reinforcement* since presentation of the reinforcer is not contingent on any particular response being shown. In one study, Skinner placed a hungry pigeon in a cage. At random intervals, a light would be switched on which was immediately followed by some food being given. This procedure prompted the pigeon to repeat whatever behaviour it was engaging in at the time of the reinforcement. So, if it happened to be pecking at its right wing just before it was reinforced, it was more likely to repeat that behaviour, and to be pecking its wing again when the next reinforcement was due. Consequently, the pigeon would spend more and more of its time pecking its right wing until it occupied most of its time doing this. Skinner believed that noncontingent reinforcement was responsible for much of the irrational and superstitious behaviour of humans.

Operant conditioning applied to therapy

Operant conditioning theorists argue that psychological problems are responses produced by reinforcement or punishment. For example, phobic behaviour may result from being punished in certain situations and/or from being reinforced for avoiding them (Lazarus *et al.*, 1965). Depression may be due to the loss of positively reinforcing behaviour (such as when a loved one dies) and/or ineffectual attempts at avoiding aversive situations (Ferster, 1973). The seemingly bizarre behaviour which is characteristic of psychosis may simply be responses which have been rewarded (Ayllon & Michael, 1959). The way to treat these problems is by reinforcing more appropriate behaviour. It may be useful to give a few illustrations of how this has been done.

The first two cases come from a report by Ayllon and Michael (1959). One patient spent so much time talking about her illegitimate child and the men who were constantly pursuing her that the other patients beat her up in an effort to keep her quiet. It was observed that this talk was being reinforced by the nurses on the ward listening to her. So the nurses were told only to attend to what she said when she discussed other matters. After about eight weeks of doing this, the amount of time she spent talking about her child and the men who followed her dropped from about 90 to 25 per cent.

The second patient usually only ate if she was spoon-fed. Since it was noticed she liked to keep her clothes clean, to encourage her to feed herself the nurses were asked to pay attention to her only when she fed herself and that if she insisted on being fed to occasionally spill some food onto her clothes. After about three weeks of this treatment, she regularly fed herself.

In another case a patient collected and hoarded the towels of the ward in her room (Ayllon, 1963). Although the nurses removed the towels from her room about twice a week, on average she kept about 20 of them in her room. The method of *stimulus satiation*, which is based on the idea that too much of a reinforcer will cause it to lose its reinforcing properties, was tried to discourage this hoarding behaviour. It was thought that if the patient was permitted to keep as many towels as possible in her room, the towels would lose their appeal. Consequently, the nurses were asked not to remove any towels from her room and to give her a towel at odd intervals throughout the day.

At first, the patient was delighted with this change in policy and spent much of her time folding and stacking the increasing number of towels in her room. However, as the pile of towels continued to grow, she became more and more distressed. During the third week of this treatment when she had over 300 towels, she complained to the nurses that she could not sit in her room all night folding towels. In the sixth week with over 600 towels in her room, she started to take a few of them out. When this happened, she was no longer given any more towels. She continued to remove the towels from her room until she had only one left. The nurses were rather sceptical about whether or not this relatively simple treatment would work since they thought that the patient's desire to hoard towels signified a very basic need for love and security which would be difficult to change. So, they were surprised when the patient showed no tendency to collect towels again over the next 12 months.

Attempts have been made to modify the behaviour of chronic schizophrenic inpatients by rewarding appropriate behaviour with tokens which can be subsequently exchanged for such items as food, drink, magazines and other privileges (Ayllon & Azrin, 1968). However, a careful study, which compared patients who were given tokens over a year for showing appropriate behaviour with those who were provided with a similar number of tokens regardless of how they behaved, found that both groups improved equally in terms of their social behaviour but that there was no change in symptoms such as disturbed speech and thought (Baker et al., 1977). In other words, the results of this study suggested that the provision of tokens neither reduced symptoms nor was responsible for the improved social behaviour.

Operant conditioning has also been used to treat various other disorders, such as agoraphobia and anorexia nervosa. In one study, three patients with agoraphobia were encouraged to go for walks outside the clinic by praising them whenever they showed a specified increase in either the distance travelled or the length of time spent outside (Agras et al., 1968). After an initial baseline period (B) during which they were observed and which was similar to the no reinforcement procedure, sessions using reinforcement (R) were systematically varied with those in which no reinforcement (N) was given (BRNR) so that the effects of reinforcement could be examined within each of the three cases. In at least two of the patients, deterioration seemed to occur when praise was not offered, suggesting that providing encouragement was solely responsible for the progress shown. Interestingly, asking patients to walk as far as possible without feeling tense and maintaining a pleasant relationship with them did not produce any improvement since this was done in the sessions with no reinforcement.

However, in a larger investigation no difference was found in 16 patients with agoraphobia who were randomly assigned to one of two treatments. One method was 'successive approximation', in which patients were given both feedback about how long they had remained outside as well as praise if they had stayed outside for at least as long as the mean time of the previous two trials. The other method was 'self-observation', in which neither of these two elements was present and patients simply had to stay outside for as long as possible without feeling tense (Emmelkamp & Ultee, 1974). It is, of course, possible that the lack of a difference between these two procedures was because the level of reinforcement did not vary sufficiently between them. The failure to check that the critical variable has been appropriately manipulated is a problem which recurs in studies evaluating the validity of psychological principles. One way of trying to ensure that the degree of reinforcement might have been less in the 'self-observation' condition would have been for the therapist to have expressed mild disappointment at the amount of progress made since it would be difficult to conceive of this as positive reinforcement. It would also have been worthwhile to have assessed the patients' perception of the level of reinforcement received from the therapist and from themselves to determine whether these sources of reinforcement differed between the two conditions.

In another study, two patients with anorexia nervosa were praised when they ate more and were given certain privileges, such as watching television and going out, when they gained weight (Leitenberg *et al.*, 1968). As a result of this treatment, their weight returned to normal and they resumed their usual activities. However, a controlled clinical evaluation found no significant difference in the amount of weight gained in 81 anorexic patients treated either with or without operant conditioning (Eckert *et al.*, 1979). One reason for the failure of operant conditioning to be more effective may have been that privileges contingent on gaining weight were only given after periods of five days. More immediate reinforcement may have led to greater improvement.

Some operant conditioning theorists have implied that operant conditioning occurs implicitly in other forms of psychotherapy where certain behaviours of the patient are reinforced or punished by the therapist (Krasner, 1962). Truax (1966a), for example, indirectly examined this question in a patient successfully treated by client-centred therapy, an approach which tries not to influence the client or patient in any particular direction and which therefore provides the most severe test for determining whether therapists unintentionally influence their patients' behaviour. Truax selected 40 sequences of therapist–client interaction (consisting of a statement by the therapist consecutively followed by one from the client and a further one from the therapist) from 85 successive sessions of client-centred therapy and looked at the extent to which nine kinds of patient statements were related to three types of therapist comments.

Therapist comments thought to be reinforcing were empathic understanding and unconditional acceptance, while those seen as being aversive were directiveness. The four of the nine patient behaviours most consistently related to these therapist responses were: (1) fresh ways of looking at old feelings; (2) insight into problems; (3) similar style of expression as therapist; and (4) greater clarity. Furthermore, three of these four patient behaviours increased over the course of therapy implying that they were selectively reinforced. Unfortunately, the relationship of these patient responses to therapeutic improvement is not made clear and in a non-experimental design such as this, the possibility exists that the patient was reinforcing the therapist rather than vice versa.

A more convincing test of verbal operant conditioning in psychotherapy was reported by Williams and Blanton (1968) who allocated non-psychotic patients to one of three treatment groups each consisting of nine 30-minute sessions. Patients were reinforced either for talking about their feelings in one condition or for expressing non-feeling statements in the other, while in the third condition they were given the usual psychotherapy. When the number of feeling and non-feeling statements in the three treatments were counted, it was found that the percentage of feeling statements increased over the nine sessions for both the patients receiving psychotherapy and for those reinforced for talking about their feelings, while they decreased for the patients reinforced for uttering non-feeling statements.

There was, however, no increase in the proportion of non-feeling statements in the patients reinforced for making these, possibly because they could not discriminate what it was about these statements which was being reinforced. The finding that the increase in feeling statements was similar for both psychotherapy patients and for those reinforced for talking about their feelings implies that the patients receiving psychotherapy were encouraged to discuss their feelings. Although this study, like the previous one, suggests that operant conditioning may be occurring in psychotherapy, it does not examine what constitutes effective psychotherapy. For example, does talking about one's feelings bring about therapeutic improvement, and if so, why should discussing one's feelings be therapeutically beneficial?

The discovery that autonomic responses could also be altered by reinforcement encouraged an interest in the study of *biofeedback* (feedback from biological processes) to treat various physiological disorders such as hypertension, tension headaches, migraine headaches and asthma (Shapiro & Surwit, 1976; Miller, 1978). For example, although successful attempts have been made to lower hypertension in the laboratory (Benson *et al.*, 1971), the failure of this effect to generalize outside it seems to have put a stop to this work (Blanchard & Epstein, 1977).

Evaluation of operant conditioning

Some problems with the theory and application of operant conditioning as originally formulated will be briefly mentioned. Firstly, Skinner's assertion that respondent responses or natural reflexes cannot be operationally conditioned is not true. There appears to be substantial evidence that autonomic responses, such as salivation, heart rate, blood pressure and electrodermal activity, can be modified by reinforcement (Shapiro & Surwit, 1976; Miller, 1978). For example, in one study a particular amplitude in the spontaneous electrical fluctuations of the skin was reinforced (Shapiro *et al.*, 1964). One group of individuals was given a reward each time this response occurred, while a second group was presented with the same number of rewards but at times when the response was absent so that any difference in the response rates between the two groups could not be due to differences in the amount of reward received. Responses which were reinforced increased in number while those which were not reinforced decreased.

Secondly, operant conditioning theory does not offer a self-contained account of learning since classical conditioning theory is used to explain how two stimuli become associated. The organism which is being operationally conditioned learns to associate a particular stimulus (the discriminative stimulus) with being rewarded (the reinforcing stimulus). This learning takes place through classical conditioning. For example, to teach a rat to press a lever (the discriminative stimulus) to obtain food (the reinforcing stimulus), the rat has to learn that food (the unconditioned stimulus in classical conditioning terms) is associated with the lever (the neutral stimulus which is to be conditioned). In other words, operant conditioning includes classical conditioning. Consequently, deficiencies in the adequacy of classical conditioning theory also hold true for operant conditioning theory. Furthermore, it is difficult to determine whether a treatment such as aversion therapy should be viewed primarily as a form of either classical or operant conditioning since both processes may be involved, although traditionally it is seen as classical conditioning. For instance, in treating alcoholism with electric aversion therapy, alcohol may be either the discriminative or the neutral stimulus, electric shock may be either punishment or the unconditioned stimulus, while avoiding alcohol may be either the operant or the unconditioned response.

Finally, much of human behaviour seems to be learned through imitation and verbal instruction, either by others or oneself. It should, of course, be pointed out that these processes can be, and have been, accounted for by operant conditioning theory. For example, learning through imitation or verbal instruction can be simply explained by arguing that children are reinforced for showing this behaviour and so learn in these ways.

Two implications follow from holding this view. Firstly, an account, which can be disconfirmed, has to be given as to why other organisms and some humans do not learn in these ways. For example, to suggest that animals have not acquired linguistic ability due to lack of appropriate environmental reinforcements during their evolutionary development simply states the obvious and does not offer a satisfactory account of the phenomenon requiring explaining.

The second implication is that if humans learn more quickly through imitation and verbal instruction, then it may be more appropriate to teach or to employ these more effective methods when trying to help people overcome their psychological problems. Such methods are usually seen as being cognitive in nature and so will be outlined in Chapters 6 and 7.

Summary

The behavioural approach, which assumes that much of human behaviour is learned, is primarily concerned with understanding the process of learning. Two major learning theories are classical conditioning and operant conditioning. Classical conditioning proposes that learning takes place through the repeated association of a previously neutral stimulus with one which naturally evokes a response, while operant conditioning holds that learning occurs through the reinforcement of responses. Psychological problems are seen as learned responses which can be changed through further conditioning. Difficulties with the classical conditioning model of phobias, however, include the failure of extinction to occur and the restricted range of phobias usually seen. The application of learning principles to the treatment of psychological disorders is known as behaviour therapy or behaviour modification. At present, there is insufficient evidence to support the view that the effectiveness of aversion therapy is primarily due to the repeated association of the aversive stimulus with the stimulus to be reconditioned or that the efficacy of psychotherapy is enhanced by including a specific operant conditioning component for modifying particular problematic behaviours.

4

Behavioural approach. II: Avoidance learning and reciprocal inhibition

Avoidance learning theory

A major difficulty with the classical conditioning theory of phobic behaviour outlined in the previous chapter is the absence of an adequate account of why some phobias do not extinguish. One theory which is widely cited as a more appropriate explanation for the failure of classically conditioned responses to diminish is Mowrer's (1947) avoidance learning theory. This theory is also known as *two-factor* or *two-process learning theory* since it holds that two kinds of learning are involved when someone learns to avoid a frightening stimulus. Firstly, the person learns to associate through classical conditioning the unpleasant experience with other stimuli present at the same time. So, for example, in Watson and Rayner's (1920) study (see Chapter 3), Albert learned to associate being frightened with the presence of the rat until he was afraid of the rat itself.

Classical conditioning:
$$CS \quad + \quad UCS \quad \rightarrow \quad CS$$
(rat) \qquad (loud noise) \qquad (fear)

Secondly, the person then learns through operant conditioning to move away from the frightening situation by being rewarded with a reduction in anxiety every time the situation is avoided. So, for instance, Albert would move away from a rat whenever he saw one and this avoidance behaviour would be reinforced by feeling less anxious as a result.

Operant conditioning:

$$S^D \rightarrow R \rightarrow S^R$$
$$\text{(rat)} \quad \text{(escape)} \quad \text{(less fear)}$$

Since the person is no longer exposed to the frightening situation, they do not come to realize that this situation is not always associated with unpleasant experiences, and so their fear of it does not extinguish.

Some theorists believe that this two-factor theory can also explain obsessive–compulsive behaviour such as frequent hand-washing (Metzner, 1963; Walton & Mather, 1963). A person who compulsively washes their hands may do so to avoid dirt which has become associated with anxiety. The hand-washing removes any dirt and so reduces anxiety. The reduction in anxiety in turn reinforces the hand-washing.

$$CS \quad + \quad UCS \quad \rightarrow \quad CR$$
$$\text{(dirt)} \quad \text{(e.g. punishment)} \quad \text{(anxiety)}$$

$$S^D \quad \rightarrow \quad R \quad \rightarrow \quad S^R$$
$$\text{(dirt)} \quad \text{(hand-washing)} \quad \text{(less anxiety)}$$

One procedure, used extensively for studying avoidance learning in animals in the laboratory, involves a shuttle-box consisting of two compartments which are separated by a barrier over which the animal can jump (Mowrer & Lamoreaux, 1942). The floor of each compartment can be electrified to give the animal a shock, while the box may also contain a light or buzzer which can be used as a signal to warn the animal the shock is coming. The animal can avoid receiving the shock by moving from one compartment to the other.

To train the animal to escape the shock, it is first put into one of the compartments. The signal (or CS) is presented, shortly followed by the shock (or UCS). When this happens, the animal may move into the next compartment which is not electrified, thereby escaping the shock. Eventually, it learns to associate the signal with the shock through classical conditioning.

$$CS \quad + \quad UCS \quad \rightarrow \quad CR$$
$$\text{(signal)} \quad \text{(shock)} \quad \text{(fear)}$$

It will then be able to avoid the shock by moving into the other compartment as soon as the signal is presented. Once it has learned to do this, it will continue to move into the other compartment whenever the signal is presented, even if it is no longer shocked for staying in the compartment where it was originally shocked.

The reason for this behaviour, according to Mowrer, is that the signal, because it has been associated with shock, makes the animal anxious. Consequently, any response which makes the animal less fearful will be reinforced. Since escaping from one compartment to the other reduces the animal's anxiety because it is no longer shocked, this avoidance response is strengthened through operant conditioning.

$$S^D \quad \rightarrow \quad R \quad \rightarrow \quad S^R$$
(signal)   (escape)   (less fear)

Animals will go on escaping into the other compartment for hundreds of trials without receiving any further shocks. For example, dogs which were given a few intense shocks to teach them to escape being shocked continued to avoid them for 650 trials without receiving any further shocks and without showing any signs of extinction (Solomon & Wynne, 1954). Although the shocks used in this study were so intense that they almost paralysed the dog's muscles, no relationship has been found between the intensity of the shock used to train the animal to make the avoidance response and the frequency with which the animal shows that behaviour (Brush, 1957).

Furthermore, once the animal has learned to avoid the shock, it will show little or no sign of fear. For example, it has been found that the dog's heart beat did not increase when the signal was presented, implying that the dog was not frightened (Black, 1959). In fact, it has been suggested that the behaviour of these animals is very similar to that of patients with obsessive–compulsive disorder (Baum, 1970). For instance, someone with a compulsive desire to wash their hands will show no fear or anxiety, even after becoming dirty, provided that they can cleanse their hands. If they cannot, however, they will become extremely agitated and anxious. Similarly, an animal which is prevented from moving from one compartment to the other will also become extremely disturbed. Moreover, punishing the animal for making the avoidance response by shocking it in the compartment to which it has escaped will not deter it from making that response. In fact, it makes the animal move even faster (Solomon et al., 1953). So punishment does not seem to be an effective way of trying to eliminate obsessive–compulsive behaviour such as hand-washing.

However, there are two main problems with this explanation of avoidance behaviour. Firstly, the animal does not appear to be anxious when responding to the warning signal. As has already been noted, the heart rate in dogs does not increase when the signal is presented (Black, 1959). And secondly, according to classical conditioning theory the association between the warning signal and the shock should extinguish unless the warning signal is repeatedly associated with the shock. For example, it has been observed that when very intense shock is used as the unconditioned stimulus, the conditioned response in rats extinguishes within 40 trials when the animal is no longer shocked (Annau & Kamin, 1961). When weaker shocks have been employed, extinction occurs even faster. In dogs, it has been shown that classically conditioned changes in heart rate extinguish within 10 trials, and that substantial extinction takes place after the first non-reinforced trial (Church & Black, 1958).

If it is assumed that fear or anxiety is the conditioned response in avoidance learning, then this response should disappear when it is no longer reinforced, which it does. After several non-reinforced trials, the animal seems to be making the avoidance response without showing any signs of anxiety. Consequently, if the anxiety response has been extinguished, then it cannot be argued that the animal is reinforced for avoidance by feeling less anxious because it is not anxious in the first place.

Avoidance learning applied to therapy

Despite the unsatisfactory nature of Mowrer's explanation of avoidance learning, the strong resistance of avoidance responses to extinction suggested that behaviour learned in this way should be more persistent than that resulting from classical conditioning. Although alcoholism has been treated with aversive classical conditioning (Lemere & Voegtlin, 1950), a method based on avoidance learning should be more effective since avoidance learning has been shown to be more impervious to extinction than classical conditioning alone.

Such an approach, called *anticipatory avoidance aversion therapy*, was developed by Feldman and MacCulloch (1965) to treat homosexual behaviour in men. Before then, there had been very few reports of aversion therapy being used to treat homosexuality. In one of the first references to this treatment, electric shocks were given to a patient while he indulged in sexually attractive fantasies (Max, 1935). The largest study conducted before that time was based on 67 patients, who in the first phase of their treatment were made to feel sick to slides of men. In the second phase, they were given testosterone and then shown films of women (Freund, 1960). However, of the 47 patients who were followed up three years after treatment had ended, only 26 per cent showed some signs of heterosexual behaviour. These 12 improved patients were followed up two years later when only 6 reported a complete lack of homosexual behaviour. Consequently, straightforward aversion therapy did not appear to be a very promising technique for the treatment of male homosexuality.

Anticipatory avoidance aversion therapy consists of presenting the patient with pictures (or films) of men. The patient is told that he will be shown a picture of a man and that several seconds later he might receive an unpleasant electric shock. At any time he wishes, he can turn off the picture with a switch, which will also stop the shock. It is made clear to him, however, that he should leave the picture on for as long as he finds it sexually attractive. The patient is successively shown pictures of increasingly attractive men (as previously rated by him) and the level of shock is raised during each presentation until he switches it off. On some of the trials, he is shown a picture of an attractive woman after turning off the picture of the man so that he learns to associate the relief of pain with attractive women. The women in the pictures gradually become less attractive so that he does not learn to associate the absence of shock with just attractive women.

This procedure is similar to that of avoidance learning in that first the neutral stimulus of men is paired with the unconditioned stimulus of shock and second the avoidance response of not looking at men is reinforced by the absence of shock. In addition, the absence of shock is associated with pictures of women.

$$
\begin{array}{cccc}
\text{Men} & + & \text{Shock} & \to & \text{Avoidance} \\
\text{(N/CS)} & & \text{(UCS)} & & \text{(U/CR)}
\end{array}
$$

$$
\begin{array}{ccccc}
\text{Men} & \to & \text{Avoidance} & \to & \text{Loss of pain} \\
\text{(S}^D) & & \text{(R)} & & \text{(S}^R)
\end{array}
$$

Since avoidance responses have been found to be highly resistant to extinction, this method should be more effective in treating homosexuality than simple classical conditioning aversion therapy of associating pictures of men with shock.

A couple of studies have compared the effectiveness of anticipatory avoidance aversion therapy, aversion therapy and a third procedure in treating homosexuality in men mainly (apart from two women). In the first study, 30 patients were randomly assigned to one of three treatments, each consisting of 24 sessions (Feldman & MacCulloch, 1971). The first procedure was anticipatory avoidance aversion therapy as previously described. The second method was classical conditioning aversion therapy in which shortly after a picture of a man was displayed, the patient received an electric shock. Following this, a picture of a female was shown. The third treatment was a form of psychotherapy in which the patients' difficulties were explored and discussed.

Although the authors claim that the two forms of aversion therapy were superior to psychotherapy, this interpretation is difficult to accept for several reasons. Firstly, the results presented suggest that these differences were not statistically significant. Secondly, only one measure of improvement was used and that was the patients' self-rating of homo- and heterosexual interest. Thirdly, the statistical analyses of the data are less than ideal in that the pretreatment means for this measure are not given so that it is not possible to check whether the patients in the three treatments were comparable in terms of their sexual preferences before treatment began. And fourthly, since there was no control group of patients who were not treated, it is not possible to tell whether the improvement that occurred in all three groups was greater than would have happened without any treatment. Consequently, a more circumspect interpretation of this study would be that the three treatments did not differ in terms of their effectiveness.

In the second study, 46 patients were randomly assigned to one of three treatments (McConaghy & Barr, 1973). The first two procedures were the same as those in the previous investigation, while the third was backward classical conditioning in which the patient received the shock before the slide of the man was shown. The authors, citing Pavlov (1927), claim that backward conditioning should produce little classical conditioning, although subsequent investigators have obtained it, particularly in humans (Levey & Martin, 1975). Patients received 14 sessions of treatment within five days and six booster sessions over the next six months. The effectiveness of treatment was tested in patients by measuring change in the volume of the penis to photographs of men and women and in self-reports of heterosexual and homosexual desires and behaviours. Although details of the statistical tests were not given, no significant differences in improvement between the three treatments were reported.

Two studies have also investigated the effectiveness of anticipatory avoidance therapy in treating alcoholism. The first study found it to be unsuccessful in the treatment of four patients (MacCulloch *et al.*, 1966), while the second study claimed it to be more effective than three control conditions (Vogler *et al.*, 1970). However, the latter conclusion can be seriously questioned on three grounds. Firstly, the attrition rate amongst patients receiving anticipatory avoidance aversion therapy seems to have been considerably higher than that in the other three control conditions. If this high attrition rate was due to the therapy itself, then this would indicate that the treatment may have been less acceptable to patients. Secondly, no evidence is presented to show that the problems of the patients in the four groups were equivalent before treatment began. And thirdly, the comparisons between conditions may have been confounded by grouping together the patients in the three control conditions and comparing them with those in the other two treatments.

The results of these studies suggest, that contrary to expectations derived from laboratory demonstrations of classical conditioning and avoidance learning, there were no differences in the efficacy of classical conditioning and anticipatory avoidance aversion therapy. One implication of these findings is that the effectiveness of these methods does not seem to depend on the kind of classical conditioning shown by animals in the laboratory. This interpretation is strengthened by the observation previously discussed that aversion therapy does not generally lead to fearful reactions (Marks & Gelder, 1967; Hallam *et al.*, 1972).

Flooding and implosion

The observation that avoidance learning in animals can be readily extinguished by preventing them from leaving the compartment in which they were originally shocked (Page & Hall, 1953; Polin, 1959) has given rise to another behavioural treatment called *flooding* (Rachman, 1966).

The essence of this method is to expose the patient to the situation of which they are frightened and ask them to fully concentrate on their feelings of fear. Exposure can be carried out either *in vivo* (i.e. in real life) or *in imagination*.

The earliest report of a patient being given flooding *in vivo* seems to have been made by an unnamed physician who treated a young woman with a phobia of being driven along unfamiliar roads by ordering her to be taken by car to his New York office (Crafts *et al.*, 1938). Although she was initially very frightened, her fear had disappeared on her way home. The first case of flooding in imagination appeared many years later when a patient, frightened of taking exams, was made to imagine for 20–30 minutes at a time the terrible events that might happen to him if he failed (such as his wife and mother crying) until he no longer felt afraid (Malleson, 1959). After a few days of this treatment, the patient overcame his fear and passed his exams.

Someone with a fear of speaking in public may be asked to imagine being in the following kind of scenario during a session of flooding.

> You are sitting at the the back of a large hall, which is full of people you don't know. The lecture has come to an end and there is still time for a few questions. There is an awkward silence in which no one seems prepared to ask anything. The speaker is beginning to look embarrassed while the audience is coughing nervously and shuffling about. You've got a question you want to ask, but you are too nervous to do so. Your heart is thumping away, your mouth is completely dry and you are having difficulty in swallowing. You raise your hand, showing that you want to ask a question. The speaker looks startled but beckons you to ask it. Half the audience turns round to look at who is going to ask something. You begin to go red. Your cheeks feel hot and flushed. As you stand up, your hands and knees start to tremble vigorously. Your legs feel weak. Suddenly, your mind goes completely blank. You've forgotten what it is that you wanted to ask. You begin to mention this while people around you start to titter. The speaker can't hear what you're saying and asks you to repeat the question. Someone in the audience shouts out you can't recall it. Almost everyone is looking at you now and roaring with laughter. You feel terribly embarrassed and try to scramble out of your seat and the hall as quickly as possible. As you do so, your coat gets caught on the armrest and you hear it tear as you struggle to get away.

The patient and therapist will construct together the scenes to be used in flooding so that they are most relevant to the patient's fears and evoke the greatest anxiety. The patient will imagine being in these situations until they no longer feel anxious, at which time they will then move on to another scenario.

Although the two terms are often used interchangeably, *implosion* (or implosive therapy) should be distinguished from flooding since the former word was originally employed to describe a method based on both avoidance learning and psychodynamic theory (Stampfl & Levis, 1967, 1973). Consequently, this distinction will be maintained here. According to the theory underlying implosion, patients are usually only initially aware of stimuli which are the least threatening. A woman, for example, with a compulsion to check if the radio has been turned off, will only feel less anxious if she has been able to verify this a number of times.

The compulsion to do this is like an avoidance response. The radio is the cue to take the avoiding action of making sure it is switched off.

$$S^D \quad \rightarrow \quad R \quad \rightarrow \quad S^R$$
$$\text{(radio)} \qquad \text{(check)} \qquad \text{(less anxiety)}$$

By reducing her anxiety in this way, the patient is less likely to become aware of the other stimuli which are associated with this compulsion. Consequently, in implosion, the patient might be asked what would happen if the radio was left on, to which she may reply the radio will short circuit and catch fire. The therapist might then ask her to imagine a scene where this happened and where the whole house burned down. When doing this, she might hear her father's voice calling her name. Now it could be the case that she associates her father's voice with the radio being left on because her father has told her off and punished her for such actions as leaving radios on. In other words, her compulsion to check whether the radio is on is related to her fear of her father, which she manages to control by checking the radio. Implosion theorists believe that compulsions like these are associated with a number of cues, many of which the patient is unaware. Ultimately, the patient's anxiety is related to various psychodynamic themes such as aggression, death, injury, rejection, loss of control and sex, which need to be exposed.

According to avoidance learning theory, anxiety is shown when the avoidance response is prevented from being made. Consequently, it might be surmised that patients who do not experience strong anxiety when undergoing either flooding or implosion are not confronting the situations most closely associated with their fears. If this is the case, then treatment should be less effective for patients who appear to be less anxious when confronting their fears. A number of studies, however, have found no relationship between the amount of anxiety experienced during treatment and the degree of improvement shown (Marks *et al.*, 1971; Watson & Marks, 1971; Boudewyns & Wilson, 1972; Hafner & Marks, 1976).

The effects of anxiety on outcome cannot be investigated by simply correlating anxiety during treatment with improvement since patients who are more seriously disturbed may also feel more anxious and so be less likely to improve. In other words, it is necessary to control for the patient's initial level of anxiety when examining these correlations.

However, none of these studies did this. A more appropriate method for determining the effects of anxiety is to conduct a true experiment (Campbell & Stanley, 1963) in which patients are assigned to two treatments at random so there is less chance of individuals in one group differing in any particular way from those in the other. The only difference between the two groups will be that patients in one treatment will be made to feel more anxious than those in the other, so that if feeling anxious is necessary for flooding, then the more anxious patients should be expected to show greater improvement.

The few studies employing this design have found no differences in outcome between the two procedures, implying that feeling anxious is not essential for effective flooding (Everaerd et al., 1973; Emmelkamp, 1974; Hafner & Marks, 1976). For example, one investigation compared the effectiveness of four treatments for agoraphobia (Emmelkamp, 1974). One method consisted of flooding, a second involved a procedure called 'self observation' in which the patient travels as far as possible without feeling anxious, a third contained both flooding and self observation, while the fourth was a waiting-list control group in which patients were told they could not be treated then but would have to wait for treatment.

The effects of the four conditions were measured in various ways, including how much time the patients stayed outside. Patients receiving the three treatments demonstrated significant improvement on a number of measures, while those on the waiting-list showed no improvement. There were no differences in outcome between flooding and self observation but the combined treatment tended to be more effective than either treatment on its own. For instance, the increase in time spent outside was zero for the waiting-list group, 45 minutes for the self observation condition, 47 minutes for the flooding condition, and 65 minutes for the combined treatment. Consequently, the results of this study and those of others suggest that feeling anxious need not be a requisite part of flooding.

While it may be more convenient to treat patients with flooding *in imagination*, it might be thought that flooding *in vivo* would be a more effective method since the patient would be exposed to the situation they were frightened of in real life. Various studies have evaluated both procedures and generally suggested that flooding *in vivo* is more effective (Crowe *et al.*, 1972; Gelder *et al.*, 1973; Stern & Marks, 1973; Watson *et al.*, 1973; Emmelkamp & Wessels, 1975).

One investigation, for example, compared the effects of flooding in imagination, flooding *in vivo*, and a combination of the two methods in treating agoraphobia (Emmelkamp & Wessels, 1975). Patients receiving either flooding *in vivo* or the combined treatment showed greater improvement on more of the outcome measures than those undergoing flooding in imagination. In general, flooding *in vivo* was the most effective method, followed by the combined procedures, and then flooding *in imagination*. The improvement shown can be most concretely illustrated by the increase in time patients remained outside without feeling tense after six sessions of treatment, which was 49 minutes for flooding *in vivo*, 29 minutes for the combined procedure, and 6 minutes for flooding *in imagination*.

One exception to the finding that flooding *in vivo* is superior to flooding *in imagination* is a study by Mathews *et al.* (1976), who also compared the efficacy of the three treatments of flooding *in vivo, in imagination* and combined. After eight sessions there were no significant differences between the three treatments on various measures, although patients in all three groups had significantly improved since the start of treatment. Two differences between previous studies and this one, which may have contributed to the conflicting findings, were that in this study patients received more sessions and these were restricted to one per week. Consequently, it is possible that flooding *in vivo* is more effective when sessions are concentrated within a shorter period and/or after fewer sessions.

If flooding works solely by extinguishing the avoidance response to an unpleasant situation, then imagining being in situations which are naturally frightening, such as burning to death or drowning, should not be expected to reduce phobias. Yet, when Watson and Marks (1971) compared flooding to such scenes with phobic ones in patients, they found that although significant improvement occurred in both treatments, there was no difference between them. It is possible that the effectiveness of these two treatments is brought about in different ways, although such an approach to explaining these results is less parsimonious than one which can account for the outcome of both methods. As we have seen when discussing the relative successfulness of classical conditioning and anticipatory avoidance aversion therapy, two apparently different therapeutic techniques may produce similar results. Since, as we shall discover, such findings are not uncommon when comparing different methods, it may be more appropriate to postpone a discussion of this important issue until later in the book.

Reciprocal inhibition theory

·An alternative treatment to flooding, which appears to be more widely used and studied, emerged from Wolpe's (1954, 1958, 1982) reciprocal inhibition theory of neuroses. Wolpe (1982) formally defines neurotic behaviour as 'a persistent unadaptive habit that has been acquired by learning in an anxiety-generating situation (or a succession of such situations) and in which anxiety is usually the central component' (pp. 9–10), where anxiety is believed to be physiologically mediated by the autonomic nervous system (p. 23).

Wolpe (1952) decided to test this idea in cats by trying to condition them to be frightened of eating in a particular situation. For this behaviour to be described as neurotic, it should also be unadaptive (in the sense that it prevented the cat from fulfilling its needs) and to persist when the original conditions no longer held. Consequently, if the cats refused to eat when hungry and when they were no longer shocked, then this behaviour could be called neurotic since it was unadaptive and persistent.

His study involved two experimental conditions. In one of them, cats were given 5–10 uncomfortable electric shocks in a cage after an auditory signal had been presented. In the other condition, cats were first taught to approach a food box in the cage when the auditory signal was played. After they had been trained to do this, they were shocked just before they were about to eat the food. The two conditions were run to see whether neurotic behaviour resulted either from simply receiving shock or from conflict between two incompatible behaviours (i.e. wanting to eat and to move away at the same time) as had been suggested by Masserman (1943).

Since both these conditions produced very similar behaviour in the cats, conflict does not seem to be necessary for bringing about neurotic behaviour and the difference between the two conditions can be ignored. When the cats were shocked, they displayed signs of fear such as trembling, hissing, rapid breathing and erect hair, which they later showed whenever they were put into the cage in which they had been shocked or when they heard the auditory signal. In other words, they had learned to associate the cage and the auditory signal with being shocked. Some of the cats showed their fear in ways which were unique to themselves. For example, one cat always breathed very rapidly, another invariably urinated, a third trembled continuously, while a fourth vigorously jerked its shoulders every few seconds.

The cats also refused to eat in the cage, even when they had not eaten for 2–3 days. Furthermore, their fear generalized to similar situations. Many of the cats refused to eat food outside the cage in rooms which looked similar to the one in which they had been shocked and would stop eating as soon as they heard the auditory signal. Although Wolpe does not give exact details as to how long their fear persisted, he does report that in 3 of the 12 cats it lasted for at least 6 months.

Having established what he believed was neurotic behaviour in his cats, Wolpe then tried to teach them to unlearn this behaviour. One way of breaking these neurotic habits would be to encourage the cats to engage in behaviour which would inhibit their anxiety and so weaken the association between anxiety and the situation which aroused it. This idea was called the *principle of reciprocal inhibition*, and was based on the observation made by the neurologist Sherrington (1906) that if the muscles which extended a limb were electrically stimulated, then the muscles which flexed it were inhibited, and vice versa. Gellhorn (1967) later suggested that the same principle of reciprocal innervation may hold for the autonomic nervous system. For example, an autonomic response such as anxiety may inhibit relaxation, while relaxation may suppress anxiety.

Wolpe noted that the cats' anxiety seemed to be inhibiting eating and so thought that eating in turn may prevent the cats from becoming anxious. Two approaches were tried to encourage the cats to eat in the cage in which they were originally shocked. Initially, attempts were made to feed the cats inside the cage. For three of them, this was done by pushing them towards some food within the cage. Although very anxious at first, they did eventually eat and after doing this a number of times, they seemed much less anxious. The other nine cats were fed by hand inside the cage because it was thought that since these cats were usually fed manually they may have learned to associate hands with food. In the end, four of the cats were coaxed to eat in this way and seemed much less anxious as a result.

Five of them, however, were still not eating inside the cage and so these cats were to be encouraged to eat outside it. Wolpe discovered that not only were these animals frightened of being put in the cage, but they were also scared of the room which housed the cage and other rooms which were similar to it.

Consequently, these cats were initially fed in a room dissimilar to the one in which the cage stood and were then gradually enticed to eat in rooms more and more similar to the original room until they were eventually eating in it. Once this happened, they were fed closer and closer to the cage until they were eating in the cage itself. By using this gradual approach, Wolpe found that he could retrain all his cats to eat inside the cage.

However, if at this stage the auditory signal which had previously preceded the shock was presented once again, the cats became very anxious and would not eat in either the cage or the experimental room. Wolpe then successfully implemented two methods to teach the cats to eat in the presence of the signal. The first approach involved feeding the cats at a distance where they would eat when the signal was being played and then to gradually reduce that distance. The second procedure was to feed the cats and shortly afterwards present the signal, very briefly at first but for longer periods subsequently. As a result of this study, Wolpe believed that the way to treat human neuroses was to gradually expose patients to situations which frightened them, while encouraging them to engage in behaviour which would inhibit the anxiety these situations evoked. He called this method of treatment *reciprocal inhibition therapy*.

Although Wolpe had demonstrated that neurotic behaviour in cats could result from experiencing a few very unpleasant events, he believed that most human neuroses did not develop in this way (Wolpe, 1958). The most common way in which anxiety becomes associated with certain situations is either through conflict which generates anxiety or through a series of mildly unpleasant events which cause anxiety to accumulate.

Reciprocal inhibition therapy

Wolpe has employed three responses mainly to inhibit anxiety. Sexual excitement is the most appropriate behaviour to use when a patient suffers from sexual anxiety. For example, a man may be unable to obtain an erection because anxiety has become associated with sexual situations. The anxiety inhibits sexual arousal. To overcome this fear, the man must be encouraged to become sexually excited in situations which are the least threatening to him. Once he is able to do this, he then tries to become sexually aroused in circumstances which evoke greater anxiety but always ensuring that this fear can be controlled by his sexual excitement.

The response of assertiveness is usually chosen to help those who are anxious about expressing their own feelings towards others. For instance, someone may be afraid to express an opinion which is different from those held by others because they are frightened of being rejected. When encouraging assertiveness, it is necessary that patients should realize that their own interests are as important as those of other people. Patients may be asked to give examples of situations in which their feelings were hurt and to say how they would have liked to have behaved. The therapist may then role play these interactions with patients so that they can practise being more assertive.

Wolpe first used assertiveness to inhibit anxiety after reading a book called *Conditioned Reflex Therapy* by Salter (1949) who argued that people should be encouraged to express themselves. However, he found that this response was not appropriate for fears of non-social situations, such as open spaces, heights or blood. Shortly after realizing this, he came across a book entitled *Progressive Relaxation* by Jacobson (1938) who advocated the use of relaxation to help cope with stress. This response was convenient for inhibiting anxiety since it could be used in a variety of situations. Initially patients were gradually exposed to the circumstances which made them anxious, but because this was not always easy to arrange, Wolpe explored the possibility of asking patients to imagine being in these situations. As long as these imaginary scenes did not arouse too much anxiety, patients could remain relaxed which was more likely to be ensured by starting off with situations that did not evoke too much anxiety and then gradually progressing to those that were most threatening.

This therapeutic procedure developed into *systematic desensitization*, which consists of four steps. The first step entails learning to think of anxiety in terms of *subjective units of disturbance* or *suds*, usually along a

100-point scale in which 100 represents the most anxiety ever felt or imaginable while zero reflects the state of utmost calm. This scale is used to assess anxiety in the subsequent three steps. The second step is *relaxation training* which involves teaching patients to relax as completely as possible. Since many patients find it difficult to relax, this training takes about six sessions to complete together with half an hour of daily practice at home. The exact procedure for relaxation training varies from therapist to therapist, but essentially entails alternately tensing and relaxing the different sets of muscles in the body so that these two states can be readily discriminated and controlled.

The third step is usually introduced in the same session as relaxation training and consists of constructing *anxiety hierarchies* of the major situations or themes of which the patient is frightened. A patient may, for example, be afraid of a number of different things such as heights, injured bodies and speaking in public. For each separate fear anxiety hierarchies will be developed consisting of a series or hierarchy of scenes which become progressively more threatening. Scenes within each hierarchy ideally should provoke increases of anxiety of 5 to 10 suds, ranging from a low degree of anxiety (i.e. 5–10 suds) to a high one (i.e. 95–100 suds). In other words, an anxiety hierarchy should contain 10–20 situations which evoke regularly increasing increments of anxiety. For example, such a hierarchy for someone with a fear of heights may begin by imagining standing on the first floor near a window and end by visualizing looking down from the window of the tenth floor.

The fourth step consists of *desensitization proper* in which the patient progressively imagines being in each of the scenes of a hierarchy while trying to remain relaxed. The patient starts off with the scene which brings about the least anxiety and does not move on to the next scene in the hierarchy until they are able to visualize the first one without feeling any anxiety. In this way, they proceed up the hierarchy until finally they are imagining being in the situation which initially terrified them the most.

Wolpe believes that all neurotic habits are unlearned through the process of reciprocal inhibition. Where these habits are not very strong, it may not be necessary to apply reciprocal inhibition very systematically in order to change them. For example, these less intense fears may disappear without professional therapeutic help if the person naturally learns to inhibit their anxiety in some way, such as by being encouraged and reassured to gradually confront situations of which they are afraid. Similarly, in forms of psychotherapy where reciprocal inhibition is neither explicitly recognized nor systematically practised, the patients' anxiety about certain problems may be inhibited by, say, the attraction they feel for the therapist. However, where the habit is well learned or the anxiety is very strong, patients will need to be specifically taught to inhibit their anxiety by formal reciprocal inhibition procedures. These procedures can be used not only for anxiety but also for other emotional problems, such as jealousy and neurotic depression, which may result from anxiety.

Empirical evaluation of systematic desensitization

The principle of reciprocal inhibition seems to imply that flooding should only be effective in cases where patients feel relaxed during the procedure. However, as already discussed, patients who were encouraged to feel anxious showed as much improvement as those who were relaxed, indicating that relaxation may not be necessary for therapeutic change. Moreover, in one study both methods proved to be more efficacious than no treatment which suggests that these techniques were effective to some extent (Emmelkamp, 1974). However, as the effectiveness of these two methods were not compared with groups of patients receiving either an equal amount of attention or an alternative form of therapy, it is not possible to ascertain whether these techniques produced greater improvement than any other form of treatment. Because this is an important point, it will be elaborated later.

None the less, if therapeutic improvement depends more on the inhibition of anxiety by an antagonistic response (reciprocal inhibition) than simple exposure to situations associated with anxiety (response prevention), then systematic desensitization should be more effective than flooding. However, if simple exposure is the means by which therapeutic gain takes place, then although both procedures should work because they expose patients to situations which were originally associated with anxiety, systematic desensitization should be slower than flooding since it is carried out much more gradually. Consequently, the relative effectiveness of systematic desensitization and flooding, like that of anticipatory avoidance and classically conditioned aversion therapy, is of potentially great theoretical interest as it may throw light on the way in which therapeutic improvement occurs.

At least five studies have compared the clinical benefits of these two methods in patients seeking therapy for phobias (Hussain, 1971; Marks *et al.*, 1971; Crowe *et al.*, 1972; Gelder *et al.*, 1973; Shaw, 1979). Generally, there were no significant differences in outcome between these two treatments. The failure to find systematic desensitization to be more effective than flooding may have been due to patients receiving insufficient relaxation training. Wolpe (1982) has suggested that part of the first six sessions in therapy should be devoted to relaxation training and that during this time patients should also practise relaxing for half an hour daily. No information was presented on the amount of relaxation training provided in one of the studies (Hussain, 1971), only one session was given in another study (Marks *et al.*, 1971) and only three sessions were provided in the remaining three studies (Crowe *et al.*, 1972; Gelder *et al.*, 1973; Shaw, 1979).

How much relaxation training is required for effective systematic desensitization, or indeed whether it is necessary at all, is not really known. One investigation comparing desensitization with and without relaxation training gave no details of the amount of relaxation training provided (Gillan & Rachman, 1974), while two others only provided one and two sessions respectively (Agras *et al.*, 1971; Benjamin *et al.*, 1972). The results of these three studies indicated that systematic desensitization with relaxation was not superior to desensitization without relaxation, although the lack of information about relaxation training in one study and only two sessions of it in the other rule them out as appropriate tests of the role of relaxation training in systematic desensitization.

Two studies have investigated the physiological effects of at least six sessions of relaxation training. One of these reported that in treating community volunteers experiencing three or more tension headaches a week, eight twice-weekly relaxation sessions produced significantly lower muscle tension in the front muscles of the head than four weekly sessions in which a placebo was given which was said to be an effective muscle relaxant (Cox *et al.*, 1975). Since the number of sessions for the two treatments was not the same, the difference in outcome may have been due to the greater number of sessions received rather than the relaxation training. The other investigation found that six weekly sessions of relaxation training did not produce greater levels of physiological relaxation than the same number of discussion sessions in patients with phobias (Mathews & Gelder, 1969). Consequently, stronger evidence is required to show that six or more sessions of relaxation training are necessary for physiological relaxation to occur.

A further difficulty in interpreting the results of these studies comparing desensitization with flooding is that in only one of them were these two methods compared with a *placebo* or *non-specific* control condition (Gelder *et al.*, 1973). The lack of such a control condition means it is not possible to ascertain in the other four studies whether these two methods were more effective than a placebo treatment. As this is an important point, it will be necessary to discuss it in more detail. It has long been acknowledged in medicine that the effects of a treatment may be due to the faith patients have in it (Shapiro, 1960). In studies evaluating the efficacy of drugs, inert substances (similar in taste and appearance to the drug being investigated and called *placebos*) have been used to assess these psychological effects (Rivers, 1908). In fact, it has been recognized that not only the person receiving the treatment should be unaware of, or 'blind' to, the nature of the substance, but also the individual administering it should not know whether the drug or the placebo was being given (Gold, 1946). This methodological innovation is known as the 'double blind' procedure. Since placebo effects have sometimes been found to be quite substantial, it has been suggested that placebo controls should be employed in studies evaluating the effectiveness of psychotherapy to assess the role of factors such as the amount of contact patients receive and their faith in the therapist and treatment (Rosenthal & Frank, 1956). The need to control for these effects has, however, been controversial (O'Leary & Borkovec, 1978; Wilkins, 1984; Parloff, 1986) and there is no consensus on what form these controls should take.

In the placebo or non-specific control condition of the study by Gelder *et al.* (1973) comparing systematic desensitization with flooding, patients were asked to free associate to images they found frightening and to describe the thoughts, feelings and other images this procedure aroused in them. They were told that this activity would lead to greater self-understanding which would help them overcome their fears. In general, there were not many statistically significant differences between the three treatments in terms of the 54 measures used to assess their effectiveness, suggesting that these two methods may not be much better than a placebo control treatment. Overall, flooding was slightly more effective than desensitization, which in turn was somewhat more effective than the non-specific control condition. Flooding was superior to desensitization and the control on three and seven of the measures respectively, while desensitization was better than the control on only four measures. Patients receiving flooding rated their ideal self as more potent and their self as both more active and potent than those having desensitization.

Compared to the controls, desensitization patients reported being frightened of fewer agoraphobic and social situations and expected to feel less anxious and to show fewer anxiety symptoms in the situation they considered most difficult prior to treatment. Finally, compared to the controls, the main phobia of the flooding patients was assessed by an independent psychiatrist as less severe and patients rated themselves more positively on the following six measures: (1) overall improvement; (2) depression; (3) progress shown in a real-life situation; (4) anxiety felt while imagining being in the situation thought to be most difficult before treatment; and (5) the anxiety and (6) number of anxiety symptoms expected in this situation.

However, the conclusiveness of these findings is limited by three potential shortcomings of the study. Firstly, when controlling for placebo effects in drug studies, it is necessary to institute a 'double blind' procedure in which neither the person administering the treatment nor taking it know if it is the drug or the placebo. Because of the nature of the placebo control used in this study, it was not possible for the therapist to be unaware of what it was. Consequently, the therapist in the placebo condition may have conveyed to the patient the impression that this treatment was less effective. To check if this occurred, patients should have been asked how much they expected to improve. As this was not done, it is possible that the slightly poorer outcome for the placebo control condition was due to the patients' lower expectancy for improvement.

On the other hand, the difference between the placebo control condition and the other two treatments may have been lessened by the fact that in the last four sessions patients in all three groups practised *in vivo* exposure. If *in vivo* exposure is the most important therapeutic component in flooding and desensitization, then since this feature was common to all three conditions, it may have reduced the differences in outcome between them. Finally, no check was carried out to see if the three treatments were practised as specified.

One problem, then, in trying to deliver a psychological version of a placebo treatment is the difficulty of keeping the therapists administering it unaware of its nature. A further problem is that a treatment considered to be ineffective by some therapists may be thought to be potentially effective by others. An interesting case in point is a study in which implosion was compared with the usual hospital treatment and a procedure called 'desensitization therapy using free association' (Boudewyns & Wilson, 1972) which was similar in many respects to the placebo control condition in the previous study. This is also one of the few clinical studies of the effectiveness of implosive therapy as developed by Stampfl and Levis (1967). In the desensitization procedure patients were trained to use muscle relaxation and self-hypnosis while visualizing the objects of their fears and to describe to the therapist whatever came to mind. Outcome was mainly measured with two patient questionnaires. Although there was a tendency for patients receiving implosion to do better than those in the other two conditions, few of the differences were statistically significant.

Lick (1975) also found no differences between systematic desensitization and two placebo or pseudotherapy control conditions in the treatment of women with snake or spider phobias and who were recruited via newspaper advertisements from the community. Before treatment, these subjects would not go nearer than about six feet towards these animals when the animals were kept in a container. In the two placebo conditions subjects were told they would be shown slides which would be presented too quickly to see what was on them but which were pictures of their phobia. If these pictures produced a physiological response, they would receive a mild electric shock. In reality, flashes of light were presented and subjects were given decreasing numbers of shocks throughout the eight sessions. In the placebo feedback condition, subjects were shown a printout of their responses after each session and told how their responses had become less marked over time, implying that they had improved. In the other placebo condition, no such feedback was given. There was also a waiting-list control condition in which subjects were told that they would be treated in several months' time when therapists became available.

After eight sessions there were no significant differences between the three treatment groups in terms of how close they approached a tarantula or three-foot boa constrictor and their pulse rate while waiting to do so, although all three were significantly more effective than the waiting-list control condition. While only one session of relaxation training was given and subjects were not clinical patients, this generally well-designed study suggests that systematic desensitization may be no more effective than placebo controls. The three treatments were seen by subjects as being roughly equivalent in terms of how effective they were expected to be. However, there was no relationship between their expectations about the effectiveness of treatment after the first session and their improvement following eight sessions, which suggests that their initial expectations did not influence the subsequent outcome. The failure to find a significant association may have been due to basing the correlations on the smaller number of subjects within each treatment rather than the whole sample.

The finding that hypnosis was as effective as systematic desensitization implies that simply telling patients that their fears may gradually disappear may be an effective method (Marks *et al.*, 1968). Hypnosis involved the usual suggestions that the patient would feel relaxed and be able to lift their arm as well as the idea that their fears would fade away. Although there was no placebo control condition and no indication of the number of relaxation sessions, there were few significant differences in outcome between the two treatments.

There is also some evidence to question whether relevant anxiety hierarchies are necessary for effective systematic desensitization. Goldfried and Goldfried (1977) compared the effects of three methods in the treatment of people with anxiety about speaking in public who were recruited via newspapers from the community. There were two systematic desensitization treatments. Although both included five sessions of relaxation training, desensitization proper was begun in the second session. In one treatment the anxiety hierarchy consisted of scenes concerned with public speaking anxiety, while in the other they were concerned with fears of flying which were irrelevant to their phobia. Subjects in this condition were told that they would be taught to cope with anxiety generally, which would begin with situations unrelated to public speaking but which would be eventually applied to it. In the third condition subjects were asked to concentrate on their feelings while imagining being in situations concerned with public speaking which were the same as those in the first desensitization group. Although there was a slight tendency for desensitization with relevant hierarchies to show significant improvement over the seven sessions on more of the various measures than the other two conditions, there were no significant differences between the three treatments at the end of treatment.

Further studies which have compared the effectiveness of systematic desensitization with other psychotherapeutic methods will be mentioned in subsequent chapters when the relevant techniques have been described.

However, some investigations have evaluated the efficacy of systematic desensitization against waiting-list or placebo-control conditions and reported conflicting results. For example, in the treatment of erectile impotence, Auerbach and Kilmann (1977) found group systematic desensitization to be more effective than a placebo control consisting of relaxation training, while Kockott *et al.* (1975) obtained no difference between systematic desensitization and either a waiting-list control or routine therapy consisting of medication and general advice.

Summary

Avoidance learning theory has been put forward to explain why phobias sometimes endure. Although this explanation is unsatisfactory partly because classically conditioned responses readily extinguish in the repeated absence of the unconditioned stimulus, the study of avoidance learning has led to the development of the behavioural techniques of anticipatory avoidance aversion therapy and flooding (and the similar procedure of implosion). While avoidant responses in animals have been found to be highly resistant to extinction, anticipatory avoidance aversion therapy appears to be no more effective than classical conditioning aversion therapy in treating disorders such as alcoholism and homosexuality. Gradual exposure as reflected in systematic desensitization has been advocated by Wolpe as a more effective method for reducing avoidant and phobic behaviour than the direct exposure characteristic of flooding. Few differences in the effectiveness of these two methods have been reported in clinical studies which have compared them. Little is known of what it is about these two techniques which might make them effective.

5

Biobehavioural approach

The learning or behavioural approach to personality is often interpreted as implying that the behaviour shown by an individual is solely a function of what has been previously acquired through reinforcement. However, early on in the development of this approach, classical conditioning theorists in particular intimated that learning was affected by constitutional or temperamental differences. Watson and Rayner (1920), for example, suggested that phobias would be more likely to persist in 'constitutionally inferior' individuals, while Pavlov (1927) observed that dogs with melancholic temperaments conditioned more quickly than those with sanguine ones. The idea that personality itself is constitutionally determined has a long history dating back to the Roman physician Galen who in the 2nd century AD suggested that temperamental differences may be due to the influence of bodily fluids. One of the most influential personality theories within this tradition today is undoubtedly Eysenck's biobehavioural approach (Eysenck & Eysenck, 1985).

Eysenck's biobehavioural theory

Eysenck (1970a) has defined personality rather broadly as the 'more or less stable and enduring organization of a person's character, temperament, intellect, and physique, which determines his unique adjustment to the environment' (p. 2). Although temperament is not clearly differentiated from personality (Eysenck & Eysenck, 1985, p. 86), the theory seems to be primarily concerned with describing and explaining per-

Figure 5.1 An example of a normal distribution.

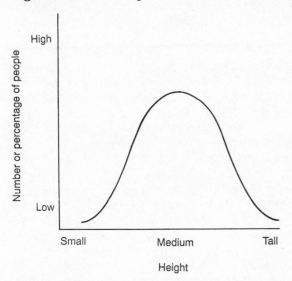

sonality in terms of temperament. Based largely on the statistical analysis of questionnaire items (Eysenck & Eysenck, 1969a), Eysenck has suggested that the major part of personality can be most parsimoniously described in terms of three fundamental characteristics or dimensions. These three dimensions have been called *extraversion, neuroticism* and *psychoticism*, while their opposite ends are referred to, respectively, as *introversion, stability,* and *impulse control.* The distinction between neuroticism and psychoticism reflects Eysenck's belief that psychological distress needs to be explained in terms of two underlying dimensions which differentiate the psychoses from the neuroses.

Individuals who show high degrees of extraversion tend to be sociable, lively, active, assertive and carefree. Those with strong levels of neuroticism have a tendency to be anxious, depressed, tense, moody and low in self-esteem, while those high on psychoticism are inclined to be aggressive, cold, egocentric and antisocial.

People vary in the extent to which they show these three characteristics, just as they do in terms of physical measures such as height or weight. For example, some people will have a high degree of neuroticism, while others will exhibit a low level of it. In fact, levels of extraversion and neuroticism, like measures of height and weight, are thought to be *normally distributed* in the population and take the form of an inverted U. An example of a normal distribution for a variable such as height is presented in Figure 5.1 where it can be seen that most people are neither very tall nor very short but are of in-between height. In the same way, the majority of individuals possess neither very high nor very low degrees of extraversion or neuroticism but show intermediate levels. In terms of extraversion, most people are ambiverts and do not show the characteristics of either extreme.

Since people do not fall into two or more very clear groups (reflecting *bimodal* or *multimodal* distributions respectively) along either of these two dimensions, it is somewhat arbitrary to designate those having more than a certain level of these qualities as belonging to a particular category. However, sometimes it is more convenient to group individuals together as being the same, even though they differ somewhat amongst themselves. For instance, people who are higher than average on extraversion may be referred to as extravert and those lower than average as introvert. Similarly, those with above average neuroticism may be called neurotic and those with below average neuroticism stable.

A person's position on any one of these dimensions is independent of their location on the other two. In other words, an individual's level of extraversion is unrelated to their degree of neuroticism or psychoticism. If we simply take the two dimensions of extraversion and neuroticism, people may be categorized as falling into one of the following four groups which Eysenck sees as corresponding to the four temperaments of Hippocrates and Galen: neurotic introvert (melancholic); neurotic extravert (choleric); stable introvert (phlegmatic); and stable extravert (sanguine).

Since people's level of neuroticism and extraversion are normally distributed, these four types of individual should be equally common. With only two levels of both neuroticism (neurotic vs stable) and extraversion (extravert vs introvert), personality can only be described in terms of four points in two-dimensional space. With three levels of each dimension, the number of types increases to nine, while with 10 degrees of each, it becomes 100. However, since these two dimensions are normally distributed, some of these types will be less frequent than others. Adding the third dimension of psychoticism will augment the number of points which can be used to depict personality. Two levels of three dimensions gives eight points in three-dimensional space, while 10 degrees of each will result in 1000 points. Although the number of individuals which can be distinguished with three 10-level dimensions is large, the ability to differentiate 10 degrees of a variable such as neuroticism and the value of doing so needs to be demonstrated.

These three dimensions are thought to have a strong hereditary component. It has been estimated that up to about 50 per cent of their variation may be genetically determined (Eaves *et al.*, 1989). These characteristics remain relatively stable over a person's lifetime and are expressed both physiologically and psychologically. These processes have been described more clearly for the longer established dimensions of extraversion and neuroticism (Eysenck, 1967) than for the more recent one of psychoticism (Eysenck & Eysenck, 1976).

Differences in extraversion are reflected physiologically in terms of the way in which the brain works. In particular, extraverts are less cortically aroused than introverts. They try to increase their level of cortical arousal by seeking further stimulation, while introverts endeavour to decrease it by avoiding additional stimulation. Psychologically, extraverts condition less well than introverts under normal conditions. Neuroticism, on the other hand, is physiologically related to the autonomic nervous system, particularly the sympathetic system which is responsible for preparing the body for action. This system is more easily activated in neurotics and once aroused tends to persist for longer than it does in stable individuals. Psychologically, neuroticism is reflected in differences in drive, with neurotics showing higher levels of drive than 'stables'. It is not yet clear what psychoticism represents physiologically and psychologically. Eysenck has tentatively suggested that physiologically it may be related to level of sex hormones, with psychotics showing higher quantities of the male hormone androgen than 'impulse controls'. Consequently, psychotics are inclined to portray more masculine characteristics than non-psychotics.

These three dimensions of personality can be used to explain psychological adjustment. People who show psychotic, psychopathic and antisocial behaviour should have higher levels of psychoticism than 'normals'. Individuals who suffer from neurotic disorders, such as anxiety, depression, phobias and obsessive–compulsiveness, should be characterized by both higher neuroticism and introversion than normals and may be categorized as being neurotic introverts. While those who experience such problems as hysteria, psychopathy, alcoholism, drug addiction, personality and sexual disorders should be high on neuroticism as well as extraversion and may be classified as being neurotic extraverts.

The disorders of neurotic introverts may be seen as resulting from overconditioning and those of neurotic extraverts as due to under-conditioning. Because neurotic introverts condition more easily, they are more likely to develop conditioned fears and anxieties. Neurotic extraverts, on the other hand, condition less readily and so are less likely to acquire the usual conditioned responses of being socialized. As a result, neurotic introverts tend to have emotional problems, while neurotic extraverts have social ones. These disparate psychological disorders require different kinds of behaviour therapy. Desensitization and flooding are the most effective treatments for the emotional difficulties of neurotic introverts, while aversion therapy is most suitable for the social problems of neurotic extraverts.

Eysenck's personality questionnaires

Having outlined Eysenck's theory of personality, it is now time to review some of the evidence relevant to it. The main method for determining and assessing the three dimensions of extraversion, neuroticism and

Table 5.1 Versions of Eysenck's questionnaires

Full title	Abbreviated title	Year	Dimensions*
Adult forms			
Maudsley Medical Questionnaire	MMQ	1952	– N – –
Maudsley Personality Inventory	MPI	1959	E N – –
Eysenck Personality Inventory	EPI	1964	E N L –
Eysenck Personality Questionnaire	EPQ	1975	E N L P
Children/junior (J) forms			
Eysenck Personality Questionnaire	JEPQ	1965	E N L –
Personality Inventory	JPI	1971	E N L P
Eysenck Personality Questionnaire	JEPQ	1975	E N L P

*N = neuroticism; E = extraversion; L = Lie scale; P = psychoticism.

psychoticism is by questionnaire. Over the years a number of different but related questionnaires have been developed to measure these three personality dimensions in both adults and children. Details of these instruments are presented in Table 5.1.

The latest version is the Eysenck Personality Questionnaire (EPQ) which in its adult form consists of 90 questions that are answered either 'Yes' or 'No' (Eysenck & Eysenck, 1975). Extraversion is measured by 21 items such as 'Are you a talkative person?' and 'Do you enjoy meeting new people?', neuroticism with 23 items such as 'Does your mood often go up and down?' and 'Do you ever feel "just miserable" for no reason?', and psychoticism with 25 questions like 'Do you enjoy hurting people you love?' and 'Do you have enemies who want to harm you?'. In addition, there is a Lie scale made up of 21 items such as 'Have you ever said anything bad or nasty about anyone?' and 'Do you always practise what you preach?'.

The Lie scale was included to try and find out if people filling in the questionnaire are answering the questions in a socially desirable way and thereby presenting an overly positive picture of themselves. There is some evidence to suggest that under normal conditions, individuals do not deliberately endeavour to portray themselves in a favourable way. The scores of children who anonymously completed a forerunner of the Junior EPQ (JEPQ) did not differ from those who were asked to sign their names and who therefore might have been expected to put themselves forward in a better light (Nias, 1972). However, when the results of the questionnaire may be used against the interests of someone, less honest answers may be expected. Candidates applying for a sought after apprentice course had higher Lie scores and lower neuroticism and psychoticism on an earlier form of the EPQ than those who had already been accepted for this course (Michaelis & Eysenck, 1971).

However, in general a high Lie score does not necessarily mean that the person is trying to present themselves favourably. Firstly, it is possible that they have a tendency to see themselves in a more positive way, even though this view may be inaccurate. In other words, they may have a false picture of themselves rather than deliberately attempting to paint such an image. Secondly, a higher Lie score may result from the form of the Lie items which are predominantly phrased in an all-or-none manner (e.g. 'Have you ever . . .' or 'Are all your . . .') in contrast to the structure of the questions assessing the three personality dimensions which tend to be stated more generally. Because the majority of items are written in this way, the Lie scale items may be interpreted in the same manner as those for the other dimensions. For example, if you generally practise what you preach, you may answer affirmatively to this question even if you do not always follow your own advice. Thirdly, a high Lie score may indicate someone with a greater degree of morality and conscientiousness than others. If this is the case, the Lie scale may constitute a fourth dimension of personality which may be more appropriately called conscientiousness, although Eysenck seems to prefer the term conformity. The evidence for viewing the Lie scale as reflecting a personality dimension will be discussed later.

To determine if the items making up the four scales of the EPQ constituted four dimensions of personality, the questionnaire (together with 11 additional items which were subsequently omitted) was given to a sample of 1796 men and 2565 women (Eysenck & Eysenck, 1976). The results were then submitted to a statistical method called *factor analysis*, which essentially groups items that are answered in a similar way. So, for example, if extraversion is a distinct personality dimension which is separate from neuroticism, then the questions which are thought to assess extraversion should be answered in a similar manner and which are unrelated to the way in which the questions assumed to be measuring neuroticism are answered. In other words, if the four scales measure four separate dimensions, then the items within each of these four scales should be grouped together.

There are a number of different methods of factor analysis which need not concern us here. However, the factors which initially emerge from an analysis can be rotated to ease their interpretation. The two most commonly used methods of rotation are *orthogonal*, in which the factors are made to be unrelated to one another, and *oblique*, in which they may be related (Bryman & Cramer, 1990). In this analysis of the EPQ, four factors were taken out and obliquely rotated. All the items of a scale (apart from one and two items of psychoticism for men and women, respectively) loaded or correlated most highly on the same factor, indicating that they were measuring the same underlying construct. For extraversion, two of the items which correlated most highly with the factor which represented it were 'Are you rather lively?' and 'Do other

Table 5.2 Correlations between the four EPQ scales for women and men

	Women			
	E	N	L	P
E		−0.14**	−0.09*	0.07
N	−0.16**			−0.15**
				0.07
L	−0.10*	−0.04		−0.19**
P	0.06	0.12**	−0.23**	
		Men		

*P < 0.05; **P < 0 .01 (two-tailed).

people think of you as being very lively?'. For neuroticism, they were 'Are you a worrier?' and 'Do you worry about awful things that might happen?'. For psychoticism, they included 'Do you think people spend too much time safeguarding their future with savings and insurances?' and 'Do you think marriage is old-fashioned and should be done away with?'. While for conscientiousness, they covered 'Were you ever greedy by helping yourself to more than your share of anything?' and 'Have you ever taken anything (even a pin or button) that belonged to someone else?'.

The relationship between the four scales were provided for a subsample of 500 women and 500 men and these are shown in Table 5.2. It can be seen from this table that some of dimensions are not independent but are significantly related to one another, although most of these correlations are small. The highest correlation for both women and men is the negative one between the Lie scale and psychoticism, which means that higher psychoticism scores tend to go with lower Lie scores. Neuroticism is also negatively related to extraversion in both sexes so that introverts tend to be neurotic. For women neuroticism is negatively correlated with the Lie score, while for men neuroticism is positively associated with psychoticism.

The distribution of the personality scores was also given and was similar for both women and men. The distribution of the scores of extraversion was negatively skewed with higher extraversion scores being more common. The neuroticism scores were more normally distributed with lower scores being slightly more common for men than for women. Psychoticism scores were strongly positively skewed with Lie scores less so, so that low scores were more common than high ones. The distribution of these personality characteristics, apart from that of neuroticism, does not appear to be clearly normal.

Few details of the group of people on which these results are based were presented, although it is clear that they were not a representative sample of the British population. However, the previous version of the EPQ, the EPI (Eysenck & Eysenck, 1965), was included, with a wide variety of other measures, in the 1984/5 Health and Lifestyle Survey which was carried out on a large, nationally representative sample of British adults (Cox *et al.*, 1987). This 57-item questionnaire, which contains the Extraversion, Neuroticism and Lie scales, was completed by a sample of 3012 women and 2475 men, together with a nine-item Framingham Type A Scale (Haynes *et al.*, 1978), the 30-item General Health Questionnaire (GHQ) (Goldberg, 1972) and a 20-item checklist of predominantly physical symptoms. The General Health Questionnaire is a measure of non-psychotic psychological distress, while the Type A Scale is thought to assess the personality of people who are most likely to suffer from coronary heart disease.

The 116 items from these questionnaires were separately factor analysed for women and men (Cramer, 1991a). The six factors, which were extracted and rotated both orthogonally and obliquely, seemed to correspond to the six variables measured by these instruments. Of the 24 neuroticism items, 18 and 20 of them, respectively, correlated most highly on the same factor for women and men; 19 and 18 of the 24 extraversion items correlated most strongly on the same factor for women and men respectively; while all 9 items of the Lie scale loaded most highly on the same factor for women and men. Two of the questions which correlated most highly with the extraversion factor were, 'Can you usually let yourself go and enjoy yourself a lot at a lively party?' and 'Can you easily get some life into a rather dull party?'. For neuroticism, these two items included 'Does your mood often go up and down?' and 'Do you often worry about things you should not have done or said?'. For the Lie scale, they were 'Are all your habits good and desirable ones?' and 'Have you ever been late for an appointment or work?'.

The relationships between the three EPI scales for women and men are shown in Table 5.3. The correlations between extraversion and neuroticism

Table 5.3 Correlations between the three EPI scales for women and men

	Women		
	E	*N*	*L*
E		0.05**	−0.15***
N	0.06**		−0.10**
L	−0.13***	−0.15***	
	Men		

**P < 0.01; ***P < 0.001 (two-tailed).

are positive and smaller than those for the previous study and are statistically significant because of the large numbers of subjects involved. The reason for these differences are not clear since both the questionnaire and the sample differ between the two studies. As the other correlations are similar in size and direction to those in the first study, it is possible that the differences are due to the sample and not the questionnaire. The distribution of scores for women and men are presented in Figure 5.2 for extraversion and in Figure 5.3 for neuroticism. These appear to be normally distributed apart for neuroticism, which tends to be slightly positively skewed. The samples are larger than those for the factor analyses and the scale correlations since less information is missing when one rather than several variables are being examined. Distributions are not shown for the Lie scale since the range of scores was very limited.

One attempt to validate the EPI involved comparing a person's description of themselves on the questionnaire with that by someone who knew them well (Gibson, 1971). There was a strong positive correlation of 0.61 between a person's extraversion score and how an acquaintance saw them in terms of that scale. In other words, people who saw

Figure 5.2 Distribution of EPI extraversion scores for women (n = 3348) and men (n = 2740).

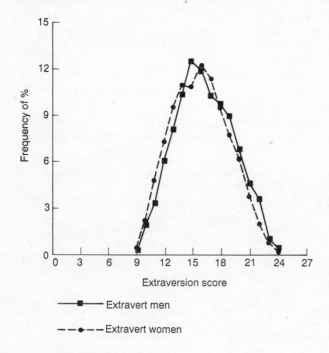

Figure 5.3 Distribution of EPI neuroticism scores for women ($n = 3363$) and men ($n = 2761$).

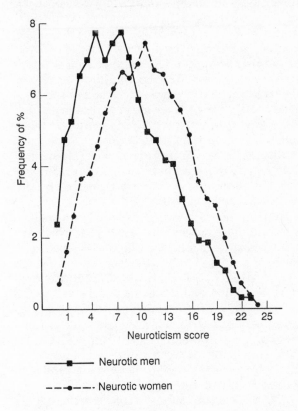

--■-- Neurotic men

--●-- Neurotic women

themselves as extraverted were also seen as being extraverted by some-one who knew them well. For neuroticism, the correlation was also significantly positive but lower at 0.44, which may have been due to people being less willing to express their neuroticism than their extra-version. For the Lie scale, there was no relationship between a person's own score and how they were seen by someone else. In fact, there was a moderately strong tendency for people to see the other person as being similar to them with respect to their Lie score, although this was not the case for the other two dimensions of extraversion and neuroticism. The fact that a person's own score on extraversion and neuroticism is not significantly related to how they rate someone else in terms of these two dimensions suggests that the similarity between a person's own score and how they are rated is not due to people choosing to rate someone who was similar to themselves.

Other personality questionnaires

A large number of personality questionnaires have been developed by other psychologists, some of which appear to be measuring concepts similar to extraversion and neuroticism. One of the earliest attempts to assess a comprehensive range of personality characteristics was by Cattell (1946). He began by examining all published questionnaires before developing his own which he called the *16PF* because it measured 16 primary or first-order personality factors. The present version of the 16PF has six parallel forms (Cattell *et al.*, 1970). There are also versions of this questionnaire which can be used with children. Subsequently, 19 other primary factors were found. Seven of these reflected normal characteristics and were measured with the 16PF Seven Scale Supplement (Marshall & Cattell, 1973). The other 12 represented psychotic aspects of personality, and together with the original 16 normal factors, were assessed by the Clinical Analysis Questionnaire (Cattell & Sells, 1974).

Factor analyses of the 16 first-order factors have resulted in a smaller number of secondary or second order factors, the first two of which are similar to extraversion and neuroticism but are called *exvia–invia* and *anxiety–adjustment* (Gorsuch & Cattell, 1967; Cattell & Nichols, 1972; Cattell, 1973; Bolton, 1977). A factor analysis of the Clinical Analysis Questionnaire produced at least two additional secondary factors of *depression* and *psychosis* (Cattell, 1973; Krug & Laughlin, 1977). In a large scale study by Saville and Blinkhorn (1976), 1158 students drawn from various British universities completed both the 16PF (Forms C and D) and the EPI (Form A). The correlation between exvia–invia and extraversion was 0.73 while that between anxiety–adjustment and neuroticism was 0.77. Since the alternate forms of the scales for these two questionnaires is also about 0.7, this finding suggests that extraversion is similar to exvia–invia and neuroticism to anxiety–adjustment.

Guilford and Zimmerman (1949) also used factor analysis to develop their Guilford–Zimmerman Temperament Survey (GZTS) which measures 10 first-order factors. In addition, three new primary factors were derived in an unpublished factor analysis of the items of the Humm–Wadsworth Paranoid Temperament Scale (Humm & Wadsworth, 1935), making 13 factors in all. Based on the correlations between these primary factors, Guilford (1975) has proposed four second-order factors called *social activity*, *introversion–extraversion*, *emotional stability* and *paranoid disposition*. However, he makes clear that his second-order factor of introversion–extraversion differs from Eysenck's in that his consists of the two primary factors of *restraint* and *thoughtfulness* while he believes Eysenck's is composed of lack of *restraint* (impulsiveness) and *sociability*.

In an attempt to determine whether the factor structure of different personality questionnaires was similar, several studies have been conducted in which items taken from various measures have been factor analysed together. Comrey and Duffy (1968) factor analysed the factor scores of 272 volunteers on the 16 factors of the 16PF, extraversion and neuroticism of the EPI, and 52 groups of items representing the seven factors of the Comrey Personality Inventory. The four second-order factors were *neuroticism, extraversion, socialization* and *empathy–hostility*, the last of which may be similar to Eysenck's dimension of psychoticism.

Eysenck and Eysenck (1969a) gave 114 items from Form A and B of the EPI, 109 Guilford items and 99 items chosen by Cattell to 600 men and 600 women. Items were grouped into 43 scales representing first-order factors and the correlations between these scales were factor analysed. The two major factors which emerged from this analysis were identified as extraversion and neuroticism.

Cattell (1946) believed that words are made up to describe important aspects of personality. Consequently, to ensure that his classification of personality characteristics was comprehensive, he worked through various lists of personality terms which he eventually managed to reduce to 36 clusters of traits. He then asked groups of people who knew each other to rate themselves on these characteristics. Factor analysis of these ratings suggested that they could be further grouped into 12 primary factors. Subsequent workers have argued that these ratings may be better described in terms of five independent factors which are measured by 20 bipolar clusters of characteristics (Norman, 1963; Digman & Inouye, 1986; McCrae & Costa, 1987). The 'big five', as they have become known, consist of *emotional stability, extraversion* or *surgency, culture, agreeableness* and *conscientiousness*. Costa and McCrae (1985) have developed the NEO Personality Inventory (NEO-PI) to measure these five factors which they respectively call *neuroticism* (N), *extraversion* (E), *openness to experience* (O), *agreeableness* and *conscientiousness*. They report that the correlation between the neuroticism scales of the NEO-PI and the EPQ was 0.84 while that for extraversion was 0.76. It remains to be seen whether agreeableness and conscientiousness respectively correspond to psychoticism and the Lie scale.

Social and emotional problems associated with personality

Eysenck has suggested that individuals with psychotic disorders such as schizophrenia and endogenous (major) depression should have higher psychoticism scores; those with neurotic disorders such as phobias and obsessions should have higher neuroticism and lower extraversion scores; those with habit problems such as alcoholism and sexual disorders should have both higher extraversion and neuroticism scores; and those with antisocial and criminal tendencies should be higher on all three scales. Eysenck (Eysenck & Eysenck, 1976; Eysenck *et al.*, 1976) has provided EPQ scores for some of these groups so that the validity of these

Table 5.4 Mean EPQ scores for five groups of men and women*

Groups	n	E	N	L	P
Men					
Normals	2312	13.2	9.8	6.8	3.8
Prisoners	1023	13.6	13.1	6.8	5.7
Neurotics	216	9.4	16.6	8.0	4.2
Endogenously depressed	58	10.0	15.9	9.7	4.1
Psychotics	104	10.7	13.4	9.6	5.7
Sexual problems	23	11.9	12.4	7.1	4.9
Women					
Normals	3262	12.6	12.7	7.7	2.6
Prisoners	71	12.3	14.6	9.0	6.4
Neurotics	332	9.5	17.9	9.6	3.3
Endogenously depressed	68	10.2	16.5	12.0	3.5
Psychotics	72	10.6	14.6	11.6	4.1
Sexual problems	25	10.0	16.3	9.4	3.6

*E = extraversion; N = neuroticism; L = Lie scale; P = psychoticism.

propositions can be examined. The mean scores for 'normal' people, prisoners, and patients diagnosed as psychotic, neurotic and endogenously depressed are shown separately for men and women in Table 5.4. As can be seen, the psychoticism scores for patients diagnosed as psychotic are slightly higher than those of patients diagnosed as neurotic and of normal people, although the difference is only a matter of a couple of items. Since psychotically ill patients should represent the extreme end of this scale as this disorder is uncommon and seriously debilitating, this small difference suggests that this scale is not a valid measure of psychotic disorder. Furthermore, there is little difference in the psychoticism scores of patients diagnosed as endogenously depressed, which is usually thought of as a psychotic disorder, and of those diagnosed as neurotic. The psychoticism scores of psychotically ill patients in the study by Verma and Eysenck (1973) were slightly higher than the reported norms for the questionnaire used (Eysenck & Eysenck, 1969b). However, other studies have found no differences between these groups, which increases the doubt that the psychoticism scale measures what its name suggests (Davis, 1974; McPherson et al., 1974). Incidentally, since the psychoticism scores of the men are only slightly higher than those of women, it is unlikely that psychoticism is related to sex differences.

Patients diagnosed as neurotic have higher neuroticism and lower extraversion scores as predicted (Eysenck & Eysenck, 1976). There is evidence, however, from follow-up studies that patients with neurotic disorders, psychotic depression, sexual disorders and anorexia nervosa show lower neuroticism and higher extraversion scores on improvement (Coppen & Metcalfe, 1965; Morgenstern *et al.*, 1965; Ingham, 1966; Kendell & DiScipio, 1968; Bailey & Metcalfe, 1969; Kerr *et al.*, 1970; Hallam, 1976; Crisp *et al.*, 1979; Lipsky *et al.*, 1980). These results suggest that patients' scores on these scales are partly affected by their psychological disorder. Furthermore, Kendell and DiScipio (1968) found that the neuroticism and extraversion scores of depressed patients differed less from those of normals when the patients were asked to try to disregard their illness when answering the questions and to answer them according to how they felt or behaved when they were their usual self. The fact that the items of the neuroticism scale have been found to form a separate and independent factor from those measuring non-psychotic psychological distress implies that these two variables are distinct (Cramer, 1991a). However, the moderately strong positive correlation found between neuroticism and psychological distress (Henderson *et al.*, 1981; Horwood & Ferguson, 1986; Cramer, 1991a) may be partly due to psychological distress affecting the way in which the neuroticism items are answered.

One way of determining the extent to which neuroticism scores may reflect temporary psychological distress is to examine the relationship of these two variables to a distressing event. It is necessary that this event is unlikely to be the result of neuroticism itself. For example, it would be inappropriate to use divorce or marital separation since both these situations may stem from neuroticism as divorce and marital dissatisfaction have been found to be associated with neuroticism (Burchinal *et al.*, 1957; Eysenck & Wakefield, 1981; Kelly & Conley, 1987). Conjugal bereavement, on the other hand, is unlikely to be associated with neuroticism since there is little or no relationship between partners' neuroticism scores (Eysenck & Wakefield, 1981; Eaves *et al.*, 1989) should mortality be related to neuroticism. In addition, death of partner is seen as being one of the most distressing events that can befall one (Paykel *et al.*, 1976; Dohrenwend *et al.*, 1978; Henderson *et al.*, 1981) and also causes considerable distress (Vachon *et al.*, 1982; Stroebe & Stroebe, 1987). Consequently, if neuroticism was found to be as strongly related as psychological distress to length of bereavement, this finding would suggest that neuroticism scores are affected by transient psychological distress. This issue was investigated in 272 widows and 94 widowers in the Health and Lifestyle Survey who had been bereaved for up to five years (Cramer, 1991d). The results for the widowers were inconclusive since neither neuroticism nor the measure of temporary psychological distress (the General Health Questionnaire) were related to duration of bereavement. However, for the widows, time after bereavement was related to neuroticism ($r = -0.14$), although less strongly than the General Health Questionnaire ($r = -0.32$). This finding implies that neuroticism scores are weakly affected by transient psychological distress.

The largest group of patients with habit disorders which Eysenck and Eysenck (1976) have provided mean EPQ scores are those with sexual problems. While these patients have higher neuroticism scores than normals, their extraversion scores are lower than normals. In other words, these patients have a tendency to be neurotic introverts rather than neurotic extraverts as predicted by the theory. Feldman and MacCulloch (1971), in their study of treating male homosexuality with aversion therapy, also found their 67 patients were inclined to be neurotic introverts. Furthermore, greater improvement was associated with a reduction in neuroticism as has been found in previous studies. Consequently, there is no evidence to suggest that patients with habit disorders are neurotic extraverts. However, it is possible that individuals who seek treatment are more likely to be both more neurotic and introverted, although there appears to be little evidence on this point.

Finally, although the prisoners have elevated neuroticism and psychoticism scores than normals, they are not higher on extraversion as postulated by the theory (Eysenck & Eysenck, 1976). However, there are various problems with testing this prediction by comparing prisoners with non-prisoners. For example, it is not known to what extent people who are imprisoned are representative of those who commit crimes. Being convicted and sent to prison are likely to be highly distressing events for many people, which may be reflected in an increased neuroticism score. The prison experience may affect the suitability of some of the items for assessing these personality dimensions. Consequently, it would be more appropriate to test this hypothesis in a survey which included a measure of antisocial behaviour.

A series of such studies have been reported by Rushton and Chrisjohn (1981), which generally found extraversion and psychoticism, but not neuroticism, to be positively associated with self-reported delinquency in secondary school and university students. The delinquency scale included 20 items such as stealing and fighting. The interpretation of the results of this study, however, are complicated by the finding that the Lie scale was negatively correlated with delinquency so that more conscientious people reported engaging in more delinquent acts. Since there was a tendency for the less conscientious to be significantly more extraverted and psychotic, it is possible that their scores on these two scales are inaccurate. In the largest sample, which consisted of 124 university students, delinquency was significantly correlated with the Lie scale ($r = -0.38$), extraversion ($r = 0.34$) and psychoticism ($r = 0.30$) but not neuroticism ($r = -0.16$). However, when the present author held constant the effect of the Lie score by partialling it out, delinquency was still significantly and positively correlated with extraversion ($r = 0.26$) and psychoticism ($r = 0.24$) but negatively related to neuroticism ($r = -0.23$).

Neurosis versus psychosis

The fact that patients diagnosed as psychotic do not score much higher on the psychoticism scale than normal individuals or those classified as neurotic implies that this scale may not be a highly discriminating measure of what is conventionally understood by the term 'psychoticism'. If this is the case, then the finding that the psychoticism items load on a different factor from those of neuroticism does not mean that psychological distress can be readily categorized in terms of these two dimensions as suggested by Eysenck. A more direct way of determining the number of dimensions needed to describe psychological disorders is to conduct a factor analysis of a wide range of patient symptoms, including both psychotic and neurotic ones. Since Eysenck views psychoticism and neuroticism as higher order factors, it is necessary that higher order factors should be extracted.

One of the few studies which has done this extracted second-order factors on responses to the Symptom Checklist-90 (SCL-90) from 300 men and 300 women patients being treated for chronic pain (Shutty *et al.*, 1986). The SCL-90, as its name suggests, is a checklist of 90 physical or psychological symptoms which is completed by the patient (Derogatis, 1977, 1983). It consists of the following nine subscales, each of which are made up of 6 to 12 items: somatization (e.g. soreness in muscle, feeling weak, heavy feeling in arms or legs); obsessive–compulsive (e.g. doing things very slowly to ensure correctness, checking and double-checking, trouble remembering); interpersonal sensitivity (e.g. feeling uneasy when watched, very self-conscious, shy and uneasy with opposite sex); depression (e.g. feeling blue, worthless, and hopeless about the future); anxiety (e.g. nervousness or shakiness inside, frightening thoughts, feeling something bad will happen); hostility (e.g. shouting or throwing things, urges to break or smash things, uncontrollable temper outbursts); phobic anxiety (e.g. afraid to travel on public transport, of being in open spaces or streets, and of going out of the house alone); paranoid ideation (e.g. feeling others will take advantage of you, are to blame for most of your troubles, and that most people cannot be trusted); and psychoticism (e.g. having thoughts that are not your own, believing someone else can control your thoughts, and other people being aware of your thoughts).

Previous studies have generally obtained five to eleven interpretable first-order factors which tend to correspond to these subscales (e.g. Derogatis & Cleary, 1977; Hoffman & Overall, 1978; Evenson *et al.*, 1980; Holcomb *et al.*, 1983). Shutty *et al.* (1986), using various factor analytic methods, suggested that 10 first-order factors provided the most meaningful solution. Five of these factors were similar to five of the subscales (obsessive–compulsive, interpersonal sensitivity, hostility, phobic anxiety, and paranoid ideation), two of them corresponded to one subscale (somatization 1 and 2), two reflected a mixture of two subscales (depression and depression–anxiety) and one was new (sleep). The absence of a psychoticism factor may have reflected the fact that 67 per cent of the people in this sample did not report these symptoms. However, Holcomb *et al.* (1983) also did not find a psychoticism factor in a sample of in-patients which included a substantial group of people with what are normally considered psychotic disorders (27 and 20 per cent of people were diagnosed as having major affective disorder and schizophrenia, respectively). A factor analysis of the correlations between the 10 factors obtained in the study by Shutty *et al.* (1986) indicated that three second-order factors may be derived. Based on the first-order factors which correlated most highly with them, these second-order factors were called cognitive distress, somatic distress and distrust. The primary factors of obsessive–compulsive, interpersonal sensitivity and depression loaded most strongly on the secondary factor of cognitive distress; the two somatization factors and that of sleep correlated most highly on somatic distress, while hostility and paranoid ideation loaded most strongly on distrust. The third factor of distrust appears most similar to Eysenck's dimension of psychoticism which incorporates hostility.

Two other studies did not carry out second-order factor analyses but did provide the intercorrelations for the first-order factors which enabled second-order factors to be computed by the present author. Holcomb *et al.* (1983) gave the SLC-90 to 451 psychiatric inpatients. Nine first-order factors were extracted. Four of these corresponded to the four subscales of depression, somatization, hostility and phobic anxiety, while the other five were called paranoia, tension, concentration difficulties, compulsion and insomnia. Four second-order factors emerged. Paranoia and hostility loaded most highly on the first factor, depression and tension on the second, phobic anxiety and insomnia on the third, and compulsion, somatization and concentration difficulties on the fourth. The first factor is similar to that of distrust in the previous study and seems to resemble what Eysenck refers to as psychoticism.

In the second study, the symptoms of 924 psychiatric patients, about 59 per cent of whom were diagnosed as psychotic, were rated by psychiatrists on a 100-item symptom checklist called the Boston City Hospital-Behavior Checklist (BCH-BCL) (Martorano & Nathan, 1972). The following 13 first-order factors were obtained from the intercorrelations of 70 of the symptoms: schizophrenic disorganization (e.g. disordered progression of thought, flight of ideas); depression (e.g. delusions of sin, guilt, self-accusation); disordered memory and consciousness (e.g. amnesia, disordered retention of thinking); mania–hypomania (e.g. increased motor behaviour, change in the quantity of psychomotor activity); catatonia (e.g. change in the quality of psychomotor activity, mutism); anxiety (e.g. previous psychiatric history, verbalizes persistent anxiety); abnormal perceptual behaviour (e.g. auditory hallucinations, hallucinations); 're-active' depression (e.g. emotions more or less pronounced in an appro-

Figure 5.4 Foulds' hierarchical model of psychological distress.

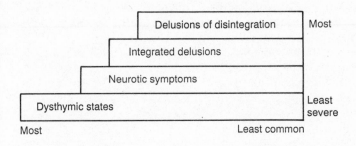

priate response to recent events, depression in appropriate response to a recent event); autism with stupor (e.g. autistic thinking, stupor); 'endogenous' depression (e.g. emotions more or less pronounced in the absence of appropriate environmental stimuli, emotions more or less pronounced than normal); abnormal affective behaviour (e.g. abnormal affect expression, increased motor behaviour); paranoid process (e.g. delusions of persecution, delusions); and abnormal cognitive behaviour (e.g. incoherent, clouding of consciousness). Four second-order factors were extracted from the intercorrelations of these factors. Paranoid process, abnormal perceptual behaviour, 'reactive' depression, abnormal affective behaviour, catatonia and autism with stupor correlated most highly on the first factor; anxiety and depression on the second; mania–hypomania and schizophrenic disorganization on the third; and abnormal cognitive behaviour, disordered memory and consciousness, and 'endogenous' depression on the fourth. No clear psychoticism factor emerges from this analysis.

An alternative model to that of Eysenck has been proposed by Foulds (1976) who suggested a hierarchical model of psychological distress, or personal illness as he calls it, where those people with psychotic disorders would also have neurotic disorders while those with neurotic disorders would not have psychotic disorders. In Foulds' scheme, there are four major classes of psychological distress which are arranged in a hierarchy as shown in Figure 5.4. The first class contains the least severe form of psychological distress, called the *dysthymic states*, and comprises the disorders of anxiety, depression and elation. The second class incorporates the next most severe form of psychological disturbance, the *neurotic symptoms*, which include those of conversion, dissociation, phobia, compulsions and ruminations. The third class consists of *integrated delusions* such as those of persecution, grandeur and contrition, while the fourth class encompasses *delusions of disintegration* such as loss of control of thoughts, feelings and actions.

Patients who have disorders in the higher classes will tend to have those in the classes below, so that a patient with delusions of disintegration will be inclined to show integrated delusions, neurotic symptoms and dysthymic states. These disorders are assessed with the Delusions-Symptoms-States Inventory (DSSI) (Bedford & Foulds, 1977). When this questionnaire was given to 480 patients, the disorders of 93 per cent of them could be arranged in this hierarchical manner (Foulds, 1976). Starting at the second level of the hierarchy, of the 168 patients who had neurotic symptoms but no delusions, 98 per cent also complained of dysthymic states. Moving to the next level, of the 106 patients with integrated delusions but no delusions of disintegration, 86 and 95 per cent respectively exhibited neurotic symptoms and dysthymic states. Finally, at the highest level, of the 45 patients with delusions of disintegration, 87 per cent had integrated delusions and 93 per cent each had neurotic symptoms and dysthymic states.

The results of two other studies using the same questionnaire supported this hierarchical model (Bagshaw, 1977; McPherson *et al.*, 1977). A third study (Surtees and Kendell, 1979), in which the disorders of 424 psychiatric in-patients were rated by psychiatrists using the Present State Examination (PSE) (Wing *et al.*, 1974), found that only 75 per cent of the patients fitted the hierarchical model. About two-thirds of patients diagnosed as having psychotic delusions did not show neurotic symptoms, as well as up to 50 per cent of those with the psychotic disorders of schizophrenia or mania. The difference between the results of this study and those of the three previous ones may have been due to the use of a different instrument or to the fact that patients did not rate their own behaviour. Eysenck's view that psychoticism and neuroticism are separate dimensions will be thrown into question if more evidence is obtained for Foulds' hierarchical model.

Genetic basis of personality

Eysenck believes the personality dimensions of extraversion, neuroticism, psychoticism and maybe even that underlying the Lie scale are strongly genetically determined (Eaves *et al.*, 1989). Before describing the results of several studies which have assessed the influence of genetic factors on these dimensions, it is necessary to outline the rationale behind some of the major methods used. One of the most common procedures for estimating the importance of hereditary factors is the *classic twin* method proposed by Galton (1883). It is based on two main assumptions. Firstly, it is presumed that identical or *monozygotic* twins are genetically the same as they have both developed from the same fertilized egg, while fraternal or *dizygotic* twins are no more genetically alike than any other two siblings as they have grown from two separate fertilized eggs. If this is the case, and if a variable is to some extent genetically determined, then identical twins should be more similar on this characteristic than fraternal twins.

Secondly, it is assumed that the environment of identical and fraternal twins is the same when they are brought up together since they were both born at about the same time and were raised together in the same family. This second assumption is more controversial. The environment of identical twins may not be the same as that of fraternal twins. On the one hand, the experiences of identical twins could be more similar than that of fraternal twins since they look alike and so may be treated similarly. If this was the case, then identical twins could be more alike because their environment was more similar. On the other hand, the experiences of identical twins may differ more than that of fraternal twins because both they themselves and other people may try to distinguish them from each other.

Unfortunately, there is little evidence as to which of these two possibilities is more likely to occur. Loehlin and Nichols (1976) in their study of 850 pairs of same-sex twins found that identical twins were more likely than fraternal twins to dress alike, have the same friends, share the same room and eat the same food. However, the extent to which they were similar in these respects was not generally related to their similarity in personality. In another study, Scarr (1968) tried to determine whether twins were seen and treated as similar due to their genetic similarity or because they were believed to be similar. If their similarity was the result of the belief that they were similar and not because of their genetic make-up, then identical twins who were mistakenly thought to be fraternal should be less alike than identical twins who were correctly recognized as such. Similarly, fraternal twins who were mistakenly believed to be identical should be more alike than fraternal twins who were accurately identified. Although the numbers of twins who were incorrectly identified was small, the results suggested that it was the genetic constitution of the twins which determined their similarity and not their mothers' belief about their genetic origin.

Despite this problem, many studies have employed the classic twin method. Four large investigations have been conducted using versions of Eysenck's questionnaire. Some 543 pairs of twins in Britain (Eaves *et al.*, 1989) and 5967 in Australia (Martin & Jardine, 1986) completed the EPQ, while in Sweden (Floderus-Myrhed *et al.*, 1980) and Finland (Rose *et al.*, 1988) 12 898 and 7144 respectively provided data on extraversion and neuroticism measured with about nine items each taken from the EPI. Genetical identity was generally determined from questions on self-reported physical similarity (such as 'In childhood were you frequently mistaken by people who knew you?' and 'Do you differ markedly in physical appearance and colouring?') which have been found to agree well with results from blood-typing tests (e.g. Cederlof *et al.*, 1961; Magnus *et al.*, 1983). The findings of these studies suggested that all four

Table 5.5 Correlations between twins for extraversion and neuroticism

Twins	n	E	N
Together fraternal	25	−0.17	0.11
Together identical	43	0.42	0.38
Apart identical	42	0.61	0.53

personality dimensions have a significant genetic component. For instance, in the Australian study, which provided the most complete information on the largest sample, the variation in these personality dimensions which was estimated to be accounted for by hereditary factors ranged from 36 per cent for psychoticism in men to 53 per cent for extraversion in men and women.

A second method for assessing the influence of genetic factors on personality is to compare the behaviour of identical twins who have been reared together with those who have been brought up apart. Since the experiences of twins who have been separated from each other at an early age are more likely to be different from those who have been raised together, separated identical twins should be less similar than identical twins brought up together. This method, incidentally, also provides further information on the problem previously discussed as to whether the similarity of identical twins is due to the similarity of their environment.

One such investigation included a questionnaire which measured extraversion and neuroticism and which was developed by Eysenck based on a factor analysis of Guilford's items (Shields, 1962). This measure was completed by 25 fraternal and 43 identical twins brought up together, as well as 42 identical twins raised apart. The correlations between twins in the three groups are shown for extraversion and neuroticism in Table 5.5. Identical twins, regardless of whether they were brought up together or apart, were much more alike than fraternal twins. However, identical twins reared apart were much more similar than those raised together, suggesting that being brought up together may reduce their similarity. Since data were not collected for fraternal twins also raised apart, it is not known whether this finding is restricted to identical twins. If it is, it suggests that the influence of genetic factors may be under-estimated in classic twin studies.

Genetic resemblance or zygosity was determined by a number of methods including blood-typing, finger-printing and similarity in physical appearance. Detailed information was collected on the family history of the twins. About half the identical twins who had been brought up apart were separated from their immediate family within three months of being born and a further quarter within two years. They were generally separated because it was felt that their mothers could not look after both of them together. Most of them, however, were brought up by other members of the same family such as the mother's uncle, aunt or grandmother. One of the biggest differences in social background was a pair, one of whom was brought up by a rich doctor in a city in South America, while the other was raised by a ship's carpenter in the countryside of Scandinavia. In another case, one twin was adopted by a middle-class builder and his warm wife who lived in a London suburb, whereas the other twin was looked after by his reserved grandmother who was married to a Chinese cook and who lived in a working-class district in the same city. Inspection of the data suggested that twins who were separated at a later age or who were brought up in similar social or cultural backgrounds were no more alike than those who were parted earlier or who were raised in more different environments.

A second more recent and larger study collected information on both fraternal as well as identical twins raised together or apart (Pedersen *et al.*, 1988). Unlike the previous study, identical twins brought up apart were not found to be more similar in either extraversion or neuroticism than those brought up together and a similar finding was reported for the fraternal twins. In other words, this study provided no evidence that being raised together reduced personality similarity.

A third method for investigating the role of genetic factors is comparing the resemblance between adopted children and their foster parents with that between children and their natural parents. The similarity between siblings can be compared with that between natural and adopted siblings. If these personality dimensions are partly genetically determined, then adopted children should be less similar in these respects to both their foster parents and the natural children of those parents. If these personality characteristics do not affect who mates with whom, then mothers and fathers should on average share none of the genes which might determine these features. However, since a child receives half its genes from its mother and half from its father, then parent and child have about half their genes in common as do two siblings or fraternal twins. Consequently, if these personality dimensions are to some extent hereditary, then the amount of similarity between these three pairs of first-degree relatives should be roughly comparable.

The correlations between various kinds of relatives are presented in Table 5.6 for these personality dimensions (Eaves *et al.*, 1989). Spouses do not resemble each other in terms of extraversion and neuroticism but are more similar with respect to psychoticism and the Lie scale. Of course, it is not known whether the extent of these similarities is due to being together. Results from another study, however, suggested that the degree of similarity between spouses on these characteristics did not change with the length of the marriage (Eysenck & Wakefield, 1981).

Table 5.6 Correlations between relatives for extraversion, neuroticism, Lie scale and psychoticism

Relationship	Number of pairs	E	N	L	P
Spouses	155	0.04	0.06	0.37	0.27
Foster parent-adopted child	208	−0.02	0.07	0.02	0.00
Parent–child	533	0.21	0.12	0.17	0.13
Siblings	409	0.25	0.04	0.31	0.16
Fraternal twins	231	0.16	0.08	0.37	0.26
Identical twins	297	0.51	0.46	0.55	0.44

There is no statistical relationship between the personality of the foster parents and that of their adopted children, although no details are given of the fostering experience of the children which may have affected these correlations. The correlations between first-degree relatives are higher than those between foster parents and their adopted kin. However, there does not appear to be a clear pattern to the results for first-degree relatives, except that least similarity is shown for neuroticism. The absence of a strong correlation between the personality of parents and their children implies that these characteristics are not largely acquired through children modelling their parents. Identical twins are obviously the most alike. The results of these methods concur in suggesting a strong genetic component to these personality factors. So far, there is little evidence for alternative mechanisms through which these personality dimensions could be acquired.

Consistency of personality over time

There is a growing body of evidence which shows that the relative position of people with respect to one another remains relatively consistent over fairly long periods of time for a number of personality characteristics including extraversion and neuroticism (e.g. Schuerger et al., 1982; Conley, 1984). In one of the few studies to investigate this issue with the EPI, this questionnaire was given to two large groups of male and female students on two occasions a year apart and the test–retest correlations were found to range from 0.72 for extraversion to 0.82 for neuroticism (Simon & Thomas, 1983). Similar results have been reported for other measures of these two personality dimensions. The Social Introversion Scale of the Minnesota Multiphasic Personality Inventory (MMPI) was shown to have a test–retest correlation of 0.74 over a 30-year period for 71 men (Leon et al., 1979). The test–retest correlations for Cattell's 16PF in a large group of men was about 0.76 for extraversion and 0.65 for neuroticism over a 10-year period (Costa & McCrae, 1977). In a subsample of this group, the test–retest correlations averaged 0.80 for the three extraversion scales and 0.72 for the four neuroticism scales of the Guilford–Zimmerman Temperament Survey over a 12-year period (Costa et al., 1980). When corrected for unreliability, these correlations rose to 0.91 and 0.87, respectively.

Physiological basis of personality

Eysenck (1967) has suggested that physiological processes may underlie the personality dimensions of extraversion and neuroticism. In particular, extraversion may be related to differences in brain activity with introverts generally showing higher cortical arousal than extraverts. Neuroticism, on the other hand, may be linked to variations in the activity of the autonomic nervous system with neurotics reflecting greater autonomic arousal than stables. Although there is some evidence that the galvanic skin response (GSR) was greater in subjects with higher neuroticism scores (Coles et al., 1971), in general little relationship has been found between neuroticism and physiological measures of autonomic arousal (e.g. Davis & Cowles, 1988). Furthermore, no strong or consistent associations have been obtained between such physiological indices and either behavioural or self-report measures of anxiety (e.g. Leitenberg et al., 1971; Lamb, 1973), despite autonomic responses being found to be greater for phobic than for non-phobic stimuli (e.g. Grossberg & Wilson, 1968; Boulougouris et al., 1971; Prigatano & Johnson, 1974).

A large number of studies have examined the relationship between extraversion and electroencephalogram (EEG) recordings of brain activity (Gale, 1973, 1983). The greater presence of *alpha-waves* while awake is thought to indicate less cortical arousal. In a review of 33 studies involving 38 EEG comparisons, extraverts were found to be less aroused than introverts on 22 of the comparisons, more aroused than introverts on five of them, and no different on the remaining 11 (Gale, 1983). Although the reasons for the variation in results are not known, it is clear that overall extraverts have lower cortical arousal as measured by the EEG than introverts. An alternative approach to assessing cortical arousal is the *averaged evoked response* in which the EEG response to a stimulus which is repeatedly presented is averaged to produce a characteristic wave. The height between the peak of the first negative wave and that of the subsequent positive wave (N_1–P_2 amplitude) is thought to indicate level of cortical arousal, with bigger amplitudes signifying greater arousal. Some studies have reported introverts as showing higher cortical arousal than extraverts on this measure (Stelmack et al., 1977; Bruneau et al., 1984). However, it is possible that these differences in arousal are due to the fact that extraverts are less interested than introverts in being on their own in the rather quiet conditions in which the EEG is usually monitored.

Conditioning and personality

Drawing upon Pavlov's (1927) idea that cortical inhibition retards classical conditioning and facilitates extinction, Eysenck (1957) suggested that extraverts should condition less readily than introverts because cortical inhibition builds up more quickly and reaches higher levels in extraverts than introverts. In a review of 12 published studies which examined the relationship between extraversion and eyeblink or galvanic skin response conditioning, half of them found that introverts did condition more easily than extraverts (Eysenck, 1965). To account for the failure to find that introverts always conditioned more readily than extraverts, Eysenck (1965) proposed that introverts condition more quickly than extraverts when reinforcement is partial, the unconditioned and conditioned stimuli are weak and when discriminatory learning is necessary. A little later, Eysenck (1967) added a fourth proviso, that introverts would condition better when the interval between the conditioned and the unconditioned stimulus is short. He also reformulated the proposition between conditioning and extraversion in terms of cortical arousal. If cortical arousal facilitates classical conditioning, then extraverts should generally condition less well than introverts because of their lower arousal.

Although this revised theory does not seem to have been the subject of much research, three studies have provided some support for it. In the first study which used partial reinforcement and relatively weak unconditioned and conditioned stimuli, it was found that subjects who showed the most eyelid conditioning on the last 60 of 300 trials were both significantly more introverted and neurotic (Piers & Kirchner, 1969). The second study compared the effects of partial versus continuous reinforcement, weak versus strong unconditioned stimuli, and short versus long CS–UCS intervals on eyelid conditioning in introverts, ambiverts and extraverts (Eysenck & Levey, 1972). The biggest difference in conditioning between introverts and extraverts was when the strength of the UCS was varied, followed by the length of the CS–UCS interval, with the performance of ambiverts being intermediate. Introverts conditioned most readily when the UCS was strong and the CS–UCS interval was short. There was little effect for partial versus continuous reinforcement. Introverts were also found to condition more easily than extraverts with a weaker UCS in a third study (Jones et al., 1981).

There is also evidence suggesting that introverts may show greater operant conditioning than extraverts (e.g. Eysenck, 1959b; Hekmat, 1971;

Gupta, 1976; Nagpal & Gupta, 1979), although some research has failed to find such an effect (Zinbarg & Revelle, 1989). Most of the studies have adopted a verbal task in which subjects are presented with a limited choice of words which have to be used to complete a simple sentence. Subjects are reinforced or punished for selecting a particular class of word such as first person personal pronouns ('I' and 'We'). The most recent study of a series carried out by Gupta found that neurotic introverts conditioned better with punishment while neurotic extraverts conditioned more readily with positive reinforcement which supported Gray's (1970) modification of Eysenck's proposition (Nagpal & Gupta, 1979).

If therapy is based on conditioning principles, then the degree of improvement with particular techniques should also be related to extraversion and neuroticism. Eysenck (1970b, 1976b) has intimated that systematic desensitization may be more effective for patients lower on both extraversion and neuroticism, aversion therapy may be more successful with those who are lower on neuroticism, while flooding may be better with those who are higher on neuroticism. However, these propositions were not made with any confidence and little theoretical justification was provided for them. A number of investigations have administered Eysenck's personality questionnaire to patients receiving various treatments. While some statistically significant relationships were obtained in some of these studies, no clear pattern of findings has emerged.

Two studies found that aversion therapy for patients being treated for transvestism (Morganstern et al., 1965) or homosexuality (Feldman & MacCulloch, 1971) was more effective for those who were less neurotic while there was no relationship with extraversion. One investigation reported that of the patients receiving either desensitization, flooding, or a nonspecific control treatment for phobias, those who were more extraverted showed greater improvement (Mathews et al., 1974). Unfortunately, the results for the separate treatments were not presented so that it is not known whether this relationship was the same for all three treatments. Another study found that flooding was significantly more successful in the treatment of phobias of more introverted patients while desensitization was more effective for more extraverted patients, although this last finding was not statistically significant (Marks et al., 1971). However, in three further studies no relationship was obtained between either extraversion or neuroticism and the effectiveness of flooding for agoraphobia (Mathews et al., 1976) and exposure for phobia (Hallam, 1976), or between extraversion and the outcome of systematic desensitization for interpersonal anxiety in students (DiLoreto, 1971). In the latter study, extraverts fared better with client-centred therapy while introverts improved more with rational–emotive therapy. Since the implementation of these two forms of therapy was criticized by their advocates (Boy and Ellis in DiLoreto, 1971), it remains to be seen whether similar relationships will be found in clinical patients treated by more experienced practitioners.

Summary

Eysenck has suggested that personality can be most parsimoniously described in terms of the four independent dimensions of extraversion, neuroticism, psychoticism and the Lie scale, which are usually measured with his self-report questionnaires. Factor analyses of these and other personality questionnaires have generally provided support for these dimensions. Identical twins have the most similar scores on these scales, indicating that these characteristics may be partly genetically determined. Since psychotic patients have generally not been shown to have markedly higher psychoticism scores, this scale does not appear to be an appropriate measure of the psychological variable which may underlie psychotic disorders. The finding that neuroticism scores of non-psychotic patients decrease with improvement implies that this measure is partly affected by transient psychological distress. While there is little evidence that higher neuroticism scores are related to greater or more sustained autonomic activity, greater extraversion scores have been found to be associated with EEG measures of lower arousal and less conditioning.

6

Cognitive–behavioural approach. I: Social learning and social skills

The fact that classical and operant conditioning are readily susceptible to cognitive control (Brewer, 1974) and that much of human learning occurs through observation and instruction implies that it may be more fruitful to turn to some of the theories which emphasize the cognitive aspects of human behaviour. However, it should be remembered that both Pavlov (1927) and Skinner (1953) argued that their principles of learning also applied to cognitive events such as thoughts and images. Indeed, Wolpe (1958) in developing what quickly became one of the most widely used behavioural techniques, namely systematic desensitization, proposed a method which was partly cognitive in that it required patients to imagine being in certain situations. Behavioural procedures which use cognitions are sometimes referred to as *covert* techniques (Cautela, 1966) since some of the behaviours they involve are not directly observable. Although the application of these techniques does not entail any additional explanatory principles, a description of some of the methods practised should prove informative.

Covert conditioning techniques

The term *covert sensitization* was first used to describe a form of aversion therapy in which patients imagined unpleasant events being associated with the behaviour they wished to eliminate (Cautela, 1966). There seem to have been very few controlled clinical evaluations of this method. One study compared covert sensitization with anticipatory avoidance aversion therapy, systematic desensitization and family behavioural counselling in treating alcoholism (Hedberg & Campbell, 1974). Patients received 17 hourly sessions over the course of 6 months and had to decide whether the aim of their therapy was either abstinence or controlled drinking. Outcome was assessed by the patient 6 months after treatment had ended. The least improvement was shown by those receiving anticipatory avoidance aversion therapy, of whom 75 per cent reported no improvement. Furthermore, only 4 of the 12 patients who had been randomly assigned to this treatment remained in it after the third session. Of those being given covert sensitization 33 per cent demonstrated no improvement, compared with 13 per cent each for those having either systematic desensitization or family behavioural counselling which were the two most effective methods.

Another covert technique which has received some controlled clinical evaluation is *thought stopping* which was first suggested by Lewis (1875) and much later was independently put forward by Taylor (1963) to eliminate compulsive eyebrow plucking. In this technique, patients are asked to imagine with their eyes closed the situation which usually sets off the compulsive act, obsessional thought or associated anxiety. They indicate when they have done this by raising one finger, whereupon the therapist shouts 'Stop!'. When patients have learned to curb these unwanted behaviours in this way, they are then instructed to control their behaviour themselves by initially shouting 'Stop!' whenever these impulses occur and later saying this to themselves subvocally. Several clinical studies have compared thought stopping with either prolonged exposure (Hackmann & McLean, 1975; Emmelkamp & Kwee, 1977) or habituation (Likierman & Rachman, 1982). In the comparison with prolonged exposure, both methods were found to be equally effective. However, in the comparison with habituation neither method appeared effective. The reason for this therapeutic failure is not clear since the treatments in the three studies appear comparable.

Social learning theory

Social learning theory proposed by Bandura (Bandura & Walters, 1963; Bandura, 1977a) postulates that much of human learning occurs vicariously through observation rather than directly through trial-and-error. Observational or vicarious learning allows complex behaviour to be acquired more quickly than through trial-and-error learning and enables the mistakes of others to be avoided. This is an obvious and important advantage when those mistakes could be dangerous or fatal such as eating poisonous substances. The greater learning achieved through modelling over shaping was shown in a study by O'Connor (1972) in which socially withdrawn nursery school children watched a

23-minute film of either dolphins performing tricks or children playing with their peers. After viewing the film, some of the children were reinforced for interacting with their peers. About three weeks later, it was found that the children who had seen the modelling film spent more time interacting with their peers than those who had watched the control film of the dolphin and who had been reinforced for playing with their peers. Moreover, for the children who had watched the modelling film, being reinforced for playing with their peers did not further increase the time they spent interacting with others.

It should be pointed out that operant conditioning theory as put forward by Skinner (1953) does not deny that learning takes place through observation or imitation. Instead, it argues that imitation itself is learned by being reinforced. For example, a young girl may be taught to clap her hands by her father clapping his hands and reinforcing her when she does this. In terms of the operant conditioning paradigm, the father clapping his hands is the discriminative stimulus, the daughter clapping her hands is the response and the father rewarding his daughter is the reinforcing stimulus.

This kind of learning was demonstrated in a study by Baer and Sherman (1964), in which young children were first presented with a talking puppet which also pressed a bar at the same time. At this stage none of the children imitated the puppet. A little later, the puppet asked the children at various points in its conversation, when it also stopped pressing the bar, whether they could do such things as nod their head, open and close their mouth and say such statements as 'Glub-flubbug', 'One–two–three-four', and 'Red robins run rapidly'. Whenever the children imitated any of these responses, they would be rewarded. The idea behind this experiment was to see if the children would also imitate pressing the bar when they had not been reinforced for doing this. Since the majority of them copied this response as well, it appears that children will imitate actions which have not been specifically reinforced.

Bandura, however, believes that while reinforcement affects whether a response is performed, it is not necessary for the learning of that response. This idea can be depicted by letting S^M signify the model being observed, C the cognitive processes through which learning occurs, S^R the observer's expectation that the observed response will be reinforced, and R^M the observer's modelled response.

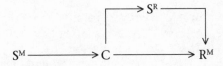

In other words, it is important to distinguish the learning or acquisition of a response from its performance, a distinction which Bandura (1965) demonstrated in the following study.

Young children, 3–5 years old, watched one of three versions of a film in which a man attacked an adult-sized doll in ways not spontaneously shown by similar children in a previous study (Bandura *et al.*, 1961). In one version, the man was rewarded for his aggressive behaviour, in another he was punished for it, while in the third he was neither rewarded nor punished. Immediately after seeing the film, the children were given an opportunity to play with various toys, one of which was the adult-sized doll in the film. It was predicted and found that children who had seen the man or model rewarded for his aggression would be more likely to show the same behaviour than those who had watched him being punished for it. However, the fact that the children who had seen the man being punished for his behaviour showed less aggression does not mean that they had not learned what they had observed. To find out if the children had learned more than they had shown, they were told that they would be rewarded for displaying each aggressive response enacted by the model. When this was done, there was no difference between the children who had watched the three films in the number of aggressive actions they reproduced. Although it is not clear from the report that the novel ways in which the aggressive responses were combined was actually recorded, the results of this study suggest that reinforcement is not necessary for learning to occur.

Observational learning is thought to involve the four cognitive processes of attention, retention, motor reproduction and motivation. First, for observational learning to occur, the observer must pay attention to the modelled behaviour. Various factors affect what is attended to such as how attractive or influential the model is. Similarly, how much is learned from a model partly depends on variables such as how complex the modelled behaviour is, how much is already known about the behaviour and differences in ability to process information. Second, what is observed needs to be remembered in order for it to be repeated later. Information is usually stored in terms of either images or words, which have to be rehearsed to be retained. People who code what they have seen into symbols and who rehearse these symbols have been found to be better at reproducing what they have observed.

This was demonstrated in a study by Bandura and Jeffery (1973) in which people were shown a series of complex movements which they had most probably never seen before. Some subjects were given either a letter or a number code to remember the movements, while other individuals were not provided with this aid. It was anticipated and largely confirmed that people provided with a code were better able to repeat the movements than those without one. Furthermore, of those not given such an aid two-thirds developed their own code to help them remember the information and these people were better at reproducing the movements.

After repeating the movements, some subjects were given an opportunity to rehearse either the movements or the code, while others were prevented from rehearsing by having to carry out another task. Subjects who could rehearse were expected to reproduce the movements better than those who could not. In addition, it was thought that people who rehearsed the codes rather than the movements would be better at repeating them since the codes could be rehearsed more frequently than the movements which also provided less time for rehearsing the code. While subjects who rehearsed the codes rather than the movements were better at reproducing the movements, there was no difference between those who were prevented from rehearsing and those who rehearsed the movements. When participants were tested a week later, those who had coded the information symbolically were better at recalling the movements than those who had not. This study demonstrated that symbolic coding, and to some extent rehearsal, improved observational learning.

The third cognitive process in observational learning involves translating the symbolic coding of information into action. This process depends on factors such as familiarity with the component responses which go to make up the observed behaviour and awareness of the accuracy with which it is repeated. Complex skills such as swimming may need to be broken down into a series of smaller, more discrete actions which may be easier to learn separately before being integrated into a coordinated sequence. Finally, motivation is important in determining not only what is performed but also what is attended to, coded and rehearsed.

According to social learning theory, much of human behaviour is self-regulated. People set standards for themselves. We reinforce ourselves if these standards are met or exceeded, and punish ourselves if we fail to achieve them. Individuals who have a high or positive opinion of themselves reinforce themselves more than those who have a low or negative opinion of themselves. A number of studies have found that individuals with poor psychological adjustment reinforce themselves less (Nelson & Craighead, 1977; Rozensky *et al.*, 1977; Barling & Fincham, 1979; Vasta & Brockner, 1979; Gotlib, 1982). Bandura believes that many people who seek psychotherapy are basically competent and relatively free from anxiety but punish themselves for not attaining a standard which is set too high for themselves. These standards can be learned through modelling as has been demonstrated by Lepper *et al.* (1975). In their second experiment, 7–10-year-old children were shown how to play one of two games in which they could receive one of four scores. There were three main conditions, in which children were presented with a model who varied in whether and how she rewarded herself. In one condition, she did not reward herself while in the other two conditions, she gave herself a penny if she achieved either the highest score or the two highest scores. After being shown these models, the children were allowed to play the game by themselves and to reward themselves with pennies whenever they felt they deserved them. It was expected and found that children exposed to the model who rewarded herself for the highest score would give themselves fewer pennies when they obtained the second highest score than those children presented with the model who rewarded herself for the two highest scores. Furthermore, these children also gave themselves fewer pennies when they received either of the two lowest scores.

Models can have one of four distinguishable effects (Rosenthal & Bandura, 1978). First, they can demonstrate new forms or arrangements of behaviour which the observer can learn. Second, they can indicate the possible consequences of behaving in certain ways. If the consequences portrayed are negative, then they can have inhibitory effects on the observer, whereas if the modelled consequences are positive, they can have a disinhibitory effect. Third, models can initiate or facilitate similar behaviour in observers. For example, yawning may cause other people to yawn. Fourth, models may provide observers with standards for rewarding themselves, particularly when the basis for such standards is unclear or ambiguous. For instance, seeing people withstand pain may increase the observer's own tolerance of pain (Craig & Neidermayer, 1974; Craig *et al.*, 1975).

Several studies have compared the effectiveness of modelling with other techniques. In one of the first such investigations, Bandura *et al.* (1969) examined the effectiveness of symbolic desensitization, symbolic modelling, live modelling with guided participation, and no treatment in reducing snake phobias in participants recruited from the community and an introductory psychology course and who were unable to hold a snake for five or more seconds. Symbolic desensitization was the term used to describe systematic desensitization *in imagination*. Only the first session, however, was devoted to relaxation training. The symbolic modelling treatment was similar to symbolic desensitization except that subjects watched a film in which children, adolescents and adults handled a snake in a gradual and increasing threatening and realistic way, rather than visualizing themselves carrying out similar actions. In other words, they were taught to relax and were instructed to remain relaxed while viewing the film. If they became anxious, they were to stop the film and to replay the scene until they no longer felt afraid. In the live modelling with guided participation treatment, subjects watched the experimenter handle the snake, initially through a one-way mirror and shortly afterwards in the same room. Subjects were then gradually encouraged to touch the snake while the experimenter held it until they could eventually handle it on their own. In general, all three treatments resulted in decreased phobic behaviour while the no treatment group showed no change. Of the three methods, live modelling with guided participation was the most effective while symbolic modelling and symbolic desensitization were equally efficacious.

Participant modelling has been found to be more effective than live modelling (Ritter, 1969; Blanchard, 1970; Bandura *et al.*, 1974, 1977) and exposure (Williams *et al.*, 1984) in treating phobias, while symbolic modelling has been shown to be superior to desensitization in alleviating dental phobias (Shaw & Thoresen, 1974) and sexual anxiety (Wincze & Caird, 1976). In the treatment of patients with obsessive–compulsive disorders, however, *in vivo* exposure was shown to be as effective as participant modelling (Rachman *et al.*, 1971, 1973; Marks *et al.*, 1975; Boersma *et al.*, 1976). Although a third study reported participative modelling to be better than passive modelling, the statistical analyses for these comparisons do not appear to have been presented and so this claim cannot be properly evaluated (Roper *et al.*, 1975). Furthermore, the order effect for these two treatments was not controlled.

While the behaviour requiring modifying and hence modelling in the treatment of simple phobias is relatively straightforward, what this behaviour is in disorders such as depression and alcoholism remains to be specified by the theory. Other theoretical perspectives have suggested that the lack of appropriate social skills or self-statements may underlie many psychological disorders. Additional studies evaluating the comparative effectiveness of modelling in correcting these deficits will be discussed later after these theories have been outlined.

More recently, Bandura (1977b) has proposed that all psychological treatments produce behavioural change by creating and strengthening patients' expectations that they can effectively cope with their psychological distress. Provided that patients have the appropriate ability and motivation to cope with their distress, these expectations will be a major determinant of what they choose to do, how much effort they will exert and how long they will sustain this effort in trying to overcome their problems. This idea is known as *self-efficacy theory*. Expectations of self-efficacy are based on information from the four major sources of *performance accomplishments, vicarious experience, verbal persuasion* and *emotional arousal*.

The most influential source of information is performance accomplishments, or past experiences of success and failure which may be used to gauge future performance. Psychological techniques which provide this information are participant modelling, performance desensitization (i.e. systematic desensitization *in vivo*), performance exposure and self-instructed performance. Vicarious experience involves watching how others cope with distressing situations and so is a less reliable guide to one's own capabilities. It covers such methods as live and symbolic modelling. Verbal persuasion is also less informative than performance accomplishments since the knowledge that one can overcome the problem depends on the opinion of others. Techniques based on it include suggestion, exhortation, self-instruction and interpretative treatments. Finally, reduced emotional arousal may convey a sense of control in that less distress is experienced. Methods which do this encompass attribution, relaxation, biofeedback, symbolic desensitization and symbolic exposure.

With respect to this fourth source of information, it should be noted that the effectiveness of flooding has not been found to be affected by emotional arousal (Everaerd et al., 1973; Emmelkamp, 1974; Hafner & Marks, 1976). Furthermore, it is not clear whether relaxation training is necessary for systematic desensitization to be effective (Agras et al., 1971; Benjamin et al., 1972; Gillan & Rachman, 1974) or for relaxation to occur (Mathews & Gelder, 1969). Consequently, there is little evidence to suggest that the effectiveness of these techniques depends on reducing emotional arousal. Since lowering emotional distress is undoubtedly the aim of these techniques, describing the therapeutic mechanism in terms of one of its outcomes is tautological and does not further our understanding of how these methods work.

The same argument can be more generally applied to Bandura's notion of self-efficacy (e.g. Eastman & Marzillier, 1984). A number of studies have been conducted which find that expectations about being able to effectively cope with a phobic situation are closely related to what is actually achieved in these settings (e.g. Bandura et al., 1977; Bandura et al., 1982; Williams et al., 1984). However, since the expectations are measured shortly before the participants confront the phobic situation, all that this finding may indicate is that individuals are able to accurately predict how they will behave in this situation. Consequently, those who have improved more will be more confident about handling these situations than those who have shown less improvement. In other words, self-efficacy may not determine improvement but may simply depend on what has already been achieved. To show that self-efficacy by itself brings about change, it is necessary to manipulate it independently of improvement through some other source of information such as vicarious learning, verbal persuasion and false or differential feedback. Some studies which have tried to manipulate subjects' expectancy of improvement through false feedback have failed to find an effect (Borkovec, 1973), possibly because expectancy itself was not successfully varied (Lick, 1975). However, in a study where perceived self-efficacy was appropriately varied through false feedback, subjects informed that they had made large reductions in muscular tension reported fewer tension headaches than those told they had only achieved a small decrease (Holroyd et al., 1984).

Social learning theory suggests that psychological disorders such as phobias can be acquired by observation as well as more directly through classical or operant conditioning. Various studies have tried to ascertain the origin of phobias. One investigation of patients with dental phobias found that all 34 of them had suffered a traumatic experience with a dentist on at least one occasion during their childhood compared with only 29 per cent of patients without such fears (Lautch, 1971). Four of them subsequently avoided dentists while the remaining 30 had a second traumatic experience in contrast to only one of the control patients. Wolpe (1982) reported that out of 40 patients with phobias, 65 per cent seem to have been classically conditioned with 81 per cent of these associated with a single traumatic event. The remaining 35 per cent were cognitively based.

Rachman (1977) has suggested that fears can be acquired through the three pathways of conditioning, vicarious learning and information or instruction. Avoidant behaviour and physiological reactions should be more characteristic of conditioned fears, which should be more effectively treated with conditioning techniques such as systematic desensitization and flooding. Subjective reports of anxiety, on the other hand, should be more common among indirectly acquired fears, which should be more amenable to cognitive methods of treatment. Ost and Hugdahl (1981) developed the Phobic Origin Questionnaire to determine the way in which fears have been acquired. The first section of this questionnaire consists of nine questions, two of which are concerned with conditioning experiences ('When you think back of your phobia and try to remember how it started, can you recall that the fear started with any specific event or situation where you experienced strong discomfort and/or anxiety?' and 'Do you think that you can trace back the start of your fear to any specific event or situation where you had been frightened or hurt?'), three with instructional learning (e.g. 'Can you recall having heard of unpleasant things in relation to the situation you now fear at the start of the phobia?' and 'Did you often read, see on TV, or hear on the radio, unpleasant things in relation to the onset of your fear?'), and four with vicarious experiences (e.g. 'Did your mother fear the same situation at the time your phobia started?' and 'Can you recall having seen some other person with intense fear and/or anxiety in relation to the situation you now fear?').

When Ost and Hugdahl (1981) gave this questionnaire to 110 patients with small animal phobias, social phobias and claustrophobia, 58 per cent of them attributed their phobias to conditioning experiences, while 17 and 10 per cent, respectively, accounted for them vicariously and through information or instruction. The remaining 15 per cent could not remember how their fears had originated. In a later report Ost (1985) noted that of 183 patients with phobias, 65 per cent recalled acquiring them through conditioning, 14 per cent vicariously and 7 per cent verbally. The results of these studies are consistent in showing that the majority of phobias appear to be acquired through classical conditioning and that only a minority are learned through observation.

Ost also investigated Rachman's two propositions about these three kinds of phobias. Before being treated for their phobias, patients were placed in their phobic situation and their heart rate, self-ratings of anxiety and their avoidant or anxious reactions to these situations were recorded. In general, however, there was no support for Rachman's suggestion that either heart rate and observed avoidance/anxiety (Ost & Hugdahl, 1981), or their changes in treatment (Ost, 1985), would be greater for the directly (i.e. conditioned) acquired phobias than for the indirectly (i.e. vicariously or verbally) acquired fears.

The methods of treating these phobias were classified as falling into three categories which were primarily concerned with changing either overt behaviour (*in vivo* exposure and social skills training), physiological responses (systematic desensitization and applied relaxation) or self-statements (self-instruction training and fading). According to Rachman, conditioned phobias should show greater improvement with behavioural or physiological methods of treatment, particularly when the outcome is measured behaviourally or physiologically. Indirectly acquired phobias, on the other hand, should improve more with cognitive methods, especially when effectiveness is assessed through self-reports. Although the results for these comparisons were not simple, they did not seem to support Rachman's proposition. Furthermore, they must be interpreted very tentatively since patients were not reported as having been randomly assigned to these treatments and insufficiently detailed statistical analyses were presented (Ost, 1985). In general, the behavioural (and less consistently, the physiological) methods of treatment produced the greatest change in observed behaviour as well as self-rated anxiety for both the directly and indirectly acquired phobias. In terms of the proportion of patients who were judged to be clinically improved, there was no significant difference between the three methods for the conditioned phobias while for the indirectly acquired phobias, the cognitive method produced the greatest change for heart rate.

Social skills training

Social skills training developed from the recognition that psychological disorders may stem from the lack of social competence (e.g. Sullivan, 1953; Zigler & Phillips, 1960; Phillips & Zigler, 1961) and from the use of role-playing to teach patients to be more assertive (Salter, 1949; Wolpe, 1958) as well as to have more satisfactory interpersonal relationships (Moreno, 1946; Kelly, 1955a, 1955b). A few studies have found that a substantial number of psychiatric patients are seen as socially unskilled (Bryant *et al.*, 1976; Trower, 1980) but in the absence of a comparable sample of normal people it is not clear whether the proportion of such patients is greater than that in nonpatients. Some studies, however, have shown that psychiatric patients tend to be less socially skilled than normal subjects. Observation of depressed patients and non-depressed patients and hospital employees interacting with a stranger of the opposite sex found that the patients as a whole were rated as being less socially skilled, as talking in a more monotonous way, as having a less pleasant facial expression and engaging in less eye contact (Gotlib, 1982). The only difference between depressed and non-depressed patients was that the latter talked more loudly. An earlier study, however, found that women students only felt more depressed, anxious, hostile and rejecting when talking over the phone to a depressed female patient rather than to a non-depressed one or to another normal woman (Coyne, 1976). It is not clear why the depressed patients had this negative effect. One impression given by listening to the taped conversations was that these women tended to disclose too much personal information about themselves. A later investigation, however, failed to replicate this finding (King & Heller, 1984). While the lack of appropriate social skills may be the cause of some patients' problems, it is possible that the two factors are unrelated or that the problems reduce the level of competence normally shown.

Social skills training usually includes the following elements: explaining the aims and methods of the treatment; drawing up a list of problematic social situations and working on them one at a time (e.g. recognizing feelings, greeting and parting, starting and ending conversations, giving and receiving compliments, being assertive, listening and self-disclosure); role-playing these situations with the therapist coaching and modelling appropriate social behaviour and providing feedback on the patient's recorded performance; and encouraging the patient to practise these actions in real-life situations outside of therapy.

The evaluation of social skills training in treating psychiatric patients has generally indicated that it is no more effective than a variety of other methods. Of studies which included a no-treatment control condition (Goldsmith & McFall, 1976; Finch & Wallace, 1977; Chaney et al., 1978; Monti et al., 1979), one found few differences between such a treatment and either systematic desensitization or social skills training (Marzillier et al., 1976). Social skills training has been shown to be as effective as flooding (Shaw, 1979) and systematic desensitization (Hall & Goldberg, 1977; Trower et al., 1978; Shaw, 1979) in treating social phobias. In psychiatric patients, it was better than social skills bibliotherapy (Monti et al., 1979) but as good as sensitivity training (Monti et al., 1980) while in depressed patients, it was no more effective than two other treatments including cognitive training (Zeiss et al., 1979), and either antidepressants or psychodynamic therapy with a placebo (Bellack et al., 1981; Hersen et al., 1984). Several studies have shown that social skills training with modelling and/or behavioural rehearsal is more successful than a similar treatment without these activities (Hersen et al., 1973; Percell et al., 1974; Goldsmith & McFall, 1975; Falloon et al., 1977; Eisler et al., 1978) although this effect has not always been found (Jaffe & Carlson, 1976; Eisler et al., 1978).

The finding that social skills improved in patients not given treatment (Marzillier et al., 1976) or receiving one which was not directly aimed at enhancing social competence (Marzillier *et al.*, 1976; Zeiss *et al.*, 1979; Hersen *et al.*, 1984) might indicate that the initial level of social skill may have been adversely affected by the patients' other problems. Indeed, further evidence is required to show that lack of social skill is primarily responsible for psychological disorder of a social nature.

Summary

Social learning theory assumes that reinforcement is not necessary for learning to occur and that much of human behaviour is acquired through observation and instruction. Observational learning or modelling enables novel and complex behaviour to be learned more quickly than operant conditioning procedures such as shaping. So far, modelling has been found to be as effective as *in vivo* exposure in treating obsessive–compulsive disorders, although the number of clinical trials conducted is relatively small. The idea that the effectiveness of psychotherapy depends on instilling and strengthening patients' expectations that they can overcome their problems needs to be studied in a context where expectations are not possibly confounded with therapeutic improvement. Modelling is also involved in social skills training, which holds that the lack of appropriate social skills may underlie much psychological distress. Although social skills training has been found to be as effective as a number of other methods in treating patients, more evidence is required that psychological distress results from the absence of appropriate social behaviour.

7

Cognitive–behavioural approach. II: Beliefs and constructs

Rational–emotive theory

A number of theories have proposed that psychological distress stems largely from inappropriate ways of thinking about our experiences. One of the most influential of these is rational–emotive theory, which was developed by Ellis (1957a, 1957b, 1962) and which argues that psychological distress is brought about and exacerbated by irrational thinking. Psychological disturbance is characterized by *inappropriate* emotions which are distinguished from *appropriate* ones. Inappropriate feelings have been defined in one of two ways. Initially, they were described as simply being more intense than appropriate feelings (Ellis & Harper, 1961), while later they were seen as differing in kind (Ellis & Harper, 1975). Examples of inappropriate feelings are anger, anxiety, depression, despair, guilt, resentment and worthlessness, while appropriate ones include annoyance, frustration, irritation, regret, sadness, sorrow and unhappiness. Regardless of how they are defined, appropriate feelings are brought about by both rational beliefs and particular events, while inappropriate feelings are caused by irrational beliefs about those events. For instance, rational beliefs about my partner leaving me will make me feel appropriately sad but not inappropriately depressed. However, irrational beliefs about this situation will cause me to feel depressed.

There are three ways of defining irrational thinking, which are not mutually exclusive. First and most broadly, an irrational belief is any statement which prevents us from achieving what we can realistically attain. Second, irrational thinking seems to have five main characteristics.

1 *Musturbation or demandingness.* Ellis uses these two terms to refer to the irrational belief that the world must be the way we would like it to be and that we must always have what we want. This characteristic can be recognized by the words 'ought', 'must' and 'should', contained in such sentences as 'This should not have happened' or 'You should not have done that'. Not caring whether our desires are met would be equally irrational since we do want them to be fulfilled. The rational alternative to musturbation is to realize that we would like or prefer our wishes to be satisfied and that we shall work towards achieving them, but that this does not therefore mean that they should or must be met.

2 *Awfulizing or catastrophizing.* These two words are employed by Ellis to describe the irrational tendency to exaggerate the way we feel when our demands are not met, which may be expressed in sentences such as, 'This is terrible' or 'I can't stand this'. One way of recognizing catastrophizing is to think of the worst possible thing that can happen to you, such as dying painfully at an early age. Give this experience the maximum rating of 100 on a 100-point scale of awfulness, and compare the present unpleasant situation you are in with this possibility. The fact that you can tolerate your current setback and that it is not the most terrible thing that could occur to you implies that you have exaggerated its effect.

3 *Overgeneralizing.* Overgeneralization is the irrational tendency to believe that what has happened has always occurred in the past or will always occur in the future. It is exemplified by such statements as 'This is always happening to me' or 'This will always happen'. Reflection on past experience will suggest that these experiences are less common than you believe and may have resulted from particular circumstances which can be changed or avoided.

4 *Global evaluating or damning.* A fourth feature of irrational thinking is the tendency to rate or evaluate people, including ourselves, as a whole. This characteristic is illustrated by such statements as 'I hate you' or 'I am useless' which imply that the whole person rather than a particular aspect of them is being judged. It is more rational to evaluate specific actions of an individual rather than to attempt the formidable task of assessing the multitude of activities which people undertake daily and of aggregating these estimates to form an overall rating.

5 *Not checking inferences.* A fifth characteristic of irrational thinking is not checking the inferences we make about our world. For example, the validity of the belief that you cannot change the way you think, feel or act can only be tested by trying to change it.

The third way of recognizing irrational thinking is in terms of some 10 to 12 specific irrational beliefs. The 12 irrational ideas listed below have been given a name and have been paraphrased as their exact wording has varied in Ellis' writings (e.g. Ellis, 1962; Ellis & Harper, 1975).

1 *Need for approval*. As adults, we should be loved and approved by people we value for everything we do.
2 *Fear of failure*. To be worthwhile, we need to be thoroughly competent, adequate and achieving.
3 *Damning*. Certain acts are bad, evil or unfair, and people who commit such acts should be severely reprimanded and punished.
4 *Awfulizing*. It is awful when things are not the way we would like them to be.
5 *No control*. Human misery is externally caused by other people and events and we have little ability to control or change our feelings.
6 *Anxiety*. We should be terribly concerned about dangerous things that might happen.
7 *Avoidance*. It is easier to avoid than to face life's difficulties and personal responsibilities.
8 *Dependence*. We need to rely on those stronger than us.
9 *Fixation*. If we were strongly affected by something in our past, then we will always be affected by it.
10 *Others' problems*. We should be upset by other people's problems.
11 *Perfectionism*. There is a perfect solution to every problem and we cannot be content until we find it.
12 *Inertia*. We can be happy by doing nothing.

Ellis provides numerous illustrations and reasons as to why these beliefs are irrational (e.g. Ellis, 1962; Ellis & Harper, 1975). Only a few examples of these will be given. For instance, with reference to the irrational belief concerning fear of failure, it is more rational to concentrate on improving our own performance than attempting to be better than others, and to learn from our mistakes than to use them as excuses for not trying. With respect to the irrationality of awfulizing, it is more appropriate to accept what we cannot change and to see misfortunes as challenges from which we may learn.

It is not easy to change irrational beliefs for some of the following reasons. Firstly, we have to realize that it is our irrational thinking which is largely responsible for our emotional distress. Secondly, we have to become aware that we hold these irrational beliefs or at least that our behaviour implies that we have these beliefs. We may be unaware of these irrational ideas because they are part of our culture and because we have learned them so well that we use them automatically. And thirdly, changing these beliefs is difficult because we may have often repeated them from an early age and they may also be partly innate.

Since irrational thinking is seen as the primary cause of many psychological disorders, any method which changes these beliefs can be used, including behavioural techniques such as exposure. Patients may be encouraged to put themselves into situations which frighten them to make them aware of the irrational thoughts that they hold and to show them that some of the consequences they fear do not result. Indeed, to check whether they have really eliminated their irrational thinking, patients may be asked to intentionally bring about (in a non-harmful way) the emotions which they want to change. For example, if someone is frightened of making mistakes while speaking in public, they may be asked to deliberately make a mistake in a public speech to see whether they can cope with the adverse reactions that it might bring. However, the predominant approach used to try to reduce patients' irrational thinking is a didactic one in which the therapist attempts to show them directly through argument that this kind of thinking is the principal cause of their emotional distress. Examples of how this has been done can be found in a volume of transcribed sessions with diverse patients (Ellis, 1971). The basic ideas of the rational–emotive theory of psychological disturbance and therapeutic change can be summarized with the abbreviation A–B–C–D–E (Ellis, 1962), where the letters stand respectively for the Activating event or experience, the Beliefs about that event, the Consequences of having those beliefs, the Disputing or Debating of those beliefs, and the Effects of disputing them.

The most usual method of assessing irrational thinking in research studies is through self-report questionnaires, of which there are a number. One of the earliest and most widely used questionnaires is the Irrational Beliefs Test (IBT) (Jones, 1969), which measures 10 of the specific beliefs previously listed (excluding others' problems and inertia). Examples of items from this test include 'I want everyone to like me' for assessing need for approval, 'I hate to fail at anything' for fear of failure, and 'I cause my own moods' for no control. Two factor analytic studies of this test on young students have provided independent support for all 10 scales apart from that for Awfulizing (Lohr & Bonge, 1982a; Cramer, 1985a). Other tests of irrationality include the Adult Irrational Ideas Inventory (Fox & Davies, 1971), the Common Beliefs Survey (Tosi et al., 1986), the Irrational Belief Scale (Malouff & Schutte, 1986), the Personal Beliefs Inventory (Hartman, 1968; Tosi & Eshbaugh, 1976), the Rational Behavior Inventory (Shorkey & Whiteman, 1977) and the Test of Irrational Ideation (Laughridge, 1971). Total scores on some of these tests correlate quite highly with one another, which suggests they may be measuring similar variables (Martin et al., 1977; Smith & Zurawski, 1983; Smith & Allred, 1986). Questionnaires have also been developed for assessing irrational beliefs about family (Roehling & Robin, 1986) and couple relationships (Eidelson & Epstein, 1982).

Clinical patients have been found to show a greater tendency to think in more extreme terms (Neuringer, 1961), to articulate more irrational concerns (Bates et al., 1990) and to score more highly on tests of irrationality than non-clinical samples (Jones, 1969; Fox & Davies, 1971; Newmark et al., 1973; Laughridge, 1975; Newmark & Whitt, 1983; Shorkey & Sutton-Simon, 1983), although this was not the case for a group of patients diagnosed as having personality disorders or mania (Newmark *et al.*, 1973; Newmark & Whitt, 1983). Suicidal patients endorse more strongly than other psychiatric patients the irrational belief of 'no control' (Ellis & Ratliff, 1986). In non-patient samples, certain specific irrational beliefs as well as overall irrationality have been generally shown to be positively associated with various measures of psychological maladjustment such as anxiety (Himle *et al.*, 1982; Smith & Zurawski, 1983), assertiveness (Lohr & Bonge, 1982b), depression (Nelson, 1977), self-esteem (Whiteman & Shorkey, 1978; Smith, 1982b; Daly & Burton, 1983) and social anxiety (Goldfried & Sobocinski, 1975; Smith & Zurawski, 1983). Over 80 per cent of both Rock and Country & Western songs of the 1970s contained irrational ideas (Protinsky & Popp, 1978). The three most common irrational beliefs were 'the need to depend on a stronger person to approve of yourself', 'external events cause you to feel good or bad', and 'anger is unavoidable', although the second belief would not appear to be irrational in Ellis' terms if simply stated in that form.

One reason why clinical patients and those who report themselves as being more psychologically maladjusted may score higher on measures of irrational beliefs is that some of the items of these tests refer to feelings of distress (Smith & Zurawski, 1983; Smith & Allred, 1986). However, the number of such items in the Irrational Beliefs Test seems to be about five, with one of them contained in the Need for Approval scale ('I often worry about how much people approve of and accept me') and the other four in the Anxiety scale (e.g. 'I have a fear of some things that often bothers me' and 'I am seldom anxious over the future'). Differences between patients and non-patients have been obtained with items which do not refer to emotional distress (Newmark *et al.*, 1973) and relationships have been reported for psychological maladjustment and other irrational belief scales which exclude such items (e.g. Goldfried & Sobocinski, 1975; Lohr & Bonge, 1982b).

An association between psychological distress and irrational thinking does not, however, demonstrate that irrational thinking exacerbates psychological distress. Such an association may reflect three other relationships. Firstly, psychological distress may bring about irrational thinking. Feeling depressed, for example, may make us think that we need the approval of others. Secondly, the relationship between these two variables may be reciprocal or bidirectional with irrational thinking leading to psychological distress and psychological distress causing irrational thinking. Believing that we need the approval of others may encourage us to feel depressed when we are rejected and being depressed may heighten our want for approval. And thirdly, the association may be an accidental or spurious one which is brought about by some other factor such as greater experience of negative events. For example, people who are more frequently rejected by others may feel both a greater desire for approval and more depressed, thereby giving the impression that need for approval and depression are related.

The only way to demonstrate that irrational thinking brings about distress is to conduct a true experiment, in which irrational beliefs are repeated by some of the participants and rational beliefs by others, and to assess the effect this manipulation has on their feelings. At least two such studies have been carried out. In one of them, subjects had to complete a difficult task (Rosin & Nelson, 1983). Before starting, half of them read irrational statements (such as 'I'm really going to look dumb in front of the experimenter if I can't do these relatively simple tasks correctly') and the other half repeated rational sentences (such as 'There is really no logical reason why I should consider myself a less competent or worthwhile person if I make a simple mistake on this task'). Individuals in the rational condition rated themselves as less anxious than those in the irrational condition.

In the second study, participants were asked to imagine being left alone by their partner at a party and were given either rational or irrational statements to read about this potentially distressing situation (Cramer & Fong, 1991). In a further attempt to determine whether inappropriate feelings were better conceptualized as quantitatively more intense emotions rather than qualitatively distinct kinds of emotions (Cramer & Ellis, 1988), subjects were asked to rate how strongly they would feel in this situation in terms of seven 'appropriate' emotions (displeasure, regret, annoyance, frustration, sadness, sorrow and un-happiness) as well as seven 'inappropriate' ones (resentment, guilt, anxiety, anger, despair, depression and worthlessness). Individuals in the irrational condition rated themselves more strongly than those in the rational condition on both the 'appropriate' and 'inappropriate' emotions, suggesting that inappropriate feelings may simply differ quantitatively rather than qualitatively from appropriate ones. The results of a clinical study on patients receiving therapy in which they were asked to say rational or irrational statements about the current problem for which they were being treated showed a similar tendency (Cramer & Kupshik, 1991). The finding that irrational beliefs may intensify negative feelings does not, of course, rule out a reciprocal effect in which distress may increase irrationality.

A number of studies have compared the effectiveness of rational–emotive therapy and similar cognitive derivatives such as systematic rational restructuring (Goldfried et al., 1974) and self-instruction training (Meichenbaum, 1977). In systematic rational restructuring, once patients understand the irrational beliefs that cause emotional distress, they then gradually work through a hierarchy of situations which make them progressively more distressed and in which they visualize themselves as being. In each situation they have to recognize and to challenge the irrational statements they are telling themselves and to replace these with more rational statements. In self-instruction training, patients are also gradually encouraged to face threatening situations by replacing irrational with rational statements, by working out how to handle these situations and by reinforcing themselves for making progress.

Since rational–emotive theory argues that decreased irrationality produces therapeutic improvement, it is important that a test of irrational thinking should also be included as an outcome measure when the therapy is being evaluated. The results of studies which have not measured irrational thinking and which have found that cognitive methods are less effective than other techniques may simply show that these other techniques are better able at changing irrational thinking (Emmelkamp *et al.*, 1978; Emmelkamp & Mersch, 1982). Several studies have demonstrated that although cognitive techniques reduce psychological distress and irrational thinking more than placebo or waiting-list control conditions (Alden *et al.*, 1978; Craighead, 1979; Kanter & Goldfried, 1979; Lake *et al.*, 1979; Lipsky *et al.*, 1980), they are generally no more effective in bringing about these improvements than other methods such as social skills training (Alden *et al.*, 1978; Zeiss *et al.*, 1979; Stravynski *et al.*, 1982), systematic desensitization (Kanter & Goldfried, 1979) or biofeedback (Lake *et al.*, 1979). In a comparison of rational–emotive therapy, self-instructional training and exposure *in vivo*, all three methods were equally effective in treating social phobia (Emmelkamp *et al.*, 1985). However, although only the two cognitive treatments produced a significant reduction in irrational thinking, there were no post-test differences in irrational thinking between the three methods. While therapeutic improvement without a change in irrationality would be evidence against the theory, reduced irrationality does not necessarily indicate support for the theory since this reduction may have been brought about by a decrease in distress. Consequently, the only way to test this theory is to compare a treatment which attempts to reduce irrationality with one which increases or leaves it unchanged, or to show that the change in irrationality precedes that in psychological distress.

Cognitive therapy

Cognitive therapy, like rational–emotive therapy, holds that emotional distress results from faulty or irrational thinking (Beck, 1967, 1976; Beck *et al.*, 1979). Different psychological disorders reflect different cognitive preoccupations. Anxiety is concerned with unavoidable danger; phobia with specific avoidable danger; paranoia with unjustified personal interference; hysteria with physiological dysfunction; obsession with doubt or warning; compulsion with actions to prevent danger; hypomania with exaggerated positive self-evaluation; and depression with personal loss or devaluation. Although cognitive therapy applies to the explanation and treatment of both neurotic and psychotic disorders, it is mainly discussed with respect to neurotic depression.

Beck explains depression in terms of the three concepts of the cognitive triad, schemas, and cognitive errors (Beck *et al.*, 1979). The *cognitive triad* consists of a negative view of the self, the world and the future and results in depressive symptoms such as depressed mood, paralysis of will, avoidance wishes, suicidal wishes, increased dependency and apathy. For example, if we think we are worthless, then we are better off dead. A *schema* (also referred to as an assumption, attitude, belief or rule) is a personal and stable way of viewing or interpreting a particular situation which is usually based on early experiences and which is activated when that situation or similar ones occur. For example, being criticized may trigger a schema of thinking yourself as worthless, which then begins to dominate your thoughts. The following schemas predispose people to become depressed (Beck, 1976).

1 In order to be happy, I have to be successful in whatever I undertake.
2 To be happy, I must be accepted (liked, admired) by all people at all times.
3 If I'm not on top, I'm a flop.
4 It's wonderful to be popular, famous, wealthy; it's terrible to be unpopular, mediocre.
5 If I make a mistake, it means that I'm inept.
6 My value as a person depends on what others think of me.
7 I can't live without love. If my spouse (sweetheart, parent, child) doesn't love me, I'm worthless.
8 If somebody disagrees with me, it means they don't like me.
9 If I don't take advantage of every opportunity to advance myself, I will regret it later.

Faulty thinking or *cognitive errors* confirms the depressed person's negative schema by systematically distorting contradictory evidence to fit in with this view. A number of cognitive errors have been identified.

1 *Arbitrary inference* is a conclusion drawn when the evidence is either lacking or contrary to it. For example, the inference that someone does not like you because they did not speak to you is arbitrary since there are other reasons for this behaviour which need to be checked such as they did not see you or were busy.
2 *Selective abstraction* is concentrating on one aspect of a situation and ignoring others. For instance, a person may focus on the mistakes they make rather than pay attention to both their mistakes and what they do right.
3 *Overgeneralization* is applying a conclusion based on one or more situations to all events, regardless of their similarity to the original situation. Being rejected by someone you are attracted to does not mean that you will always be rebuffed by such people.

4 *Magnification* or 'catastrophizing' is exaggerating the importance of an event. Failing a test is unfortunate but not the worst thing that can happen to you.
5 *Personalization* is assuming personal responsibility for events over which you have little control. For example, it is inappropriate to blame yourself for someone's death through illness.
6 *Absolutistic dichotomous thinking* is categorizing experiences into one of two extremes such as good and bad, or right and wrong.

Cognitive therapy treats psychological disorders by trying to change the patient's distorted thoughts or cognitions and the negative schemas that underlie them. It is a highly structured, directive and graduated approach which uses a variety of behavioural and cognitive exercises and homework assignments to help patients identify, monitor, test and correct the negative thoughts which underpin their main symptoms, and to carry out activities which give pleasure and mastery.

Various questionnaires have been devised to measure different kinds of dysfunctional thinking. The most frequently used test is the 40-item Dysfunctional Attitudes Scale which was designed to assess the underlying schemas or irrational beliefs associated with depression (Weissman, 1979). It incorporates items such as 'I am nothing if a person I love doesn't love me' and 'If I fail at my work, then I am a failure as a person', which seem similar in nature to those employed to measure Ellis' irrational beliefs. Tests developed to assess the more overt, negative automatic thoughts or self-statements related to depression include the Automatic Thoughts Questionnaire (Hollon & Kendall, 1980), the Cognition Checklist (Beck *et al.*, 1987) and the Cognitive Response Test (Watkins & Rush, 1983). The Cognitive Beliefs Questionnaire (Krantz & Hammen, 1979) and the Cognitions Questionnaire (Fennell & Campbell, 1984) attempt to measure cognitive errors, while the Cognitive Style Test (Wilkinson & Blackburn, 1981; Blackburn *et al.*, 1986) endeavours to assess the negative cognitive triad. Depressed patients show higher scores on the Dysfunctional Attitudes Scale than anxious patients (Blackburn *et al.*, 1986; Clark *et al.*, 1989), non-depressed psychiatric patients (Hamilton & Abramson, 1983; Dobson & Shaw, 1986), normal subjects (Hamilton & Abramson, 1983; Blackburn *et al.*, 1986; Dobson & Shaw, 1986; Hollon *et al.*, 1986; Zimmerman *et al.*, 1986; Peselow *et al.*, 1990) and other depressed patients who have recovered (Blackburn *et al.*, 1986; Hollon *et al.*, 1986), but not schizophrenic patients (Hollon *et al.*, 1986; Zimmerman *et al.*, 1986). In addition, depressed patients show lower scores on this scale with improvement (Hamilton & Abramson, 1983; Eaves & Rush, 1984; Silverman *et al.*, 1984; Peselow *et al.*, 1990).

Cognitive therapy has been evaluated in the treatment of non-psychotic depression where it has been found to be as effective as antidepressants (Blackburn *et al.*, 1981; Kovacs *et al.*, 1981; Murphy *et al.*, 1984a) and sometimes more so (Rush *et al.*, 1977, 1982; Blackburn *et al.*, 1981; Simons *et al.*, 1986). It has also been shown to be as effective as social skills training (Miller *et al.*, 1989a, 1989b) and more effective than Lewinsohn's behavioural treatment of depression, an attention-placebo and a waiting-list control (Shaw, 1977), standard hospital treatment which included pharmacotherapy (Miller *et al.*, 1989a, 1989b), and the early stages of routine general practice treatment (Teasdale *et al.*, 1984). The finding that antidepressants were associated with reduced scores on the Dysfunctional Attitudes Scale (Peselow *et al.*, 1990) and that there was no difference in the improvement in the scores of the Cognitive Response Test, the Automatic Thoughts Questionnaire and the Dysfunctional Attitudes Scale between patients receiving cognitive therapy and antidepressants (Simons *et al.*, 1984) suggests that these beliefs may be changed by non-psychological means.

In the treatment of bulimia nervosa, variants of cognitive therapy have been found to be more effective than a waiting-list control condition (Lacey, 1983; Connors *et al.*, 1984; Lee & Rush, 1986; Wolchik *et al.*, 1986; Freeman *et al.*, 1988; Agras *et al.*, 1989), self-monitoring (Kirkley *et al.*, 1985; Agras *et al.*, 1989) and short-term focal psychotherapy (Fairburn *et al.*, 1986). However, while it remains unclear whether cognitive therapy with response prevention is superior to cognitive therapy on its own (Wilson *et al.*, 1986; Agras *et al.*, 1989; Leitenberg & Rosen, 1989), the effectiveness of behaviour therapy was not found to be enhanced by adding cognitive therapy (Freeman *et al.*, 1988). Cognitive behavioural therapy has also been shown to be more effective than a discussion group in treating opiate addiction (Abrams, 1979).

Personal construct theory

Two major ideas underpin Kelly's (1955a, 1955b) personal construct theory. The first is that it is useful to think that people act like scientists in trying to understand the world. The beliefs that we hold about ourselves and the world around us are analogous to the theories held by scientists. Whenever we are confronted with a particular situation, we have certain expectations about what is likely to happen, which are similar to the scientist's hypotheses or predictions. Like scientists who conduct experiments to test their predictions, we act to see if our expectations are upheld. If these predictions are confirmed, our beliefs are strengthened. If they are disconfirmed, we may either try again or change our expectations. Our basic aim is to develop a set of beliefs which will help us anticipate what will most probably happen in any situation. People's beliefs, like scientific theories, differ in the extent to which they allow us to make accurate predictions.

Secondly, Kelly assumes that although there is an objective world, each of us interprets it differently, a view he calls *constructive alternativism*. As with scientific theories, some interpretations are more useful than others in enabling us to predict events. A good or useful interpretation is testable, valid and permits us to anticipate events in new situations. One way of viewing psychological disorders is to see them as interpretations which fail to predict reality. In other words, people with psychological problems have beliefs which do not allow them to anticipate events with much accuracy.

Although Kelly presented his theory formally in terms of a *fundamental postulate* and eleven *corollaries*, these propositions will be mentioned in the course of outlining his ideas. The fundamental postulate, which states that 'A person's processes are psychologically channelized by the ways in which he(she) anticipates events', has already been introduced in terms of the theory's underlying notion that it may be useful to try and understand human behaviour as a consequence of attempts to predict what is likely to occur. The idea that each of us interprets the world differently is conveyed in the *individuality corollary* (1), which says that

Persons differ from each other in their construction of events.

On the other hand, we also share certain views. This point is acknowledged in the *commonality corollary* (2), which postulates that

To the extent that one person employs a construction of experience which is similar to that employed by another, his(her) psychological processes are similar to those of the other person.

Having similar attitudes, however, is not sufficient for a constructive relationship to occur. For this to happen, it is necessary that the people involved have some understanding of how the others see events. This idea forms the *sociality corollary* (3), which proposes that

To the extent that one person construes the construction processes of another, he(she) may play a role in a social process involving the other person.

To make sense of our experience, we look for events which recur since these events are more predictable and constitute a more stable world. This idea is expressed as the *construction corollary* (4), which is

A person anticipates events by construing their replications.

Since no two events are exactly the same, we have to determine in what ways they are similar and different by comparing them with at least a third event. For example, to find out whether Sally and Ann are the same in terms of being tall, we have to contrast them with Jane who is short. The way we judge two events to be similar to each other but different from a third one is called *construing* and the means by which we do this are referred to as *constructs*. Constructs are bipolar concepts, having both a *similarity* and a *contrast* pole, such as tall-short or good-bad. This assumption is articulated in the *dichotomy corollary* (5) that

A person's construction system is composed of a finite number of dichotomous constructs.

The pole that is being used is known as the *emergent* pole, while the contrasting pole is called the *implicit* pole. Constructs differ from concepts in that concepts are only concerned with similarities between events, while constructs involve both similarities and contrasts.

Although we may readily recognize that many concepts are bipolar (e.g. warm–cold, up–down, female–male), we are also familiar with concepts which imply gradations of characteristics. For example, if we take the bipolar construct 'black–white', we know that many things in the world are neither black nor white but shades of brown or grey. Degrees of characteristics can be construed by combining constructs of quality, such as 'black–white', with those of quantity, such as 'more–less'. If we use the construct 'black–white' in conjunction with that of 'more–less', then we have a 4-point scale, namely more black, less black, less white and more white.

Constructs are not necessarily verbal. We place verbal labels on them to convey our ideas to other people, but we can also communicate our constructs by the way we act. A construct is only revealed by the pattern of choices that a person makes and is not necessarily indicated by the verbal labels used to symbolize it. In fact, many people are unable to articulate the constructs they use to anticipate events. For instance, we are able to make fine discriminations among a broad spectrum of colours, but we may be unable to name the constructs we use to do this. Furthermore, people may use the same words to refer to different constructs. For example, one person may employ the construct 'friendly–unfriendly' to refer to individuals who readily smile, while another may use it to describe people who initiate conversation.

Every construct has a focus and range of convenience. This proposition is known as the *range corollary* (6), which states that

A construct is convenient for the anticipation of a finite range of events only.

A construct's focus of convenience refers to those events which it has been optimally designed to handle, while its range indicates those events to which it could apply. For example, the construct 'threadbare–plush' most probably has as its focus of convenience materials made of cloth. Its range of convenience could be extended to include such events as ideas or plans, but it is unlikely to apply to objects such as spades, sausages or tables. Constructs are organized hierarchically, with superordinate constructs incorporating subordinate ones. For instance, the superordinate construct 'warm–cold' may include subordinate ones such as 'friendly–

unfriendly' and 'sympathetic–unsympathetic'. This assumption forms the *organization corollary* (7) which asserts that

Each person characteristically evolves, for his(her) convenience in anticipating events, a construction system embracing ordinal relationships between constructs.

Although a person's behaviour may appear inconsistent from moment to moment, consistency may exist at a higher level. For example, while a parent may seem to be behaving inconsistently by kissing their child one minute, smacking them another, and ignoring them a little later, this parental behaviour may be consistent when viewed in terms of a higher-order or superordinate construct such as 'rewarding the child when good' versus 'punishing the child when bad'. The idea that constructs may be incompatible with one another is expressed in the *fragmentation corollary* (8), which says that

A person may successively employ a variety of construction subsystems which are inferentially incompatible with each other.

Constructs differ in terms of their *permeability*, as described in the *modulation corollary* (9) which states that

The variation in a person's construction system is limited by the permeability of the constructs within whose range of convenience the variants lie.

A permeable construct can be applied to new events or elements, whereas an impermeable one is restricted to certain elements. Constructs which are widely applicable are called *comprehensive*, while those which are limited are known as *incidental*. For most people the construct 'good–bad' would be a comprehensive one, while that of 'tidy–untidy' would be relatively incidental. *Tight* constructs lead to unvarying predictions, while *loose* ones result in varying ones. For example, if the construct 'moral–immoral' was a tight construct, it might produce the invariant prediction that a person construed as immoral would also be disliked. If, on the other hand, this construct was a loose one, then on some occasions it would lead to predicting that an individual construed as immoral would be disliked, while at other times it would result in the prediction that the person would be liked. A *core* construct is fundamental to a person's sense of identity, whereas a *peripheral* one is less central to it. Core constructs are difficult to alter but once changed have far reaching repercussions.

As we experience new events, we may have to change our construct system to handle these new experiences. This proposition is expressed in the *experience corollary* (10) which states that

A person's construction system varies as he(she) successively construes the replication of events.

New events which may cause us to make major changes to our construct system are accompanied by one of the following six reactions: anxiety, fear, threat, guilt, aggression and hostility. Anxiety is when we become aware that the events which we experience lie outside the range of convenience of our construct system. We feel anxious when we are unable to construe events and so cannot anticipate what is likely to happen. We do not experience anxiety if we are able to construe events but our predictions turn out to be wrong. For example, we may be anxious when we go to the doctor knowing that there is something seriously wrong with us, but not knowing what it is.

Fear, on the other hand, is when we recognize that an incidental change in one of our core constructs is imminent. If the doctor, for instance, tells us that we have appendicitis and that our appendix will have to be removed, then our anxiety may turn into fear. We may be frightened of the pain that may result from the operation. If we believe that the operation may be dangerous, then we would feel threatened, since threat is the realization that a comprehensive change in one of our core constructs is imminent. If we thought we might die during the operation, we would feel threatened. Guilt is experienced when we recognize we would not have anticipated our actions from our core constructs. For example, a woman who has defined herself as a mother will feel guilty if she cannot have children. Aggressiveness is when we actively explore the validity of our construct system and try to extend and elaborate it to include more new events, while hostility is an attempt to change events to confirm our predictions. For instance, parents who beat their children may be trying to validate their prediction that children should always be obedient when they are not. Other emotions can be interpreted in a similar way. For example, the concept of 'being in love' may be thought of as a relationship in which two people are aggressively elaborating their construct systems by experimenting with their understanding of each other.

There are two ways in which we can change our constructs or construct systems. The first is the *C–P–C cycle*, which involves the sequence of *circumspection*, *preemption* and *control*. In the first stage of circumspection, we consider the number of ways in which the situation may be construed. For example, if it is a Friday night, we may construe the evening as one for studying, going to a party or watching television. The next stage of preemption is concerned with narrowing our choice down to two major alternatives, while the final stage of control entails deciding which of the two alternatives is most likely to lead to the *extension* and *definition* of our construct system. The principle governing which alternative is selected in this situation is stated in the *choice corollary* (11), which reads

A person chooses for him(her)self that alternative in a dichotomized construct through which he(she) anticipates the greater possibility for extension and definition of his(her) system.

Definition refers to choosing the construct pole which in the past has led to the more accurate prediction of events similar to the present one and which therefore has the higher probability of correctly predicting the present situation. If the prediction is correct, the construct becomes more explicit by having successfully made another prediction. In contrast, extension involves selecting the alternative which has the greater probability of expanding the construct to include new events. Consequently, the probability of success is less, but if the prediction is correct, the construct becomes more comprehensive. Definition, then, is the more certain and cautious alternative to extension. As both definition and extension elaborate a construct by providing more information about its validity, neither is seen as being better than the other. The second way constructs may change is through the *creativity cycle*. This cycle starts with the loosening of constructs and ends with their tightening. For example, we might try doing something unusual on Friday evening such as writing a short story.

People with psychological problems use constructs which do not help them to predict events. Furthermore, they are unable to change their constructs to enable them to make better predictions. This inability to generate valid predictions is handled in one of four ways called *constriction*, *dilation*, *tightening* and *loosening*. Constriction tends to be found in people who are depressed and who have narrowed and limited their field of attention to a small area. By doing this, the apparent incompatibilities between events is reduced. Dilation, on the other hand, is more likely to characterize people who are manic and who have endeavoured to broaden their perceptual field to incorporate as many events as possible. Tightening is inclined to occur in people who are obsessive–compulsive and who make the same predictions regardless of the situation in which they find themselves. Loosening is more likely to exist in people who are thought-disordered and who use the same construct to produce very different predictions.

The aim of personal construct psychotherapy is to explore the way in which patients construe the world and to help them develop constructs which will enable them to make more accurate predictions about events. Therapy involves finding out how the views of patients affect how they behave, suggesting new ways of seeing themselves, trying out some of these suggestions within the relatively safe bounds of the therapy situation, and reporting back on how these changes have affected their lives outside of the therapy sessions. A case study of the way in which a stutterer was treated is available in Fransella (1972). In general, patients are encouraged to try out new ideas about themselves and to experiment with their lives. A variety of different techniques may be used, including those from other therapeutic approaches such as free association, dream analysis and systematic desensitization. However, three methods which spring directly from personal construct theory are the *repertory grid* (or Rep Test), *self-characterization* and *fixed-role therapy*.

1 *Repertory grid*. The person completing the repertory grid may be asked to write down the names of not more than about 30 people whom they know or have known personally such as their partner, their mother, their father, someone they got on well with, someone they did not understand, a person they admired and so on. These people are called *elements* and normally include a reference to oneself. The next step may involve selecting three of these people and saying in what way two of them are similar to each other and different from the third. For example, the partner and mother may be seen as both being warm while the father is viewed as aloof. This construct of 'warm–aloof' is written down and then applied to all the people or elements listed. This procedure is repeated with different triads or groups of three people until not more than about 30 constructs have been elicited. These data form a matrix or grid of information, with the constructs as rows and the elements as columns. The way in which these people are construed can be determined by examining the relationships between the constructs. More sophisticated forms of analysis include factor analyzing these construct relationships, which groups together constructs similarly used. The procedure for obtaining grids also varies widely. For example, elements may be presented in dyads and need not be people, while constructs may be provided rather than elicited.

2 *Self-characterization*. Self-characterization is another technique for finding out how someone construes the world and entails inviting that person to write something about themselves according to the following instructions, where the name of the person is substituted for Harry Brown (Kelly, 1955a, p. 323).

> I want you to write a character sketch of Harry Brown, just as if he were the principal character in a play. Write it as it might be written by a friend who knew him very *intimately* and very *sympathetically*, perhaps better than anyone ever really could know him. Be sure to write it in the third person. For example, start out by saying 'Harry Brown is . . .'

The idea behind writing the characterization in the third person is to make the exercise less threatening.

3 *Fixed-role therapy*. Fixed-role therapy may be used when the patient seems to be making little progress in trying out new constructs. Its aim is to show patients that if they behave differently, then their ideas about how other people relate to them may also change. For example, if we believe that others like rather than dislike us, then we may be less inclined to avoid them. Based on the patient's self-characterization, the therapist will write another description called the *fixed-role sketch*, which to make it less threatening lies ideally about midway between the patient's self-characterization and its exact opposite. If the patient finds this role credible and acceptable, then they are asked to enact it

as completely as possible for a fixed period of about three weeks, after which time they can revert back to their usual self. During this period the patient sees the therapist fairly frequently to review what has happened and what has been learned. The purpose of this exercise is to teach patients that they have the ability to behave differently, that as a consequence it is possible to change, and that the way they construe the world partly depends on how they act.

The most commonly studied proposal of personal construct theory has been the notion that the construing of thought-disordered schizophrenics is looser than that of either normal people or patients with other psychological disorders. This idea was initially tested by Bannister (1960, 1962), who found support for it, apart from a group of patients with depression who did not differ from the thought-disordered schizophrenics in the first study (Bannister, 1960). Although this finding has been widely replicated (Bannister & Fransella, 1966; Bannister & Salmon, 1966; McPherson & Buckley, 1970; Bannister *et al.*, 1971; Williams, 1971; Frith & Lillie, 1972; Haynes & Phillips, 1973; McPherson *et al.*, 1973, 1975, 1978; Heather, 1976; Harrison & Phillips, 1979; van den Bergh *et al.*, 1981), its interpretation has varied.

Kelly described loose construing in four main ways (de Boeck, 1981). Firstly, constructs applied to elements can vary. Secondly, constructs can be extended to elements which are normally not covered. Thirdly, elements can be construed roughly and not precisely. And fourthly, the relationship between constructs and the manner in which they are applied to elements may change. Bannister (1960) seems to have defined looseness in the last way as weak relationships between constructs, which was measured by two indices (Bannister & Fransella, 1966). *Intensity* was based on the sum of the squared correlations between all possible constructs within a grid administered twice, while *consistency* was the correlation between the correlations of the constructs in the first and second grid. Two other measures of consistency are *element consistency* (Frith & Lillie, 1972), which is the average of the squared correlations between the elements on constructs in the first and second grids, and *internal consistency* (Haynes & Phillips, 1973), which is a more complex measure derived from the relationships between constructs within a grid. It has been found that the difference between thought-disordered schizophrenics and non-thought-disordered schizophrenics and normals is due more to element consistency (Frith & Lillie, 1972; van den Bergh *et al.*, 1981, who excluded normals) and internal consistency (Haynes & Phillips, 1973; Harrison & Phillips, 1979) than intensity or consistency, although this finding has not always been obtained (McPherson *et al.*, 1973).

It was suggested by Bannister and Salmon (1966), and confirmed, that thought-disordered schizophrenics should show more looseness of construing with 'psychological' constructs (e.g. kind, mean and friendly) than with 'physical' ones (e.g. tall, thin and small). A number of studies have replicated this finding (McPherson & Buckley, 1970; Williams, 1971; McPherson *et al.*, 1975, 1978; Heather, 1976; Harrison & Phillips, 1979), although in three of the more methodologically complete studies this effect was only found for either consistency (McPherson *et al.*, 1978) or intensity (Harrison & Phillips, 1979; van den Bergh *et al.*, 1985).

It has been pointed out by Radley (1974) that Bannister's (1962) intensity score is similar to both Adams-Webber's (1970) and Bieri's (1955) cognitive complexity or differentiation measure. People who are cognitively complex sort the elements differently on each construct, so that their constructs are not highly related. In other words, they are loose in Bannister's terms. Although the evidence for the predictive value of cognitive complexity does not appear to be strong (Adams-Webber, 1979), the conceptual similarity between cognitive complexity and loose construing implies that thought-disordered schizophrenics are high on both. One way of resolving this apparent paradox is to suggest that although the constructs of normals are closely related, this closeness is reflected within groups of constructs which are themselves weakly related (Radley, 1974).

Two methods have been proposed for measuring the organization of constructs within a grid. Landfield's index of *construct ordination* is based on the extent to which a person adopts the optimal strategy of employing each rating level an equal number of times (Landfield & Schmittdiel, 1983). Klion (1988) found that, compared to non-schizophrenic psychiatric patients, the construing of schizophrenics was characterised by both low construct relatedness (i.e. looseness) and low ordination. However, the relevance of this finding to previous ones was marred by the fact that the critical variable of thought disorder was not measured. The second measure is Makhlouf Norris' tripartite articulation index (Makhlouf Norris *et al.*, 1970), in which grids can be classified as *articulated* (containing two or more primary clusters of constructs with linking constructs), *monolithic* (consisting of a single primary cluster) and *segmented* (comprising two or more primary clusters without linking constructs). Articulated grids reflect cognitive complexity and non-articulated (i.e. monolithic and segmented) ones represent cognitive simplicity. Ashworth *et al.* (1982), using a slightly modified version of this index, found no differences among various diagnostic groups, including samples of patients who were schizophrenic, physically ill or who had recovered from depression. Once again, however, thought-disorder was not assessed.

This study also included another measure of cognitive simplicity based on the amount of variance accounted for by the first, or first three, principal components (Slater, 1977). Greater variance explained by these components indicates that the constructs are more closely related and so may indicate greater cognitive simplicity. The variance of the largest three components (but not of the largest component) was, however, significantly bigger in the depressed than in the schizophrenic patients.

An interesting attempt to validate or tighten the loose construing of thought-disordered schizophrenic inpatients over a two-year period was carried out unsuccessfully by Bannister *et al.* (1975). An effort was made to select the most highly related constructs of one group of patients and to strengthen them with validating experiences, while a control group received no such treatment. However, after two years of fortnightly 1–2 hour sessions, the treated group showed no discernible improvement. In general, few studies have investigated the effectiveness of personal construct therapy. Fixed-role therapy was found to be more effective than no treatment and slightly more effective than rational–emotive therapy in treating anxiety about public speaking in students (Karst & Trexler, 1970), while personal construct therapy was shown to be superior to no treatment in dealing with psychological problems in the elderly (Viney *et al.*, 1989). A modification of fixed-role therapy was used in the cognitive treatment of depression, which was found to be as efficacious as the other two therapies evaluated in the study by Zeiss *et al.* (1979). However, as fixed-role therapy was only part of the cognitive package used, this study did not enable its specific effects to be assessed.

Summary

Rational–emotive and cognitive therapy theory are more limited theories in that they are primarily only concerned with explaining psychological distress which they see as resulting from irrational or dysfunctional thinking. Characteristics of this kind of thinking include negative self-evaluation based on highly selective experiences, overgeneralization, exaggeration and making arbitrary or untested inferences. Therapy involves changing these illogical ways of thinking through instruction, debate and behavioural exercises. While this approach has been found to be as clinically effective as other methods against which it has been evaluated, more direct evidence is needed that inappropriate thinking is a cause rather than a concomitant of emotional distress and its relief. Personal construct theory is a more general theory of human behaviour and holds that psychological disorders are a function of constructs which do not accurately predict events. Most of the clinical research has concentrated on whether the constructs of thought-disordered schizophrenics are more loosely related than those of other groups of patients and non-patients. Little research has been conducted on the effectiveness of personal construct therapy.

8

Psychoanalytic approach

Psychoanalysis, which refers both to a theory of human behaviour and a method of psychological treatment, was initially put forward by Sigmund Freud, who continually worked on his ideas until his death in 1939. As is recognized by the theory itself, some of these ideas will be dismissed by many people as being implausible because they deal with experiences which Freud believed are repressed. However, despite this caution, his approach remains influential and needs to be properly evaluated. To help appreciate these ideas, it may be useful to briefly trace their development as described by Freud (1910) himself.

Development of psychoanalysis

As a medical specialist in nervous diseases, one of the more common problems Freud was required to treat was hysteria. In hysteria, the patient seems to be suffering from a physical symptom, such as being paralyzed in one arm or not being able to see, when there does not appear to be anything physically wrong with them. At that time, most doctors thought that hysteria was due to either some kind of physical degeneration of the nervous system or a form of malingering, in which the patient pretended to be ill. Freud first came to realize that this problem may be psychological when he saw a French doctor called Charcot produce and remove hysterical symptoms under hypnosis. Charcot would first hypnotize a patient who had hysteria and then give them a post-hypnotic suggestion, such as not being able to move their left arm and also not remembering that they had been given this instruction. When the patient was brought out of hypnosis, they could neither move their left arm nor recall why they were unable to do this. The only way to remove this paralysis was to re-hypnotize the patient and tell them that when they awoke they would be able to move their arm once more. Charcot, unlike Freud, believed that the particular suggestibility of these patients was due to the nature of their nervous system.

Subsequently, Freud worked with Breuer, who had used hypnosis to treat patients with hysteria, including a young woman referred to as Anna O. One of Anna's symptoms was refusing to drink water from a glass, even when she was very thirsty. The only way she would quench her thirst was by eating watery fruits such as melons. She also suffered from short bouts of confusion, when she would mutter to herself. During some of these spells, Breuer would hypnotize her and ask her to tell him what was troubling her. One day she recounted that she had seen her friend's dog drink water from a glass. Although this behaviour disgusted her, she hid her feelings so as not to upset her friend. However, after recalling this incident, she asked for something to drink and her fear of drinking water from a glass disappeared.

Anna called this treatment the *talking cure*, which has become the colloquial name sometimes used to refer to psychological treatments in which patients spend much of their time talking about their feelings. Based on cases such as these, Freud thought that hysterical symptoms would clear up if patients could remember when they first occurred and if they could also express the feelings they experienced but did not show at the time. He went on to suggest that these hysterical symptoms were caused by repressing memories of events associated with strong feelings which had not been expressed. The release of emotion that came with recalling the event was called *abreaction* and the technique employed to bring it about was referred to as *catharsis* or *cathartic hypnosis*, which Breuer and Freud (1893–1895/1955) initially adopted to treat a number of patients with hysteria.

Freud eventually gave up the use of hypnosis because he found that he could not hypnotize most of his patients and that, when he could, they were not always able to remember the origin of their symptoms. Furthermore, the therapeutic effect of recalling these events under hypnosis appeared temporary (Freud, 1916–1917/1961). Freud then tried asking patients to recollect when their symptoms first began since he remembered seeing Bernheim demonstrate that patients given post-hypnotic suggestions could recall these when he insisted and assured them that they could. Freud called this method *waking suggestion* or the *pressure* technique since he would sometimes put his hand on the patient's head to encourage them to remember.

Although this method was successful in helping patients recall their earlier experiences, Freud found it hard work. Patients often seemed to be resisting remembering these events, as if they were still actively repressing these memories. Sometimes the patient would only produce single words rather than meaningful sentences. When this happened, Freud would work with the patient to try to find out what the original traumatic experience had been. The first time this occurred was with an obsessive and phobic woman, who could only come up with the following words: 'concierge', 'nightgown', 'bed', 'town' and 'farm-cart'. When asked what these words meant, she recounted an event which happened when she was younger, in which her sister began acting in a strange way one night. Her sister had to be held down by the concierge and was taken away into town on a farm-cart (Breuer & Freud, 1893–1895/1955).

As a result of experiences like these, Freud began to encourage patients to say whatever came into their mind, no matter how silly, trivial, or unpleasant it might seem. This method became known as *free association* and was the basic technique that Freud subsequently employed to trace the events surrounding the origin of the patient's symptoms. He also practised this method on himself, and it has been said that all of his most fundamental discoveries came from his own self-analysis, which was mainly carried out between 1897 and 1901 but which he continued for the rest of his life (Jones, 1953).

The events which Freud found to be most commonly associated with the start of the patient's symptoms were forbidden sexual encounters (Freud, 1933/1964a). Many of his patients recalled having been seduced in early childhood by their opposite-sex parent. At first Freud believed that these incestuous experiences were true, but he found it increasingly difficult to accept that incest was so widespread. Gradually he realized that patients were remembering fantasies that they had had as children and not real events. These fantasies were at first consciously denied and suppressed, and then unconsciously repressed. When they emerged as the result of therapy, these repressed fantasies, or *screen memories* as Freud called them, could no longer be distinguished from other recollections. Because these memories were so frequently reported, Freud believed that young children must have strong sexual feelings towards their opposite-sex parent. The patient's symptoms partly reflected that these feelings had not been successfully repressed and were a compromise between an unfulfilled unconscious desire and an attempt to repress it. For example, a paralyzed hand may indicate a desire to masturbate which has been inhibited through paralysis.

Psychosexual development

Freud thought that psychological processes were based on biological development and that since these connections were unconscious, they would have to be inferred (Freud, 1940/1964b). The early years in our lives are particularly important because we are totally dependent on other people for survival (Freud, 1926/1959). Because of this vulnerability, what we experience then makes a profound impression on us. The most important people or *objects* at that stage will be those individuals who look after us, which are typically our parents. Consequently, our relationships with these people will be heavily invested with emotion, which consists primarily of aggression and sexuality. The way in which we express these feelings depends largely on how we have learned to satisfy them in early childhood, during which five gradually emerging stages of what is known as psychosexual development can be discerned (Freud, 1933/1964a).

Oral stage
The first of these psychosexual stages, which occurs in the first 18 months or so of life, is called the *oral stage* since the main source of satisfaction is seen as being the mouth. Young children appear to derive most pleasure from putting things into their mouths. At this stage, children have little control over themselves and are largely at the mercy of their biological drives which need to be satisfied. These drives, which constitute the *id*, are classified as belonging to one of two *instincts*. The *life* instinct (or *libido*) includes all those forces which preserve and reproduce life, while the *death* instinct covers those powers which ultimately destroy life. Love and hate, for example, spring respectively from these two drives.

The id operates by means of the *pleasure principle*, in which pain is avoided and pleasure sought. When the drives or demands of the id are not met, tension increases which is experienced as unpleasant. The id can reduce this tension either directly by reflex action (such as sneezing, coughing or blinking) or indirectly through *wish fulfillment*, in which an image of what is wanted is evoked. For example, if we are hungry in the absence of food, we will think about food which will temporarily satisfy the id since it cannot distinguish real objects from their images. Dreams and psychotic hallucinations are examples of attempts to fulfill wishes. For instance, if we want to urinate when asleep, the id may reduce this tension with a dream in which we urinate. Psychological needs, however, unlike their biological counterparts, need not be met immediately but can be postponed.

The newborn child gradually learns to distinguish itself from its surroundings through the development of part of the id into the *ego*. The ego is governed by the *reality principle*, which seeks to determine what is real and what is imaginary through the process of *reality-testing*. The ego, for instance, decides when the id should be satisfied by eating or by the image of food. It is through the ego that we become *conscious* of the world, although the id always remains totally *unconscious* to us. Between the conscious and the unconscious lies the *preconscious* which consists of events we are not immediately aware of but which is readily accessible to us such as the date of our birthday. Freud believed we were conscious of only a very small part of our lives. To illustrate the extent of the three levels of consciousness, he used the analogy of a spotlight sweeping the darkness of the night, in which the spot of light is our conscious, its range is our preconscious, and what is left is our unconscious. In other words, only a very small part of our psychic life is open to awareness. The rest is shrouded in darkness.

The increase in tension, which occurs when the instinctual drives of the id are not met, is experienced by the ego as *anxiety*. If the ego cannot satisfy an impulse of the id, then the ego allows the impulse to develop until the id experiences the increased tension as unpleasant. The pleasure principle of the id then *represses* the object to which the impulse is directed. The energy associated with that impulse is changed into anxiety. When the ego represses an id impulse in this way, it loses control of that impulse and also has to continue to expend a certain amount of psychic energy to ensure that the impulse remains repressed. One of three outcomes may occur when the ego is unable to successfully repress an id impulse. First, the ego may experience an *anxiety attack*, in which it is overcome with anxiety. Second, the ego may collaborate with the impulse to form a *symptom*, which is a partial expression of the impulse. And third, the ego, through the process of *reaction formation*, acts in the opposite way to the impulse.

Because young children are so dependent on other people for their survival during the first year of their life, they become anxious whenever their protector, which is usually the mother, leaves them. This fear is known as *loss of love* or *loss of the loved object*, as the people children love are referred to as *objects* or *love-objects* and the relationships children have with them as *object-relations*. The way in which children's psychological needs are met during the oral stage has important consequences for their relationships with others and their outlook on life. If their needs are either not sufficiently or too easily fulfilled, they will tend to cling to the ways they have tried to satisfy them. For example, children who are unable to tolerate their mother being away may endeavour to handle this anxiety by generally becoming emotionally detached from other people. Alternatively, they may cope by becoming very dependent on others, so that they are constantly seeking emotional support from people.

Fixation is the term used to refer to behaviour which is associated with needs being either frustrated or too easily satisfied during early childhood. Abraham (1924/1949) suggested that people partially fixated at the oral stage may show more extreme signs of some of the following characteristics or their opposites: optimism, dependence, demandingness; impatience; restlessness; talkativeness; sociability; generosity; cruelty; suggestibility; envy; and greediness. At a more basic level, people whose oral needs have not been appropriately met will indicate this by what they do with their mouth. For example, if they are anxious, they may demonstrate this by smoking, chewing, biting or playing with their lips.

Anal stage
In the first stage of their lives, children are primarily concerned with satisfying their oral needs. Gradually, however, their focus of attention shifts from their mouth to their anus. Once children have coped with the problems of feeding, they become more interested in the function of excretion. This transition from the oral to the *anal stage* occurs in the second year of their life. At this stage, children seem to take a great delight in and make a fuss about going to the toilet. They may have to be discouraged from playing with their faeces, which they see as being their first creative product and which they may proudly present to their mother. The manner in which children learn to control their anal feelings has an important effect later on in their life. Some children, for example, may express the pleasure they felt during this period by being productive. Freud (1933/1964a) thought that people fixated at this stage were more likely to show the three characteristics of orderliness, parsimony and obstinacy, or their opposites.

Phallic stage
As children learn to control their anal feelings, their centre of attention moves from their anus to their genitals. This shift usually takes place in the third year of their life, where they show a keen interest in sexual matters such as asking where babies come from and how boys differ from girls, together with playing with their genitals and showing them to others. Up until this stage, both boys and girls tend to direct their affection to the person most responsible for looking after them, which is usually the mother. They tend to dislike anyone they see as a rival competing for the same resources. However, boys and girls differ in how they learn to control their sexual feelings towards others.

During the phallic stage, boys' feelings towards their mother become sexual, which she usually discourages. Boys also become increasingly aware of how they differ from girls, although they may not know how these differences have developed. However, they come to believe that if they continue to show sexual feelings toward their mother, they will become similar to girls by their father cutting off their penis. To cope with this *castration anxiety*, they become like, or *identify*, with their father so that he is less likely to threaten them and they will also be more likely to win the affection of their mother. At the same time, they repress their sexual feelings toward their mother because they find these too threatening. This stage is sometimes referred to as the *Oedipal stage* in boys after the classical Greek story of Oedipus who unknowingly killed his father and married his mother.

It is through identifying with their father that sons develop a *super-ego*, which like the ego is largely unconscious. The super-ego develops from the ego, with the son taking on the attitudes and values of the father. Before the super-ego appears, children can only be controlled with rewards or punishment as they have no sense of morality. However, with the development of the super-ego, children's behaviour comes under the influence of their parents' values, and through them those of society. The super-ego continues to evolve throughout our life, incorporating the influence of people important to us. Since it includes the death instinct, it exerts a powerful effect on our behaviour, which we tend not to ignore. The three functions of the super-ego are to observe the way we behave, act as our conscience and strive for perfection. The anxiety that the ego experiences as the result of a threat from the super-ego is known as *moral anxiety*, to distinguish it from *neurotic* and *realistic anxiety* emanating from threats from the id and the external world respectively. It is the task of the ego to satisfy the demands of the id and the super-ego in accordance with reality.

The development of girls during the phallic stage is more complicated than that of boys because firstly, their attention moves from their clitoris to their vagina, and secondly, their affection shifts from their mother to their father. Initially girls also direct their sexual feelings towards their mother. When they notice that males have a penis, they begin to feel that their own genitals are inferior in comparison and stop playing with them to avoid reminding themselves of their own inadequacy. Although they do not know why they have no penis, they tend to blame their mother for their apparent castration and as a consequence, their love for her weakens and is often replaced with resentment. When girls discover that their mother also lacks a penis, they turn their attention to their father who has what they want.

This *penis envy* increases the daughter's love for her father, and in order to win her father's affection she identifies with her mother. However, although girls are frightened of losing their mother's love, this fear is not as great as boys' castration anxiety and so daughters identify less strongly with their mothers than sons do with their fathers. As a result, girls have a weaker super-ego than boys. Girls cope with their feelings of sexual inadequacy in one of three ways. Firstly, they may become sexually inhibited because they realize that their clitoris will not become a penis. Secondly, they may reject their feminity and develop a masculine complex, particularly if they are constitutionally so predisposed. Thirdly, and most commonly, they may substitute their desire for a penis with one for a baby, particularly a son who will have the sought-after penis.

Latent stage
The phallic stage is followed by the *latent stage* in about the fifth year of life. During this phase, children do not seem to be interested in sex and spend much of their time playing with children of their own sex. This

apparent lack of interest in sex is due to the anxiety they experienced over it during the preceding phallic stage. Little girls repress their sexual desires because they feel sexually inferior, while little boys do so because they are frightened of being castrated by their father.

Genital stage
Children regain their interest in sex in the final stage of psychosexual development when they become sexually mature and this interest continues throughout their life. It is during the *genital stage* that the woman's desire for a penis is usually fulfilled by her becoming pregnant and having a child. Freud thought that human sexual development was unique in that it was diphasic. It consisted of two phases, the phallic stage and the genital stage which were separated by the latent stage in which little interest in sex was shown.

Psychological disorders

Freud (1916–1917/1961) believed that psychological disorders resulted from three factors whose relative influence varied. Firstly, constitutional or genetic factors were important, although as their effects were difficult to determine, he had little to say about them. Secondly, certain early experiences in childhood were seen as being especially critical in predisposing individuals to develop particular disorders. And thirdly, precipitating factors in later life would subsequently bring about these disorders.

Four main precipating causes of neurotic disorders were elaborated (Freud, 1912/1958b). The most common reason for neurosis is frustration, particularly that of not being loved. When our desires are continuously frustrated, we may turn away from the real world and seek satisfaction in our fantasy life, particularly our earlier fantasies. If these fantasies cannot be met, symptoms will form which result from the conflict between expressing and repressing a forbidden and unfulfilled wish. Frustration does not inevitably lead to neurosis. Two constructive alternatives to neurosis are to relieve tension either by actively trying to obtain our desires or by substituting or *sublimating* them for other more accessible sources of satisfaction. A second cause for neurosis is the failure to exchange one kind of satisfaction for another, such as the inability to transfer our love from our parents to our partner. A third reason is inadequate development which does not enable a person to move beyond childhood to meet the demands of adulthood, while a fourth factor is an increase in sexual drive or libido which cannot be satisfied.

Freud endeavoured to classify psychological disorders in terms of their underlying characteristics and causes. Disorders which do not result from conflict were called *actual neuroses*, of which he described three kinds, although he recognized that they did not often exist in their pure forms.

Excessive masturbation by dissipating sexual energy causes *neurasthenia*, characterized by such symptoms as tiredness, headaches, constipation, flatulence and indigestion. Sexual frustration (brought about by practices such as coitus interruptus) or sexual abstinence, on the other hand, leads to the accumulation of sexual tension which produces *anxiety neurosis* with its symptoms of general irritability, anxiousness and anxiety attacks. The cessation of satisfactory sexual activity results in *hypochondria*, typified by an excessive concern with one's own health.

Disorders which involve conflict include the *psychoses* and the *psychoneuroses*. In a psychosis, a conflict exists between the ego and the external world, in which the ego tries to replace an aspect of reality it does not recognize with its own version, resulting in delusions, hallucinations and paramnesias (where events are remembered which have not occurred or words are recalled but not their meanings). In a psychoneurosis, on the other hand, the conflict takes place within the internal world of the person, where the ego does not lose touch with reality but replaces one version of it with another. Two kinds of psychoneurosis can be distinguished. The *narcissistic neuroses* are based on a conflict between the ego and the super-ego, while the *transference neuroses* are centred on a conflict between the ego and the id.

Individuals with narcissistic neuroses have regressed to behaviour which occurred in their first year of life. These neuroses develop in people who are fixated at the early part of the oral stage where the ego directs its feelings towards itself rather than towards other people. The three main narcissistic neuroses are *melancholia*, *paranoia* and *dementia praecox*. In melancholia, with its symptoms of severe depression, self-reproach and worthlessness, the ego directs its sense of loss onto itself. In paranoia, with its delusions of persecution, the ego tries to protect itself from hidden threats by perceiving them as stemming from others. While in dementia praecox, the ego seeks to re-establish contact with others.

Individuals suffering from transference neuroses, on the other hand, have regressed to a stage in which they can distinguish their own feelings from those of others. The three principal forms of transference neuroses are *anxiety hysteria* or *phobia*, *conversion hysteria* and *obsessional neurosis*. Phobias result from a partly repressed sexual impulse which has been displaced onto another object. Freud (1926/1959) illustrates the way in which phobias arise with the case of a 5-year-old boy called Little Hans, who was frightened that horses were going to bite him. According to Freud, Hans (like all boys) was really afraid that his father was going to castrate him. However, because he had not successfully repressed this castration anxiety, he continued to be frightened of his father. To cope with this fear, he displaced it onto the more acceptable object of horses, thereby enabling him to love his father without feeling threatened and to lessen the anxiety he felt by only becoming anxious when he saw a horse. The instinctual impulse which was repressed was Hans' hostility to his father. Animal phobias were generally caused by fear of castration in boys and the loss of being loved in girls, whereas agoraphobia was more a fear of being tempted to seek sexual satisfaction.

The symptoms of conversion hysteria, such as hysterical blindness, are often associated with attempts to repress certain sexual feelings. For example, a person who develops hysterical blindness may be trying to prevent themselves from becoming sexually excited by watching the sexual activity of others. Breuer cites the case of a 12-year-old boy who came home from school one day feeling unwell and who spent the next few days in bed refusing to eat (Breuer & Freud, 1893–1895/1955). He only recovered when he had told Breuer that on his way home that day he had gone into a public toilet where a man had shown him his penis and asked him to put it into his mouth. The boy's refusal to eat seemed to reflect his reluctance to have the stranger's penis placed in his mouth.

Obsessional neurosis also represents an attempt to avoid threatening sexual feelings by regressing to the anal stage where excessive efforts are made to keep clean. Obsessional rituals can revolve around any activity associated with sexual arousal such as going to sleep, washing, dressing and walking about. Freud (1916–1917/1961) presents the case of a 19-year-old woman, who spent about two hours carrying out various obsessional rituals before going to bed, which she claimed was to ensure that there would be no noise to keep her awake but which Freud interpreted as attempts to ward off sexual feelings directed primarily towards her father. For example, amongst other activities, she stopped or removed all the clocks and watches in her room so that she would not stay awake by their ticking. She also put all the flower-pots and vases on her writing table so that they would not fall over in the night and break. Freud interpreted these actions as endeavours to prevent certain sexual thoughts and feelings from being experienced. The ticking of the clocks and watches might remind her of the throbbing of a sexually excited clitoris, whereas the breaking of the flower-pots and vases reflected her fears about losing her virginity.

Therapy

Freud believed that the most important aspect of his treatment was the relationship between the patient (analysand) and the therapist (analyst), which would be a recreation of the important relationships that patients had had in early childhood. This therapeutic relationship was called *transference* since patients would transfer to the therapist their feelings about the significant figures in their early life, who were typically their parents. Only patients capable of forming such relationships could be successfully influenced by the therapist and so psychoanalysis was only suitable for the transferences neuroses where these relationships could develop.

The aim of psychoanalysis is to help patients to use their psychic energy more constructively by releasing energy tied up in repressing certain instinctual feelings through making them aware of what these feelings are. Neurotic symptoms result from an unconscious conflict between an id impulse seeking expression and the ego trying to repress it. The object in psychoanalysis is to make patients aware of this conflict and to resolve it more satisfactorily, which can only be done with the help of the therapist. Patients become aware of what they are repressing by following the *fundamental rule* of psychoanalysis which is to say anything that comes to mind, no matter how silly, disagreeable or irrelevant it may seem. They normally do this while lying on a couch with the therapist out of sight so that the therapist cannot influence what the patient says. Therapists should not show patients any sympathy since this makes it more difficult for patients to realize that they are transferring their feelings onto the therapist. Psychoanalysis takes about one hour a day for 5–6 days per week for an indefinite period of time, which may last three or four years.

Five factors or *resistances* work against therapists trying to help their patients recall their repressed feelings (Freud, 1926/1959, 1911–1915/1958a). First, patients by continuing to keep their symptoms may receive *secondary gains* from their illness such as being given sympathy and not having to work. Second, the ego will go on repressing any instinctual feeling it finds too threatening to express. Third, as the transference relationship with the therapist develops, patients find it difficult to free associate because they are now reliving or re-enacting their unresolved conflict with the therapist. Since the transference neuroses are based on unresolved Oedipal feelings towards the parents, involving both love and hate, patients will now express these strong feelings towards the therapist. These positive and negative feelings are described as positive and negative transference, respectively, with negative feelings generally appearing later on in therapy than positive ones.

This is the most crucial stage in therapy and is sometimes referred to as a *transference neurosis*. In handling this stage, it is essential that the therapist neither dismisses the patient's feelings nor goes along with them. Rejection of the patient's love will cause the unresolved feelings to be more strongly repressed, while its reciprocation will lead to the feelings being expressed without the repressed material being recalled. What the therapist does is to point out to patients the nature of their feelings and to help them remember the experiences that have been repressed. Strong feelings of attraction or repulsion on the part of the therapist towards the patient is known as *counter-transference* and should not be expressed.

A fourth resistance is the id's *compulsion to repeat* certain experiences, which is reflected in the tendency of patients to repeat with the therapist their earlier unresolved feelings towards their parents. To overcome this resistance, the reason for this behaviour is pointed out to patients and they are encouraged to go on free associating, a process known as *working through*. Finally, the sense of guilt and need for punishment emanating from the super-ego makes patients feel that they should continue to suffer and that they have no right to improve.

Therapists make use of all that patients say and do in trying to understand the feelings that have been repressed. Patients' recollection of their dreams is thought to be a particularly important source of information since this material is less subject to repression. Dreams, like symptoms, represent in a distorted form the gratification of an unfulfilled wish. The dream that is remembered is the *manifest* content, while the unconscious wishes which it reflects is the *latent* content. The latent content is transformed into the manifest content by a process called *dream-work* and the changes that occur are known as *dream-distortion*. Distortion takes place in five main ways. First, the manifest content is a *condensed* version of the latent material. Second, the latent elements are *displaced* onto manifest elements which may have little resemblance to them. Third, the latent elements are *dramatized* or transformed into visual images. Fourth, an attempt to make sense out of these visual images occurs through *secondary revision*. And fifth, the latent elements are sometimes represented by *symbols* which can be more readily recognized. The usual way of interpreting a dream requires the patient to free associate to some of the manifest elements of the dream in order for the therapist to become aware of their significance, which often can only be done with considerable knowledge about the patient.

Patients' insight into their own behaviour is normally helped by the interpretations of their therapist, although these are not usually made until a strong transference between patient and therapist has been established and they have to be sensitively and carefully handled. In suggesting interpretations, it is important that the patient should be close to making the same interpretation themselves. If this is not done, the patient may find the suggestion too threatening and so may reject it anyway.

Empirical evaluation of psychoanalytic ideas

Although it is often said that Freud's theories are unscientific because they cannot be tested, his ideas have received considerable empirical attention (e.g. Eysenck & Wilson, 1973; Fisher & Greenberg, 1977; Kline, 1981; Masling, 1983). However, only a few topics of direct clinical relevance, and which have been the subject of a number of studies, will be reviewed here.

Incest

There has been a recent surge of research interest in child sexual abuse, which helps address the question as to whether Freud may have been wrong in thinking that the accounts that many of his patients gave of having been sexually seduced by the opposite-sex parent in early childhood were a reflection of their own fantasies rather than that of real experiences (Masson, 1984). Although such memories are obviously difficult to verify and patients may be reluctant to report such experiences, surveys of the prevalence of parent–child incest in patients will serve to establish the extent to which this potential cause of psychological disorder may have been overlooked. While the present evidence indicates that incest is associated with psychological distress, such experiences are relatively uncommon (Lukianowicz, 1972; Rosenfeld, 1979; Russell, 1983; Sedney & Brooks, 1984; Nash & West, 1985; Finkelhor *et al.*, 1986, 1990; Herman *et al.*, 1986; Bryer *et al.*, 1987; Mullen *et al.*, 1988; Swett *et al.*, 1990).

For example, in two recent studies psychiatric patients were asked to complete a questionnaire in which the following kind of question on sexual abuse was included: 'Have you ever been pressured into doing more sexually than you wanted to do? (By sexually we mean being pressured against your will into forced contact with the sexual part of your body or his/her body.)'. In a sample of 66 female psychiatric in-patients, only 6 (i.e. 9 per cent) reported such an experience with their father or stepfather before the age of 16 (Bryer *et al.*, 1987), while in a study of 125 male psychiatric outpatients, none of them was described as having had such contact with their mothers before the age of 18 (Swett *et al.*, 1990). Furthermore, the extent of incest in non-clinical samples has not been found to be much lower than that in clinical patients. In a representative community survey of 930 women in the San Francisco area, only 4.6 per cent said they had had sexual experience with their father or stepfather before the age of 18 (Herman *et al.*, 1986). In a survey of 530 female and 266 male social science students in New England, five of the women (i.e. less than 1 per cent) reported a sexual experience with their father before the age of 12 and two of them with a stepfather, while none of the men had had sexual contact with their mothers (Finkelhor, 1979). At present, therefore, there is little evidence to suggest that parent–child incestuous experiences are common in either clinical or non-clinical samples.

Defence mechanisms

The ways in which the ego prevents itself from being overwhelmed with anxiety are called *defence mechanisms*. An outline of the various conceptions of defence presented in Freud's writings can be found in the literature (Rapaport, 1967; Leeuw, 1971). However, it should be noted that it was Freud's daughter who presented the first systematic account of over 15 defence mechanisms (Freud, 1937). At present, there is little consensus on the number of defence mechanisms and their distinguishing characteristics.

The most influential and persistent endeavour to study defence mechanisms empirically has been based on the work of Vaillant (1971, 1976). Eighteen defence mechanisms were defined as being mutually exclusive and were grouped into one of four levels of increasing psychological maturity and adaptiveness. The lowest level consists of three *narcissistic* defences, including *delusional projection* (e.g. believing that other people are trying to harm you when they are not) and *psychotic denial* (e.g. acting as if a dead person is alive). The next level contains five *immature* defences, incorporating *projection* (e.g. attributing meanness to others but not recognizing it in oneself) and *acting out* (e.g. being self-destructive). The third level has five *neurotic* defences, encompassing *displacement* (e.g. hitting the dog rather than the boss) and *reaction formation* (e.g. despising someone you really like). The highest level holds five *mature* defences, including *sublimation* (e.g. venting your anger by chopping wood) and *suppression* (e.g. minimizing the pain you feel).

In one study, about 20 brief descriptions or vignettes were prepared, from extensive information collected over 30 years, on how each of 95 men had behaved at times of crisis or conflict in their lives (Vaillant, 1976). Two judges, who independently rated these vignettes for the defence mechanisms shown by 50 of the men, achieved good agreement for some of the defences (e.g. projection, passive aggression and hypochondriasis) but not for others (e.g. dissociation, fantasy and sublimation). The reliability of the narcissistic defences could not be estimated since these were seen as being absent. The presence of these defence mechanisms were then correlated with an independent measure of psychosocial adjustment and a composite index of psychiatric illness. The immature defence mechanism of projection was associated with psychiatric illness and poor adjustment, while the mature defence mechanism of suppression was related to the absence of psychiatric illness and good adjustment. The maturity of defences, measured as the proportion of mature to immature defences, was also correlated with the lack of psychiatric illness and good adjustment.

Fifteen years later and using somewhat different measures, maturity of defences and (to a lesser extent) the presence of suppression before the age of 50 years was associated with psychosocial adjustment and satisfaction with life assessed at 50–65 years of age in an extended sample of 173 men (Vaillant & Vaillant, 1990). In another study, the presence of the 15 non-narcissistic defence mechanisms was rated on material collected from a two-hour interview on 307 47-year-old men dealing with difficulties in their relationships, physical health and work (Vaillant *et al.*, 1986). A rating of mental health, based on the same interview, was positively correlated with the five mature defences, negatively related to the six immature defences (including dissociation which was previously grouped with the neurotic defences), and generally unrelated to the four neurotic defences.

The Defense Style Questionnaire, which consists of 67 statements assessing 24 defence mechanisms and 10 Lie items (Bond *et al.*, 1983), was given to 131 of these men about seven years later (Vaillant *et al.*, 1986). Of the 67 statements, 42 were judged by three raters to correspond to one of Vaillant's 15 defence mechanisms; 50 per cent or more of the items measuring these defence mechanisms were found to be significantly related to the same defence mechanism as judged from the interview material seven years previously, suggesting that these defence mechanisms may be identified by questionnaire. An 88-item revised version of this questionnaire (Bond, 1986) was given to 413 adults, including 142 psychiatric outpatients (Andrews *et al.*, 1989). A factor analysis of the results provided some support for Vaillant's notion that defence mechanisms could be grouped together into three categories corresponding to immature, neurotic and mature defences. Unfortunately, this idea was not directly tested since the items were labelled and grouped together in terms of either Bond's 25 defences or those listed in *DSM-III-R* (see pp. 393–5). In addition, a factor analysis of the items rather than the scales would have been preferable since this would have checked the factorial validity of the scales themselves. Psychiatric out-patients scored higher on the immature and neurotic defence factors and lower on the mature defence factor than the two normal groups.

Psychoanalytic psychotherapy

Because of the length of time it might take, Freud (1919/1955) recognized that psychoanalysis could never be used to treat many people and that a shorter and more directive form of therapy would have to be devised. The development of such an approach is usually attributed to Alexander and French (1946), who believed that psychoanalysis was an appropriate method for finding out how psychological problems arose and how they should be treated, but once this was known, the use of this rather time-consuming and indirect technique was no longer necessary. They produced an approach called *psychoanalytic therapy*, in which patients are usually seen once a week, sit opposite the therapist and are encouraged to talk about their problems, which the therapist tries to interpret in terms of psychoanalytic principles.

The few studies which have attempted to evaluate the effectiveness of psychoanalysis have essentially been surveys (e.g. Knight, 1941; Ellis, 1957c; Barendregt, 1961; Heilbrunn, 1966; Hamburg *et al.*, 1967; Aronson & Weintraub, 1968). Since these investigations have not used appropriate control groups, the relative efficacy of this treatment still has to be determined. However, some controlled trials have been conducted on various forms of psychoanalytic therapy with a few mixed results. It has been found to be less effective than cognitive–behavioural therapy with depressed outpatients (McLean & Hakstian, 1979) and client-centred therapy with alcoholic male inpatients (Ends & Page, 1957); as effective as behaviour therapy (Patterson *et al.*, 1971; Miller *et al.*, 1972; Sloane *et al.*, 1975), antidepressants (McLean & Hakstian, 1979; Bellack *et al.*, 1981; Hersen *et al.*, 1984), tranquillizers and placebos (Brill *et al.*, 1964), social skills training (Bellack *et al.*, 1981; Hersen *et al.*, 1984), relaxation training (McLean & Hakstian, 1979), client-centred therapy (Meyer, 1981), carbon dioxide treatment (Harris, 1954), cognitive–behavioural therapy with opiate addicts (Woody *et al.*, 1983, 1987) and supportive psycho-therapy with non-chronic schizophrenic in-patients (Gunderson *et al.*, 1984); and more effective than behaviour therapy (Ends & Page, 1957), drug counselling (Woody *et al.*, 1983, 1987), attention control (Ends & Page, 1957) and waiting-list control (Brill *et al.*, 1964; Miller *et al.*, 1972; Sloane *et al.*, 1975).

The process of psychoanalysis and psychoanalytic therapy can be simplified by breaking it down into four interrelated steps. The patient (1) collaborates with the therapist in (2) disclosing their personal feelings and experiences, which results in the patient (3) acting out towards the therapist their unresolved childhood conflicts with their parents. With the help of appropriate interpretations from the therapist, the patient's (4) realization that their psychological problems stem from these early unresolved feelings enables them to redirect their psychological energy in more constructive and fulfilling ways.

Lately, more assiduous efforts have been made to investigate empiri-cally the relationship between some of these process variables and therapeutic outcome. Most of the research has concentrated on the collaborative relationship between the patient and the therapist, which has been variously referred to as the *therapeutic alliance* (e.g. Zetzel, 1956; Marziali *et al.*, 1981), the *working alliance* (e.g. Greenson, 1965; Horvath & Greenberg, 1986) or the *helping alliance* (e.g. Luborsky, 1976; Morgan *et al.*, 1982). This alliance has been measured by independent judges rating recorded excerpts of therapy sessions and by patients and/or therapists completing questionnaires. Rating methods include the Penn Helping Alliance Rating Method (Morgan *et al.*, 1982; Alexander & Luborsky, 1986), the Vanderbilt University Therapeutic Alliance Scale (Hartley & Strupp, 1983), and the Therapeutic Alliance Scale (Marziali *et al.*, 1981; Marmar *et al.*, 1986), amongst others (Allen *et al.*, 1985; Clarkin *et al.*, 1987; Frank & Gunderson, 1990). Three self-report measures, on the other hand, are the Penn Helping Alliance Questionnaire (Luborsky *et al.*, 1985; Alexander & Luborsky, 1986), the Therapeutic Alliance Scale (Marmar *et al.*, 1986) and the Working Alliance Inventory (Horvath & Greenberg, 1986; Tracey & Kokotovic, 1989).

A number of studies have found that the therapeutic alliance, measured early on in therapy by patients, therapists or external judges, is positively related to therapy outcome when patients' pretreatment psychological distress is controlled (Morgan *et al.*, 1982; Luborsky *et al.*, 1983; Allen *et al.*, 1985; Marmar *et al.*, 1986; Clarkin *et al.*, 1987; Gerstley *et al.*, 1989; Frank & Gunderson, 1990). For example, one study involved 31 men (with antisocial personality disorder) who were being treated for opiate addiction with either cognitive–behavioural or psychodynamic individual therapy (Gerstley *et al.*, 1989). The therapeutic alliance, assessed by both patient and therapist with the Penn Helping Alliance Questionnaire after the third session, was positively associated with therapeutic outcome about one year later. Another investigation was based on 143 patients who were hospitalized for non-chronic schizophrenia and who received either psychodynamic or supportive individual therapy (Frank & Gunderson, 1990). The therapeutic alliance, as judged by the therapist during the first six months of treatment, was positively related to certain improvements two years later.

Controlling for patients' initial level of psychological disturbance is essential in these studies since this control makes it less likely that the relationship obtained between the therapeutic alliance early on in therapy and subsequent outcome is simply due to the fact that patients who are less seriously disturbed are better able to form a therapeutic alliance and are also more likely to show greater improvement. Without this control, any association found between the therapeutic alliance and outcome may be spurious and a result of the tendency of the severity of psychological distress at pretreatment to be positively related to distress at post-treatment (e.g. Luborsky *et al.*, 1971; Luborsky *et al.*, 1980). Ideally, however, it is preferable to control for the patient's level of psychological disturbance at the time the therapeutic alliance is assessed (rather than earlier) to ensure that it is not psychological distress at the point that the alliance is measured which is responsible for the alliance–outcome relationship (Cramer, 1991b). Few studies have done this (e.g. Allen *et al.*, 1985).

Furthermore, some of the therapeutic alliance measures may be inadvertently assessing therapeutic outcome as recognized by Morgan *et al.* (1982). For example, one of their helping alliance rating scales is 'The patient feels changed by the treatment. Example: "I am improving." or "I am less anxious."'. They argue, however, that when this item was omitted, the alliance–outcome correlations remained essentially unchanged. The same assurance needs to be given for the results obtained with the patient helping alliance questionnaire, which contains more of such potentially contaminating items, (e.g. 'I believe that the treatment is helping me', 'I have been feeling better recently', 'I can already see that I will eventually work out the problems I came to treatment for' and 'I feel now that I can understand myself and deal with myself on my own (that is, even if the therapist and I were no longer meeting for treatment appointments)'. The most parsimonious solution to this problem would be to omit such items.

Despite controlling for patients' pretreatment psychological functioning, the non-experimental design of these studies means that the causal nature of the relationship between therapeutic alliance and outcome cannot be established with any certainty since a multitude of other uncontrolled factors (such as age, intelligence and socio-economic status) may account for this association. The only way in which causality can be determined is through a true experimental design in which patients have been randomly assigned to different levels of therapeutic alliance.

The other three process variables have received less empirical attention. More recent studies have failed to find any association between degree or depth of self-exploration and therapeutic outcome (e.g. Sloane et al., 1975; Strassberg et al., 1975; McDaniel et al., 1981). For instance, in the study by Sloane et al. (1975), four 4-minute tape-recorded segments taken from the fifth interview of patients receiving either individual psychoanalytic or behaviour therapy, were independently rated on Truax and Carkhuff's (1967) depth of self-exploration scale and found not to be related to therapeutic outcome about nine weeks later.

A few studies have investigated the relationship between therapeutic outcome and the frequency or accuracy of transference interpretations by the therapist. Marziali (1984) found that five out of nine outcome measures were positively related to the average number of transference interpretations which referred to the patient's feelings towards both the therapist and other people. Transference interpretations were independently measured by raters from tape recordings of the therapy sessions. The proportion of transference interpretations in the study by Piper et al. (1986) were generally not associated with 17 outcome measures. However, the correlations between therapist–parent transference interpretations and the five outcome measures shown are low and positive and may not be significant because of the relatively small numbers of patients. Assessing accuracy rather than frequency of transference interpretations, Crits-Christoph et al. (1988) reported a positive correlation between therapeutic outcome (which included controlling for patients' pretreatment distress) and the accuracy of transference interpretations independently rated in two early sessions.

The therapeutic value of recalling early events in childhood was indirectly and superficially examined in the study by Sloane et al. (1975) when patients were asked for their impressions of therapy one to two years after finishing treatment. Patients had to rate the importance of 32 characteristics of therapy in bringing about therapeutic improvement (listed in Cross et al., 1982). The item which most clearly reflected the significance of early experiences was the statement, 'By explaining the relationship of your problem to early events in your life'. However, this feature was not seen as very important by patients who found therapy very helpful.

Some psychodynamic writers have suggested that treatments like behaviour therapy which do not appear to be concerned with unearthing the psychological conflicts underlying psychological disorders (such as phobias) will lead to *symptom substitution* in which the original symptom is replaced with a new one (e.g. Friedman, 1959). Long-term follow-ups of phobic patients who have been treated with behaviour therapy have reported little evidence of the development of new disorders (Marks, 1971; Emmelkamp & Kuipers, 1979; McPherson *et al.*, 1980; Munby & Johnston, 1980). However, whether the failure of symptom substitution in behaviour therapy constitutes an appropriate criticism of the validity of psychoanalysis depends on two issues. Firstly, some doubt exists as to whether psychoanalytic theory postulates that the direct treatment of psychological disorders will cause symptom substitution (Weitzman, 1967). Freud (1955/1919) himself stated that it is necessary to persuade phobic patients to confront their fear in order to help them recall the appropriate material for resolving the phobia. Secondly, it needs to be ascertained whether awareness of underlying conflicts takes place in behaviour therapy and if so, whether it is responsible for the improvement which occurs.

Summary

Freud postulated that much of our behaviour is influenced by how we satisfied our oral, anal and sexual desires in early childhood. The three transference neuroses of phobias, conversion hysteria and obsessive–compulsiveness were considered to result from the failure to repress and redirect early sexual impulses. The aim of psychoanalysis as a method of treatment is to help patients to rechannel these desires in more appropriate ways by recalling these early experiences. Psychoanalytic therapy is a shorter and more direct form of psychoanalysis in which attempts are made to interpret the patient's problems primarily in terms of unresolved feelings towards important figures in the person's early life. Effective therapy involves the patient establishing a working relationship with the therapist in which these problematic feelings are experienced towards the therapist and their origin recalled. Psychoanalytic therapy has been found to be as effective as many of the treatments with which it has been compared and some attempts have been made to test the process through which it is thought to work.

9

Person-centred approach

The person-centred approach was originally called client-centred theory by Rogers (1946, 1951), who developed it from his experience of trying to help people with psychological problems. Rogers preferred the term *client-centred* to patient-centred since it reflected his belief that people, and not therapists, knew what was best for themselves and so should be primarily responsible for directing the course of therapy. The term client is now often used by therapists, other than client-centred ones, to refer to people who seek or receive psychotherapy. Since he believed that this approach applied not only to psychotherapy but also to other spheres of human activity such as education and social relationships (Rogers, 1959, 1961a), it seemed more appropriate to refer to it more generally as *person-centred* (Meador & Rogers, 1979).

Person-centred theory

According to the theory, people have one basic motive or *actualizing tendency*, which directs all activities necessary for survival and for trying to control the environment. The ultimate aim of this tendency is to make us independent of our surroundings. Part of it, the *self-actualizing tendency*, develops an awareness of ourselves as being separate from our environment and leads to the formation of the *self-concept* or the view we have of ourselves as individuals. The tendency to actualize ourselves works best when we are fully aware of our own feelings. Since our whole body intuitively knows what is good and bad for us, we should learn to trust and to act on these intuitive feelings.

Individuals who are fully self-actualized will show a number of characteristics. They will be open to their experience, which may be conflicting and which they do not feel has to be described in preconceived categories. By being aware of all their feelings, they are less likely to be self-destructive since they recognize that these destructive urges are only part of what they feel at any one moment, which will also include constructive desires. They act according to how they feel at the time, making use of all the information of which they are aware. Because each moment is seen as being new, they are unable to predict exactly how they will behave in the future.

Although people seeking psychological help may present what appear to be different problems, the fundamental cause of these difficulties is that they have lost awareness of their own true feelings and that their concept or understanding of themselves is different from their true feelings. In other words, their self-actualizing tendency (or self-concept) is discrepant from their actualizing tendency. As they are not conscious of their underlying feelings, they experience a sense of dissatisfaction with themselves, which is expressed in such sentiments as 'I just don't feel like myself anymore', 'I don't want people to know the real me' and 'I don't know who I really am'.

Because of the self's need for consistency, we will try to make our experience consistent with our self-concept by distorting or denying this experience when the discrepancy between our self-concept and our underlying experience (as reflected in the actualizing tendency) is not too great. Any experience which is anticipated or subceived as being inconsistent with the self-concept is seen as threatening and is felt as anxiety. In other words, we feel anxious when we are subconsciously aware that we are experiencing a feeling which is inconsistent with our self-concept. If we have to defend ourselves from having certain feelings, then we will be less aware of all of our feelings because we will always be seeking to protect ourselves from the threatening ones. This defensive attitude is characterized by such neurotic or *intensional* behaviour as a reluctance to test ideas, confusing fact with evaluation, relying on beliefs rather than experience, overgeneralizing and all-or-none thinking. When, however, the discrepancy is too great to be denied or distorted, we will become aware of our incongruent experience and our self-concept will become disorganized. As a result, we will behave erratically. Sometimes we will act in a manner which is consistent with our self-concept, while at other times we will behave in a way which is congruent with our previously denied experiences. When this happens, our behaviour may seem characteristic of the odd and bizarre actions shown by people with psychotic disorders.

A discrepancy between the self and underlying experiencing results from people being given *conditional* rather than *unconditional positive regard* or love when they were young. Children, as part of their self-actualizing tendency, have a need for positive regard which is so strong that they will often disregard their other needs in order to feel loved and accepted by someone who is important to them. If children only receive love from their parents (or other significant people) when they experience what their parents want them to, then this conditional love will cause their feelings and their concept of themselves to reflect their parents' desires rather than their own. These children will only regard themselves positively when they have experiences which have also been positively regarded by others. They will dislike themselves when they have feelings which have not been accepted by others. On the other hand, if children feel loved by their parents regardless of what they experience, then this unconditional love will make them feel positive about themselves and they will not ignore their own psychological needs.

The only conditions necessary for people to become more aware of and to accept their underlying feelings is for them to enter into a relationship with someone who shows them, and whom they perceive as showing them, the three therapeutic or *core conditions* of *unconditional acceptance*, *empathy* and *genuineness* (Rogers, 1957). Although Rogers initially stated that these were the only conditions required for therapeutic improvement to occur, later on Rogers and Truax (1967/1976) acknowledged in response to Ellis' (1959) critique that these conditions were likely to be highly desirable rather than necessary or sufficient. Unconditional acceptance is also known as unconditional positive regard, non-possessive warmth or respect; empathy as empathic understanding or accurate empathy; and genuineness as congruence. All three conditions are necessary for therapeutic improvement to occur since their presence is mutually dependent on one another. The relationship between the core conditions and therapeutic improvement is a linear one, in which higher levels of these conditions lead to greater improvement. In other words, the effectiveness of psychotherapy does not depend on the use of specialized techniques or knowledge. It is simply a function of the ability of the therapist to genuinely understand and accept the feelings of the client.

For clients to become aware of feelings they find threatening, they should feel unconditionally accepted by their therapist. If they only sense that they are conditionally accepted, then they are unlikely to explore and express feelings which are frightening and of which the therapist may also disapprove. Therapists unconditionally accept their clients because they believe that only clients can know what their own feelings are and that through such self-awareness their clients will behave more constructively. If the therapist cannot unconditionally accept a client, then these feelings should be shared with the client so that they can be worked through. If, however, the therapist does not feel unconditional positive regard for many clients, then they should undergo therapy themselves since the therapist's ability to accept others depends on the extent to which they accept themselves. If they do not approve of themselves, they will find it difficult to accept others.

For clients to feel unconditionally accepted, they must sense that the therapist really understands their feelings. If they believe that the therapist is not aware of who they are, then they may doubt whether the therapist would continue to accept them if they expressed some of the more negative and undesirable feelings they had. The therapist helps clients become conscious of feelings they have denied by trying to put themselves in their client's shoes (but without becoming the client) and tentatively suggesting to them what they might be feeling. For example, if the therapist senses that the client is angry, then the therapist does not become angry but tries to understand what meaning this feeling has for the client and conveys this meaning to them. The therapist concentrates on what the client is feeling at that particular moment rather than what they might be talking about. For example, it is more important to grasp what the client feels about their father than to correctly remember what the father may have done to the client. If the therapist can express what the client is only vaguely aware of, then the client will find it easier to acknowledge and to express these feelings.

For clients to feel unconditionally accepted and understood, they must see the therapist as being genuine or congruent in both the sense that the therapist is aware of and accepts his or her own feelings and that these feelings are apparent to the client. If the client does not feel that the therapist is genuine, then they will also feel that the unconditional acceptance and the understanding is not real. Therapists need to be aware of their own feelings since it is through this experience that they understand the client. If the therapist is not open to their own feelings, then they will also not be able to understand the client. Being genuine, however, does not mean that the therapist has to tell the client all their feelings. What it entails is that the therapist does not hide anything from the client and that there is no contradiction between what is said and what is felt. For example, if therapists feel angry, they should be aware of this feeling even though they may not think it is necessary to express it verbally. If they believe that it is therapeutically useful to discuss it, then they may mention it but without passing judgement on the client. For example, they may say something like 'I'm feeling angry at this moment. I wish I didn't feel this way, but I do'. In fact, the feeling may dissipate when expressed in this way.

After listening to many hours of recorded sessions of therapy, Rogers (1961b) proposed that when the three core conditions were present therapeutic change could be seen as occurring in seven gradual stages in seven related aspects of the client's behaviour, which became increasingly indistinguishable.

1 *Relationship to feelings.* At the beginning of therapy, clients generally do not recognize their feelings as their own. Gradually, they acknowledge these feelings as their own, but can only talk about them in the

past where they are seen as being bad and unacceptable. Later on, they describe these feelings as they arise, even though they find them frightening. Finally, they express them as they change from moment to moment while being able to accept them.

2 *Manner of experiencing.* Similarly, clients become progressively more aware of what they are experiencing, these experiences become less remote to them, and they are increasingly used as a guide to understanding themselves.

3 *Degree of incongruence.* Clients also become increasingly aware of the discrepancy or incongruence between what they feel deep down and of what they are aware. They are progressively better able both to recognize and to reduce this incongruence more quickly.

4 *Communication of self.* Initially, clients are very reluctant to talk about themselves in therapy. Gradually, they feel safe to discuss themselves impersonally as if they were an object. Ultimately, they are no longer aware of themselves but express what they feel at any one moment.

5 *Personal constructs.* Clients gradually think about their experiences in less rigid ways. They hold beliefs more tentatively and check them against further experiences.

6 *Relationship to problems.* They become increasingly aware that their problems are their own and that they have the sole responsibility for solving them.

7 *Manner of relating.* At first, clients are frightened of being themselves with the therapist. They ask how they should behave in order to act more appropriately. Slowly, they begin to take more risks in what they say and they are prepared to give reasons as to why they cannot trust the therapist. Eventually, they feel free to express their feelings as they occur in the relationship.

Although seven consecutive stages can be discerned in these seven behaviours, most people who seek psychotherapy are in Stage (3), where they describe their feelings as being remote from themselves and in the past. They talk about themselves in terms of how other people relate to them rather than in terms of what they themselves feel. Furthermore, they recognize that although their views are rigid, they have conflicting feelings. Most of the therapeutic improvement is restricted to behaviour that is characteristic of Stages (4) and (5), so that the full range of behaviour embodied in the seven stages is not usually observed in therapy.

The person-centred view of effective therapy is perhaps most succinctly summarized in the *process equation of psychotherapy*, which states that (Rogers, 1961b, p. 40):

The more the client perceives the therapist as real or genuine, as empathic, as having an unconditional regard for him (her), the more the client will move away from a static, unfeeling, fixed, impersonal type of functioning and the more (s)he will move toward a way of functioning which is marked by a fluid, changing, acceptant experiencing of differential personal feelings.

Self-esteem and psychological disorder

Person-centred theory holds that people with psychological disorders do not value themselves. This lack of self-esteem or self-acceptance results from the discrepancy between their self-concept and their underlying feelings. To assess self-esteem, person-centred theorists used Stephenson's (1953) Q-technique to develop the Butler–Haigh (1954) Q-sort. This instrument consists of 100 items (e.g. 'I feel uncomfortable while talking with someone' and 'I often kick myself for the things I do') taken from what clients had said about themselves in client-centred therapy and rewritten to further clarify their meaning (for the full list of items, see Ends & Page, 1957). Each statement is printed onto a card and individuals have to twice sort these 100 cards into nine piles. The first time they do this as a self-sort, in which they describe themselves in terms of those statements which are most and least like them as they presently see themselves. They have to put a specified number of statements into each of the nine piles, so that they are distributed in a quasi-normal way (i.e. 26 statements have to be placed in pile 5, 21 each in piles 4 and 6, 11 each in 3 and 7, 4 each in 2 and 8, and 1 each in 1 and 9). The second occasion is the ideal-sort, in which they describe themselves as they would ideally like to be. Each sort takes about 45 minutes to complete. The measure of self-esteem is the correlation between the two sorts. The more positive the correlation is, the more similar the two sorts are and the less the discrepancy is between the self and the ideal self. In other words, people with high self-esteem see themselves as being more similar to the way they would like to be than those with low self-esteem.

If the Q-sort is a valid index of self-esteem, then according to person-centred theory people with psychological problems should have lower self-esteem than those without them and therapeutic improvement should be reflected in increased self-esteem. A number of studies have generally found that therapeutic improvement is associated with greater self-esteem as measured by the Q-sort (Butler & Haigh, 1954; Ends & Page, 1957; Shlien et al., 1962; Butler, 1968; Truax et al., 1968). An exception to these results may have been due to the high self-esteem of clients before therapy which was similar to that of normals (Phillips et al., 1965). Other investigations using similar discrepancy measures have also reported an increase in self-esteem with psychotherapy, drugs and electro-convulsive treatment (Laxer, 1964; Keilson et al., 1979; Rush et al., 1982; Blackburn & Bishop, 1983; Sheehan, 1985). Psychiatric patients should have lower self-esteem than non-patients. Normals have been reported as having higher self-esteem than depressed and neurotic patients (Friedman, 1955; Hillson & Worchel, 1957; Hewstone *et al.*, 1981; Ashworth *et al.*, 1982; Axford & Jerrom, 1986), although not always higher than schizophrenic patients (Friedman, 1955; Hillson & Worchel, 1957; Ashworth *et al.*, 1982).

At the same time as the Q-sort was developed, a similar measure called the Index of Adjustment and Values was created by Bills *et al.* (1951). This instrument consists of 49 adjectives (e.g. acceptable, accurate and alert) selected initially to reflect characteristics which frequently occur in client-centred interviews. Subjects are asked to rate themselves in terms of firstly how often these characteristics are like them (their self concept), secondly how much they like being this way (their self-acceptance concept), and thirdly how much they would wish to be like this (their ideal-self concept). Self-esteem or adjustment is the discrepancy between the self and ideal-self concept. A strong correlation has generally been noted between the discrepancy score and the self-acceptance rating, indicating that a single self-rating may be an equivalent but quicker measure of self-acceptance than the discrepancy score (Bills *et al.*, 1951; Crowne *et al.*, 1961; Korner *et al.*, 1963; Medinnus & Curtis, 1963; Spitzer *et al.*, 1966; Viney, 1966). The discrepancy score on this measure has also been shown to be moderately strongly correlated with that of the Q-sort (Shlien, 1962; Winkler & Meyers, 1963).

More direct questionnaire measures of self-esteem not involving discrepancy scores have also shown an increase in self-esteem with psychotherapy (Percell *et al.*, 1974; Connors *et al.*, 1984; Wolchik *et al.*, 1986; Freeman *et al.*, 1988). One of the shortest such questionnaires is the Rosenberg (1965) Self-Esteem Scale which consists of 10 items (e.g. 'On the whole, I am satisfied with myself' and 'I wish I could have more respect for myself'). Low self-esteem on this measure (or a shortened version of it) has been found to be associated with greater psychological distress in a number of large-scale community surveys (Rosenberg, 1965; Kaplan & Pokorny, 1969; Ilfeld, 1978; Ingham *et al.*, 1986) and also with wider self-ideal discrepancy scores (Silber & Tippett, 1965).

Person-centred theorists have suggested that people who accept themselves tend to be more accepting of others. This idea was initially supported in terms of the nature of the comments made by individuals during client-centred therapy in two studies which examined the same ten cases (Sheerer, 1949; Stock, 1949). Subsequently, the same relationship was obtained in normal subjects with two questionnaires designed to measure these two attitudes (Phillips, 1951; Berger, 1952; McIntyre, 1952; Omwake, 1954). Self-ideal discrepancy measures of self-acceptance have also been shown to correlate with acceptance of specific others such as father (Suinn, 1961) and child (Medinnus & Curtis, 1963).

Therapeutic effectiveness of the core conditions

Several clinical studies have compared the efficacy of client-centred therapy with other forms of therapy (Heine, 1953; Ashby *et al.*, 1957; Ends & Page, 1957; Shlien *et al.*, 1962; Kiesler *et al.*, 1967/1976b; Truax, 1970; Meyer, 1981). However, since person-centred therapists believe that the effectiveness of therapy depends on the nature of the therapist–client relationship and not on therapeutic technique, these comparative studies do not provide an appropriate test of the importance of this relationship. More relevant is the substantial research which has examined the association between the presence of these therapeutic qualities and treatment outcome and which has been periodically reviewed (e.g. Gurman, 1977; Mitchell *et al.*, 1977; Watson, 1984; Orlinsky & Howard, 1986). Some of the more important conditions for testing this hypothesis have been outlined elsewhere (Cramer, 1990a, 1990b).

The presence of the core conditions have been assessed by questionnaire and by ratings of recorded segments of therapy sessions. Two questionnaires specifically designed for measuring these therapeutic qualities are the Relationship Inventory (Barrett–Lennard, 1962, 1964) and the Relationship Questionnaire (Truax & Carkhuff, 1967). Unlike the Relationship Questionnaire, the Relationship Inventory appropriately distinguishes unconditionality of regard from level of regard so that regard may be high or low as well as conditional or unconditional. However, no consideration is given as to how these two scales should be used together to measure unconditional positive regard (Cramer, 1989). In addition, the items have been written to assess only one quality at a time so there are four distinct sets of questions.

In the revised version (reproduced in Cramer, 1986b), each of the four scales consists of eight positively and eight negatively worded items to assess the qualities of level of regard (e.g. 'S/he feels deep affection for me' and 'S/he is indifferent to me'), unconditionality of regard (e.g. 'Depending on my behaviour, s/he has a better opinion of me sometimes than s/he has at other times' and 'Whether I am in good spirits or feeling upset does not make her/him feel any more or less appreciative of me'), empathy (e.g. 'S/he nearly always knows exactly what I mean' and 'S/he may understand my words but s/he does not see the way I feel') and congruence (e.g. 'S/he expresses her/his true impressions and feelings with me' and 'I believe s/he has feelings s/he does not tell me about that are causing difficulty in our relationship').

Although these four scales have been generally found to be moderately and positively correlated (Gurman, 1977), factor analyses of the correlations between the items suggest that the four qualities can be distinguished by individuals in their relationships with therapists (Lietaer, 1976) and close friends (Cramer, 1986a, 1986b) and that the questions are not simply measuring a global evaluation of these relationships (Mills & Zytowski, 1967).

Ratings of these three qualities have also been made by trained observers, normally using the nine-point accurate empathy and five-point non-possessive warmth and genuineness scales of Truax and Carkhuff (1967) on a number of 2–4 minute segments taken from different portions of tape-recorded therapy sessions. However, since person-centred theorists have explicitly stated that it is the client's perception of these charac-teristics which brings about therapeutic improvement, their assessment by others can only be justified if their judgments are similar to those of the client. Agreement between clients and others on the presence of these qualities has generally not been high in either clinical (Barrett-Lennard, 1962; Bozarth & Grace, 1970; Mitchell *et al.*, 1973; Kiesler *et al.*, 1967/1976c) or non-clinical samples (Burstein & Carkhuff, 1968; McWhirter, 1973). Consequently, an adequate test of this person-centred proposition should include the client's assessment of the core conditions. Incidentally, the finding that agreement on these qualities between normal individuals and others is no higher than that for clients implies that the low correspondence for clients is not due to their emotional distress interfering with their judgement.

Clients' perception of the core conditions have been assessed mainly in individual rather than group therapy. The measurement of these qual-ities is more problematic in group therapy, where the most therapeutic member of the group may not necessarily be the therapist and where this person may change in the course of treatment. Studies which have assumed the therapeutic member to be the therapist have generally reported no relationship between these conditions and outcome (Truax, 1966b; Hansen *et al.*, 1968; Roback & Strassberg, 1975), while those which have assigned equal weight to all group members have found an association (Clark & Culbert, 1965; Culbert, 1968). This problem does not arise in research on individual therapy where there is only one therapist.

Studies which have investigated the association between the core conditions measured early on in therapy and the subsequent outcome of individual therapy have produced mixed results. Only a few studies have generally found support for such a relationship for some of the therapeutic qualities (Barrett-Lennard, 1962; Kurtz & Grummon, 1972; Saltzman *et al.*, 1976; Bennum & Schlinder, 1988), while others have not (Kiesler *et al.*, 1967/1976a; van der Veen, 1967; Mitchell *et al.*, 1973; Sloane *et al.*, 1975; Ford, 1978; Hoogduin *et al.*, 1989). The fact that cognitive–behaviour therapy administered by computer was found to be as effective in reducing depression as the same treatment given by a therapist and more effective than a waiting-list control implies that therapeutic improvement may occur with minimal therapist contact (Selmi *et al.*, 1990). Similar results have been obtained for self-directed desensitization for dealing with phobias (Baker *et al.*, 1973; Rosen *et al.*, 1976). However, snake-phobic students who followed an automated desensitization procedure in which the taped voice of the therapist was warm showed less snake avoidance than those in the condition where the voice was cold, which did not differ from the no-treatment group (Morris & Suckerman, 1974a). At present, it is not clear to what extent a therapist who shows the core conditions may facilitate therapeutic improvement. One study found less snake avoidance in students given systematic desensitization with a warm than a cold therapist which in turn was equivalent to no treatment (Morris & Suckerman, 1974b), while in another study no difference was obtained for exposure treatment of acrophobia with a warm or cold therapist which were both more effective than no treatment (Morris & Magrath, 1979).

Since the core conditions are thought to be present in varying degrees in all relationships, it follows from person-centred theory that people with relationships having higher levels of these qualities will generally be more self-accepting and better adjusted psychologically than those with relationships which are lower in these characteristics. Such an association has been reported using the Relationship Inventory (Hollenbeck, 1965; van der Veen & Novak, 1971; Quick & Jacob, 1973; Cramer, 1985b, 1987, 1989, 1990c, 1990d). Although these findings are in keeping with the proposition that the core conditions facilitate psychological adjustment, three other causal relationships are plausible. Firstly, the causal direction may be reversed with psychological adjustment bringing about either the perception of or the actual presence of higher levels of the core conditions. Secondly, the causal relationship may be reciprocal with the core conditions producing and also being produced by psychological adjustment. And thirdly, the association between the core conditions and psychological adjustment may be spurious, resulting from other factors such as socio-economic status or physical health.

One way of exploring the causal nature of the association between two variables in a non-experimental way is to conduct a longitudinal study, in which the two variables are measured at the same points in time. If the correlation between the first variable (e.g. core conditions) at time 1 and the second variable (e.g. psychological adjustment) at time 2 is more positive than that between the second variable (i.e. psychological adjustment) at time 1 and the first variable (i.e. core conditions) at time 2, then this result suggests that the first variable (i.e. core conditions) has temporal predominance over the second one (i.e. psychological adjustment). Some initial support for the temporal predominance of the core conditions over psychological adjustment comes from a study in which this pattern was obtained for the Rosenberg's Self-Esteem score of a small sample of students and the total Relationship Inventory score of their closest relationship measured 15 weeks apart (Cramer, 1988, 1990e).

Further evidence for an association between psychological adjustment and the core conditions arises from studies which have asked questions about similar characteristics (Vanfossen, 1981; Burbach *et al.*, 1989; Cramer, 1990f, 1991c). However, in a large scale nationally representative survey of some 2050 women and 1873 men in Britain, the correlation between psychological distress (as measured by the 30-item General Health Questionnaire) and the adequacy of family support (as assessed by such items as 'There are members of my family who make me feel loved' and 'There are members of my family who accept me just as I am') was generally found to be unexpectedly very low, apart from in the better qualified youngest age group where it was higher (Cramer, 1991c).

Summary

Person-centred theory holds that young children's desire for love is so strong that they will disregard their other needs in order to satisfy it. If this love is only given when children do or feel what others want them to, then their self-concept will not reflect who they are and will cause them to be dissatisfied and to become psychologically disturbed. The bigger the discrepancy between their self-concept and their underlying feelings, the more seriously disturbed they will be. To help them become aware of their basic feelings and to accept them, it is necessary that they enter into a relationship with someone who they feel genuinely and unconditionally accepts and understands them. Consequently, the effectiveness of psychotherapy is seen as being primarily dependent on the extent to which the client perceives the therapist as showing the three core conditions of unconditional acceptance, empathy and genuiness. Although patients have been found to be less self-accepting than non-patients, there is little evidence to suggest that the client's perception of these core conditions early on in therapy is related to their subsequent outcome.

10

Towards a common approach?

The existence of numerous and diverse approaches to psychotherapy creates the difficulty of knowing which methods to advocate and to use for treating psychological distress. The immediate solution to this problem would be to apply those procedures found to be the most effective. However, no clear consensus has emerged on which techniques have been shown to be the most successful. As we have seen, a large number of studies have been carried out evaluating the effects of alternative treatments on patients referred for psychotherapy. So far, no attempt has been made to summarize the results of these studies and it is now time to consider how this has been done.

Summarizing outcome research

Three different methods used to try to encapsulate the findings of the literature on therapeutic outcome include the qualitative *narrative review* and the quantitative *box score* analysis and *meta-analysis*. The traditional method has been the narrative review in which greatest weight may be given to those studies evaluated as being the most methodologically adequate (e.g. Rachman, 1971; Rachman & Wilson, 1980). The advantage of such reviews is that attention can be paid to the particular drawbacks of individual studies which may be taken into account in later research. Their disadvantage is that, when studies are of comparable quality or have different weaknesses, they convey little idea of what the research may reveal in general.

As the body of studies on a particular topic increases substantially, some method of quantifying the results of these studies is helpful in providing an overview of the findings. The simplest method is box score analysis where the number of comparisons or measures giving a certain result are counted. Luborsky *et al.* (1975), for example, tallied the number of comparisons in which behaviour therapy was reported as being more effective than other forms of psychotherapy, less effective and no different. There were 19 comparisons from 12 studies on patients being treated in general for neurotic disorders. Of these, six favoured behaviour therapy while the remaining 13 did not differentiate between the two treatments. A further breakdown of these box scores can be provided. For instance, Luborsky *et al.* (1975) also noted that all six studies which found behaviour therapy to be more effective used very brief therapies and that five of them were of relatively poor methodological quality.

A more sophisticated quantitative method is meta-analysis where the size, rather than simply the direction, of the difference between two treatments is calculated (e.g. Smith & Glass, 1977; Smith *et al.*, 1980). This measure is known as the *effect size* and is the mean difference between the standard and the comparison treatment divided by the standard deviation of the comparison treatment. An effect size of +1 means that 84 per cent of the people in the comparison treatment will fall below the mean of those in the standard treatment, while an effect size of +0.5 denotes that 69 per cent will do so. In the first meta-analysis ever carried out on psychotherapy outcome studies, Smith and Glass (1977) calculated 833 effect sizes from 375 studies. They presented average effect sizes for 10 types of therapy, which were strongest for systematic desensitization (0.91), rational–emotive therapy (0.77) and behaviour modification (0.76). There was only a very weak tendency for larger effect sizes to be associated with less adequate experimental designs.

Greater details of what they did was provided in a second and expanded analysis which covered 1766 effect sizes from 475 studies (Smith *et al.*, 1980). Effect sizes were greatest for cognitive therapies (2.38), hypnotherapy (1.82), cognitive-behavioural therapy (1.13) and systematic desensitization (1.05). As would be expected, differences between treatments became smaller when they were grouped together into broader categories. So, the average effect size for the behavioural therapies (e.g. systematic desensitization, cognitive and cognitive–behavioural therapies) was 0.98 compared to 0.85 for the verbal therapies (e.g. hypnotherapy, psychodynamic and gestalt therapy). Larger effect sizes were associated with the more *reactive* the outcome measure was judged to be in terms of the extent to which it closely reflected the goals and values of the investigator. When the reactivity of the measures was statistically controlled, the difference between the effect size of the behavioural (0.91) and verbal (0.88) therapies was further reduced. It would have been informative if the same statistical adjustment had been made to the effect sizes of the more clearly differentiated categories of therapies.

Since these original studies, various other meta-analyses have been published. Andrews and Harvey (1981), for example, selected only those studies used by Smith *et al.* (1980) which were based on patients seeking treatment for neurotic disorders. Of these 81 studies, the average effect size was largest for the category of cognitive and gestalt therapies (1.20) followed by behaviour therapy (0.99) and cognitive–behaviour therapy (0.77). No reason was given for including gestalt therapy with the cognitive therapies which was not done by Smith *et al.* (1980) and which therefore makes it difficult to compare the results of the two analyses. Shapiro and Shapiro (1982) conducted a meta-analysis of 143 outcome studies, of which only 21 overlapped with those examined by Smith *et al.* (1980). Mean effect sizes were greatest for covert behavioural techniques (1.52), modelling (1.43) and flooding (1.12). Berman *et al.* (1985) restricted their analysis to 25 studies comparing cognitive therapy, systematic desensitization or their combination. There was no difference in the effect size of these two treatments, regardless of whether these comparisons were based on student volunteers or clinical patients. The final example is that of Bowers and Clum (1988) who found an effect size of 0.55 between behavioural techniques and placebo controls.

The results of these quantitative reviews point to the greater effectiveness of behavioural and cognitive therapies over other approaches. Despite this superiority, the authors of many reviews of psychotherapy outcome studies report that the effectiveness of many psychological treatments is similar (Luborsky *et al.*, 1975; Smith *et al.*, 1980; Stiles *et al.*, 1986). Indeed, as we have seen, many well-designed studies have found few differences between conceptually dissimilar therapies (e.g. Madill *et al.*, 1966; Marks *et al.*, 1968; Patterson *et al.*, 1971; Gelder *et al.*, 1973; McConaghy & Barr, 1973; Emmelkamp & Ultee, 1974; Marks *et al.*, 1975; Sloane *et al.*, 1975; Boersma *et al.*, 1976; Baker *et al.*, 1977; Emmelkamp & Kwee, 1977; Hall & Goldberg, 1977; Eckert *et al.*, 1979; Shaw, 1979; Zeiss *et al.*, 1979; Stravynski *et al.*, 1982; Woody *et al.*, 1983, 1987; Gunderson *et al.*, 1984; Hersen *et al.*, 1984; Emmelkamp *et al.*, 1985; Freeman *et al.*, 1988; Miller *et al.*, 1989a, 1989b).

Common basic factors

The fact that all forms of psychotherapy appear to be effective to some extent have led some commentators to suggest that their successes may result from the features that they share rather than those which differentiate them. In one of the earliest papers on this theme, Rozenzweig (1936) proposed that four factors common to diverse methods of psychotherapy were catharsis, the therapist's personality, the theoretical consistency of the therapy and the provision of an alternative, if only partial, explanation of the problem.

Later, Frank (1973) argued that patients seeking psychotherapy suffered from the common problem of demoralization which arose from being unable to deal with a pressing problem or having failed to meet expectations of either themselves or others. This loss of confidence in themselves made them more prone to distressing feelings such as anxiety, depression and resentment. Morale is restored by the four features of the therapeutic relationship, setting, rationale and task which are shared by all psychotherapies and which operate through the five interrelated processes of insight, hope of relief, experience of success, social integration and emotional arousal.

The essential aspect of the therapeutic relationship is that patients must feel that their therapists are competent, that they genuinely care for their patients and that they believe that their patients can overcome their problems. The setting in which therapy occurs enables patients to explore their ideas and feelings in a secure environment in which they will not be endangered. The rationale of the therapy, which is enhanced by its insusceptibility to disproof, provides patients with an explanation for their distress, goals to be reached and procedures for achieving them, all of which should be acceptable to them. The therapeutic procedure allows therapists to demonstrate their professional competence in its use and a means for influencing patients. It also offers a face-saving device for patients to change their symptoms when they wish to do so.

These four features activate five interdependent processes which bring about therapeutic improvement. Firstly, they give patients an opportunity for experiential learning or insight in which they become aware of the discrepancy between their assumptions about the world and reality. The realization of this discrepancy provides a strong motive for changing their behaviour in terms of their new cognitive understanding of their situation. Secondly, a hope of relief is created by patients' faith in the effectiveness of the therapist and the treatment, which is reinforced by the therapist. Thirdly, the therapeutic procedure provides patients with a series of success experiences, which enhance their sense of competence. Fourthly, patients' relationship with their therapist and other patients give them a common conceptual framework in which they realize that their problems are not unique and that others care for and understand them. Finally, for reasons which are not clear, emotional arousal is thought to be important for therapeutic change. However, as we have already seen in our discussion of flooding, emotional arousal in the form of anxiety does not facilitate the effectiveness of this treatment (Everaerd *et al.*, 1973; Emmelkamp, 1974; Hafner & Marks, 1976). Consequently, there is no evidence to support the role of this fifth factor.

Efforts to determine which therapeutic factors are most commonly perceived by patients as having helped them overcome their problems

have included asking patients to describe these in terms of either individual sessions (Elliott, 1985; Elliott *et al.*, 1985; Lietaer & Neirinck, 1986;
Elliott & Shapiro, 1988; Llewelyn *et al.*, 1988) or therapy in general
(Murphy *et al.*, 1984b). In a study of mainly cognitive–behavioural therapy, the two therapeutic factors found to be most highly and consistently
related to outcome were talking to an understanding person and being
given advice (Murphy *et al.*, 1984b). A taxonomy developed for describing
events occurring within sessions which are seen by patients as being
helpful (Elliott *et al.*, 1985) had the following nine categories: (1) Personal
Insight; (2) Interpersonal Insight; (3) Awareness; (4) Problem Clarification;
(5) Problem Solution; (6) Involvement; (7) Understanding; (8) Reassurance;
and (9) Personal Contact. However, so far little research has been published
relating the presence of these categories of events to outcome.

Compatibility between approaches

While some therapists have sought to reconcile diverse forms of therapy
by suggesting that their effectiveness may depend on common factors
which they share, other writers have sought to combine different
approaches in various ways. As was noted in the first chapter, surveys on
the theoretical orientations of clinical and counselling psychologists have
found that a majority of those who replied saw themselves as eclectic.
In other words, these respondents did not adhere to any one particular
theoretical approach. In an attempt to find out what practitioners meant
by the term eclectic, Garfield and Kurtz (1977) asked every other person
who had described their theoretical orientation in a previous survey as
eclectic what they understood by this term. They grouped the responses
into four main categories. About 47 per cent of the respondents employed
whatever theory or method seemed best for the client; 14 per cent
amalgamated many different theories or aspects of theories; 12 per cent
used two or three theories; while 6 per cent thought no theory or set of
theories were totally adequate. When these clinicians were asked what
two theoretical orientations were most characteristic of their views, various
combinations were offered of which the most popular was psychodynamic
and learning theory.

While some have argued that different theoretical viewpoints are
irreconcilable (Eysenck, 1959a; Yates, 1983; Messer, 1989), others have
proposed some of the following ways in which two or more theoretical
perspectives can be held simultaneously. Constructs in distinct theories
have been related to each other (Kubie, 1934; Miller, 1948; Shoben,
1949; Dollard & Miller, 1950), such as Pavlovian inhibition and psychoanalytic repression (French, 1933). Important phenomena observed in
one treatment, such as transference and resistance, have been seen as
occurring in another approach, such as behaviour therapy (Weinberg &

Zaslove, 1963; Crisp, 1966; Rhoads & Feather, 1972). Elements of two separate approaches have been combined into one treatment (Stampfl & Levis, 1967, 1973; Feather & Rhoads, 1972a, 1972b; Wachtel, 1977, 1987; Bieber, 1980). Different therapeutic approaches have been recommended for different problems (Marks & Gelder, 1966; Lazarus, 1976, 1989), such as systematic desensitization for unadaptive autonomic habits like phobias and operant conditioning for undesirable motor habits like nail biting (Wolpe, 1982). Finally, different theoretical techniques have been proposed as acting at different stages in therapeutic change (Prochaska & DiClemente, 1982, 1984; Ryle, 1984; Beitman, 1987, 1989).

Three comprehensive frameworks for including different techniques will be briefly outlined. Although these models do not generally offer sufficiently clear guidelines on which techniques to use with what problems and with what patients, they illustrate schemes which attempt to draw together various features of different therapies. Working within social learning theory, Lazarus (1973, 1976, 1989) has developed an approach called *multimodal behaviour therapy*, which he describes as *technical eclecticism*. Technical eclecticism is based on a broad theoretical framework (social learning theory) but uses specific and replicable techniques taken from any approach to treat particular problems. Multimodal behaviour therapy holds that patients usually suffer from a multitude of specific problems which need to be treated by a number of specific techniques. The problems can be thought of as concerned with seven processes or modalities: (1) *B*ehaviour (e.g. compulsions, habits); (2) *A*ffect (e.g. anger, anxiety, depression); (3) *S*ensation (e.g. aches, dizziness, pain); (4) *I*magery (e.g. disturbing recollections of unpleasant events); (5) *C*ognitions (e.g. irrational beliefs, misinformation); (6) *I*nterpersonal relationships (e.g. dependence, suspiciousness); and (7) Biological factors (e.g. intoxication, lack of exercise, inappropriate diet). If biological factors are subsumed under the rubric *D*rugs, then these seven areas can be more easily remembered with the amusingly ironic acronym *BASIC ID* which is intended to highlight the idea that this less abstract approach is more appropriate than the traditional psychoanalytic view. A Modality Profile is drawn up for the patient, as illustrated in Table 10.1 (adapted from Woolfolk, 1974), which includes proposed treatments for the problems initially identified in each area. It is not clear, however, on what basis these techniques are advocated.

Transtheoretical therapy is being developed by Prochaska and his colleagues. In a comparative analysis of 18 major theories of psychotherapy, five general processes of change were identified, which operated at both an experiential and an environmental level (Prochaska, 1979). These five general change mechanisms were consciousness raising (providing information), catharsis (emotional release), choosing (awareness of alternatives), conditional stimuli (behavioural or environmental change) and contingency control (changing consequences). In a study of smokers

Table 10.1 An example of a modality profile from multimodal behaviour therapy

Modality	Problem	Proposed treatment
Behaviour	Non-fluent and quiet speech; lack of eye contact	Behavioural rehearsal with modelling and videotaped feedback
Affect	Fear of husband Anger	Desensitization Gestalt awareness exercises
Sensation	Muscular tension	Relaxation training
Imagery	Unrealistic images of retaliation	Autohypnosis with success imagery
Cognition	Defeatist self-talk	Replace with positive self-talk
	Irrational beliefs about inferiority of women	Rational disputation and bibliotherapy
Interpersonal relationships	Lack of interpersonal sensitivity	Teach perception of non-verbal cues
	Control of husband by passivity	Negotiation of needs with relationship therapy
	Reinforcement by husband of passivity	Train husband to reward assertiveness
Drugs	Periodic depression	Discuss possible use of drugs with doctor

who had successfully given up smoking without treatment and smokers receiving treatment, four stages of change were recognized (DiClemente & Prochaska, 1982): (1) contemplation (thinking about change); (2) decision-making/determination (deciding to change); (3) action (actively changing one's behaviour and/or the environment); and (4) maintenance (maintaining the changes).

Prochaska and DiClemente (1982) have suggested that certain change processes are more important for effecting improvement at different stages of therapy. Their proposed transtheoretical therapy model of change is shown in Figure 10.1. The process of becoming more aware of the need and possibility for change (consciousness raising) is important during the stage of thinking about change (contemplation). The process of expressing feelings (catharsis) helps bridge the gap between thinking about change (contemplation) and deciding to change (determination). Realizing alternative ways of behaving (choosing) is prominent during

Figure 10.1 Transtheoretical therapy model of change.

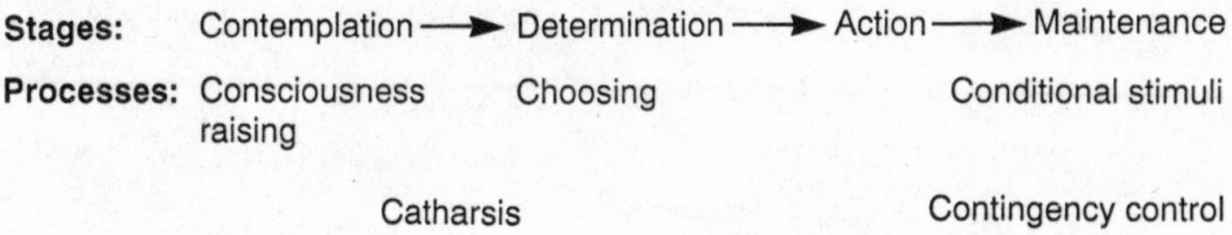

Stages: Contemplation ⟶ Determination ⟶ Action ⟶ Maintenance

Processes: Consciousness   Choosing   Conditional stimuli
raising

                Catharsis   Contingency control

the determination stage, while modifying one's behaviour, the environment and/or the consequences of one's behaviour (conditional stimuli and contingency control) occurs most readily during the stages of active attempts at change (action) and maintaining those changes (maintenance).

Empirical investigation of this model has begun. Questionnaires have been devised to assess both stages and processes of change. A 32-item Stages of Change Questionnaire has been developed on 150 outpatients seeking therapy (McConnaughy et al., 1983) which measures the stages of pre-contemplation (assessed by items such as 'As far as I'm concerned, I don't have any problems that need changing' and 'I'm not the problem one. It doesn't make much sense for me to be here'), contemplation (e.g. 'I have a problem and I really think I should work on it' and 'I'm hoping this place helps me to better understand myself'), action (e.g. 'I am doing something about the problems that had been bothering me' and 'Anyone can talk about changing; I'm actually doing something about it'), and maintenance ('It worries me that I might slip back on a problem I have already changed so I am here to seek help' and 'I thought once I had resolved the problem I would be free of it, but sometimes I still find myself struggling with it'). Decision-making did not emerge as a distinct stage and so was eliminated from further consideration.

A Processes of Change Questionnaire has also been devised to measure the ten change mechanisms and a few others including the availability and use of a helping relationship (Prochaska & Norcross, 1983b; Prochaska et al., 1988). Factor analyses of a questionnaire specifically developed for smokers trying to give up smoking resulted in a 40-item Processes of Change Questionnaire which assessed the following ten processes which corresponded better to an experiential–behavioural distinction rather than an experiential–environmental one (Prochaska et al., 1988).

The five experiential processes were Consciousness-Raising (measured by items such as 'I recall articles dealing with the problems of quitting smoking' and 'I recall information people have personally given me on how to stop smoking'), Dramatic Relief (e.g. 'I tell myself I can choose to smoke or not' and 'I tell myself I am able to quit smoking if I want to'), Self-Liberation (e.g. 'Dramatic portrayals of the evils of smoking affect me personally' and 'I react emotionally to warnings about smoking

Table 10.2 Beitman's integrative model of individual psychotherapy

Elements	Engagement	Pattern search	Change	Termination
Goals	Develop trust	Define dysfunctional behaviour	Establish new pattern	Practise separation
Techniques	Empathy	Listening	Interpretation	Mutual agreement
	Effective suggestions	Role-playing	Modelling	
Content	Presenting problems Distrust	Interpersonal style Emotion	Responsibility	Fears of relapse
Resistance	To trust	To pattern search	To change self	Recurrence of symptoms
Transference	To surface features of therapist	Interpersonal patterns of patient	Fear of losing therapist	Hold on to or reject therapist
Counter-transference	To surface features of patient	Interpersonal patterns of therapist	Fear of losing patient	Hold on to or reject patient

cigarettes'), Social Liberation ('I notice that non-smokers are asserting their rights' and 'I find society changing in ways which make it easier for the non-smoker'), and Counterconditioning (e.g. 'When I am tempted to smoke, I think about something else' and 'I do something else instead of smoking when I need to relax or deal with tension').

The five behavioural processes were Stimulus Control (e.g. 'I remove things from my home that remind me of smoking' and 'I keep things around my place of work that remind me not to smoke'), Self-Reevaluation (e.g. 'My dependency on cigarettes makes me feel disappointment in myself' and 'I get upset when I think about my smoking'), Environmental Reevaluation (e.g. 'I stop to think that smoking is polluting the environment' and 'I consider the view that smoking can be harmful to the environment'), Reinforcement Management (e.g. 'I am rewarded by others if I don't smoke' and 'I reward myself when I don't smoke'), and Helping Relationship (e.g. 'Special people in my life accept me the same whether I smoke or not' and 'I have someone who listens when I need to talk about my smoking').

Finally, Beitman (1987, 1989) has suggested that psychotherapy consists of four stages. The first stage consists primarily of the therapist and client learning to work together (engagement). The second stage involves defining the patterns of behaviour to be changed (pattern search). The third stage encompasses trying to change those behaviours and maintaining the changes made (change) and the fourth stage is concerned with ending therapy (termination). Each stage comprises the six elements of goals, techniques, content, resistance, transference and counter-transference. Examples of these elements in the four stages are shown in Table 10.2.

Summary

The presence of different psychotherapies for treating psychological disorders makes it difficult to rationally decide which approach should be adopted. A large number of studies have been conducted comparing the effectiveness of various treatments for the problems of both clinical and non-clinical volunteers. Although meta-analytic reviews of a wide range of outcome studies have shown a tendency for the more directive forms of psychotherapy to be more effective, there are numerous individual studies which find few and small differences between seemingly dissimilar treatments. Attempts to reconcile these different approaches have included the suggestion that the effectiveness of these distinct treatments depends on the factors that they have in common rather than on those that differentiate them. Other efforts at reconciliation have tried to relate features of different theories in various ways. The success of these ventures remains to be determined.

References

Abraham, K. (1949). The influence of oral eroticism on character-formation. In D. Bryan & A. Strachey (Trans.), *Selected Papers of Karl Abraham*, pp. 393–406. London: Hogarth Press. (Original work published 1924)

Abrams, J. L. (1979). A cognitive–behavioral versus nondirective group treatment program for opioid-addicted persons: An adjunct to methadone maintenance. *International Journal of the Addictions*, **14**, 503–511.

Adams-Webber, J. R. (1970). An analysis of the discriminant validity of several repertory grid indices. *British Journal of Psychology*, **61**, 83–90.

Adams-Webber, J. R. (1979). *Personal Construct Theory: Concepts and Applications*. New York: Wiley.

Agras, W. S., Leitenberg, H. & Barlow, D. H. (1968). Social reinforcement in the modification of agoraphobia. *Archives of General Psychiatry*, **19**, 423–427.

Agras, W. S., Leitenberg, H., Barlow, D. H. *et al.* (1971). Relaxation in systematic desensitization. *Archives of General Psychiatry*, **25**, 511–514.

Agras, W. S., Schneider, J. A., Arnow, B. *et al.* (1989). Cognitive–behavioral and response-prevention treatments for bulimia nervosa. *Journal of Consulting and Clinical Psychology*, **57**, 215–221.

Alden, L., Safran, J. & Weideman, R. (1978). A comparison of cognitive and skills training strategies in the treatment of unassertive clients. *Behavior Therapy*, **9**, 843–846.

Alexander, F. & French, T. M. (1946). *Psychoanalytic Therapy*. New York: Ronald Press.

Alexander, L. B. & Luborsky, L. (1986). The Penn Helping Alliance Scales. In L. S. Greenberg & W. M. Pinsoff (eds.), *The Psychotherapeutic Process: A research handbook*, pp. 325–366. New York: Guilford Press.

Allen, J. G., Tarnoff, G. & Coyne, L. (1985). Therapeutic alliance and long-term hospital treatment outcome. *Comprehensive Psychiatry*, **26**, 187–194.

American Psychiatric Association. (1987). *Diagnostic and Statistical Manual of Mental Disorders* (rev. 3rd edn.) (DSM-III-R). Washington: APA.

Andrews, G. & Harvey, R. (1981). Does psychotherapy benefit neurotic patients? A reanalysis of the Smith, Glass, and Miller data. *Archives of General Psychiatry*, **38**, 1203–1208.

Andrews, G., Pollock, C. & Stewart, G. (1989). The determination of defense style by questionnaire. *Archives of General Psychiatry*, **46**, 455–460.

Annau, Z. & Kamin, L. J. (1961). The conditioned emotional response as a function of intensity of the US. *Journal of Comparative and Physiological Psychology*, **54**, 428–432.

Aronson, H. & Weintraub, W. (1968). Patient changes during classical psychoanalysis as a function of initial status and duration of treatment. *Psychiatry: Journal for Study of Interpersonal Processes*, **31**, 369–379.

Ashby, J. D., Ford, D. H., Guerney, B. G., Jr. & Guerney, L. F. (1957). Effects on clients of a reflective and a leading type of psychotherapy. *Psychological Monographs: General and Applied*, **71** (24, Whole No. 453).

Ashworth, C. M., Blackburn, I. M. & McPherson, F. M. (1982). The performance of depressed and manic patients on some repertory grid measures: A cross-sectional study. *British Journal of Medical Psychology*, **55**, 247–255.

Auerbach, R. & Kilmann, P. R. (1977). The effects of group systematic desensitization on secondary erectile failure. *Behavior Therapy*, **8**, 330–339.

Axford, S. & Jerrom, D. W. A. (1986). Self-esteem in depression: A controlled repertory grid investigation. *British Journal of Medical Psychology*, **59**, 61–68.

Ayllon, T. (1963). Intensive treatment of psychotic behavior by stimulus satiation and food reinforcement. *Behaviour Research and Therapy*, **1**, 53–61.

Ayllon, T. & Azrin, N. H. (1968). *The Token Economy: A Motivational System for Therapy Rehabilitation*. New York: Appleton–Century–Crofts.

Ayllon, T. & Michael, J. (1959). The psychiatric nurse as a behavioral engineer. *Journal of Experimental Analysis of Behavior*, **2**, 323–334.

Azrin, N. H. & Holz, W. C. (1966). Punishment. In W. K. Honig (ed.), *Operant Behavior: Areas of Research and Application*, pp. 380–447. New York: Appleton–Century–Crofts.

Baer, D. M. & Sherman, J. A. (1964). Reinforcement control of generalized imitation in young children. *Journal of Experimental Social Psychology*, **1**, 37–49.

Bagshaw, V. E. (1977). A replication study of Foulds' and Bedfords' hierarchical model of depression. *British Journal of Psychiatry*, **131**, 53–55.

Bailey, J. E. & Metcalfe, M. (1969). The MPI and the EPI: A comparative study on depressive patients. *British Journal of Social and Clinical Psychology*, **8**, 50–54.

Baker, B. L., Cohen, D. C. & Saunders, J. T. (1973). Self-directed desensitization for acrophobia. *Behaviour Research and Therapy*, **11**, 79–89.

Baker, R., Hall, J. N., Hutchinson, K. & Bridge, G. (1977). Symptom changes in chronic schizophrenic patients on a token economy: A controlled experiment. *British Journal of Psychiatry*, **131**, 381–393.

Bandura, A. (1965). Influence of models' reinforcement contingencies on the acquisition of imitative responses. *Journal of Personality and Social Psychology*, **1**, 589–595.

Bandura, A. (1977a). *Social Learning Theory*. Englewood Cliffs, NJ: Prentice-Hall.

Bandura, A. (1977b). Self-efficacy: Toward a unifying theory of behavioral change. *Psychological Review*, **84**, 191–215.

Bandura, A. & Walters, R. H. (1963). *Social Learning and Personality Development.* New York: Holt, Rinehart & Winston.

Bandura, A. & Jeffery, R. W. (1973). Role of symbolic coding and rehearsal processes in observational learning. *Journal of Personality and Social Psychology,* **26,** 122–130.

Bandura, A., Ross, D. & Ross, S. A. (1961). Transmission of aggression through imitation of aggressive models. *Journal of Abnormal and Social Psychology,* **63,** 575–582.

Bandura, A., Blanchard, E. B. & Ritter, B. (1969). Relative efficacy of desensitization and modeling approaches for inducing behavioral, affective, and attitudinal changes. *Journal of Personality and Social Psychology,* **13,** 173–199.

Bandura, A., Jeffery, R. W. & Wright, C. L. (1974). Efficacy of participant modeling as a function of response induction aids. *Journal of Abnormal Psychology,* **83,** 56–64.

Bandura, A., Adams, N. E. & Beyer, J. (1977). Cognitive processes mediating behavioral change. *Journal of Personality and Social Psychology,* **35,** 125–139.

Bandura, A., Reese, L. & Adams, N. E. (1982). Microanalysis of action and fear arousal as a function of differential levels of perceived self-efficacy. *Journal of Personality and Social Psychology,* **43,** 5–21.

Bannister, D. (1960). Conceptual structure in thought-disordered schizophrenics. *Journal of Mental Science,* **106,** 1230–1249.

Bannister, D. (1962). The nature and measurement of schizophrenic thought disorder. *Journal of Mental Science,* **108,** 825–842.

Bannister, D. & Salmon, P. (1966). Schizophrenic thought disorder: Specific or diffuse? *British Journal of Medical Psychology,* **39,** 215–219.

Bannister, D. & Fransella, F. (1966). A Grid Test of Schizophrenic Thought Disorder. *British Journal of Social and Clinical Psychology,* **5,** 95–102.

Bannister, D., Fransella, F. & Agnew, J. (1971). Characteristics and validity of the Grid Test of Thought Disorder. *British Journal of Social and Clinical Psychology,* **10,** 144–151.

Bannister, D., Adams-Webber, J. R., Penn, J. R. & Radley, A. R. (1975). Reversing the process of thought disorder: A serial validation experiment. *British Journal of Social and Clinical Psychology,* **14,** 169–180.

Barendregt, J. T. (1961). *Research in Psychodiagnostics.* Paris: Mouton.

Barling, J. & Fincham, F. (1979). Psychological adjustment and self-reinforcement style. *Journal of Genetic Psychology,* **135,** 287–289.

Barrett-Lennard, G. T. (1962). Dimensions of therapist response as causal factors in therapeutic change. *Psychological Monographs: General and Applied,* **76** (43, Whole No. 562).

Barrett-Lennard, G. T. (1964). The Relationship Inventory: Forms OS-M-64, OS-F-64 and MO-M-64 plus MO-F-64. University of New England, Australia.

Bates, G. W., Campbell, I. M. & Burgess, P. M. (1990). Assessment of articulated thoughts in social anxiety: Modification of the ATTS procedure. *British Journal of Clinical Psychology,* **29,** 91–98.

Baum, M. (1970). Extinction of an avoidance response following response prevention (flooding). *Psychological Bulletin,* **74,** 270–284.

Bebbington, P., Hurry, J., Tennant, C. *et al.* (1981). Epidemiology of mental disorders in Camberwell. *Psychological Medicine,* **11,** 1–18.

Beck, A. T. (1967). *Depression: Clinical, Experimental, and Theoretical Aspects.* New York: Hoeber.

Beck, A. T. (1976). *Cognitive Therapy and the Emotional Disorders*. New York: International Universities Press.

Beck, A. T., Rush, A. J., Shaw, B. F. & Emery, G. (1979). *Cognitive Therapy of Depression*. New York: Guilford.

Beck, A. T., Brown, G., Steer, R. A. *et al.* (1987). Differentiating anxiety and depression: A test of the cognitive context-specificity hypothesis. *Journal of Abnormal Psychology*, **96**, 179–183.

Bedford, A. & Foulds, G. A. (1977). Validation of the Delusions-Symptoms-States Inventory. *British Journal of Medical Psychology*, **50**, 163–171.

Beitman, B. D. (1987). *The Structure of Individual Psychotherapy*. New York: Guilford Press.

Beitman, B. D. (1989). Why I am an integrationist (not an eclectic)? *British Journal of Guidance and Counselling*, **17**, 259–273.

Bellack, A. S., Hersen, M. & Himmelhoch, J. (1981). Social skills training compared with pharmacotherapy and psychotherapy in the treatment of unipolar depression. *American Journal of Psychiatry*, **138**, 1562–1567.

Benjamin, S., Marks, I. M. & Huson, J. (1972). Active muscular relaxation in desensitization of phobic patients. *Psychological Medicine*, **2**, 381–390.

Bennum, I. & Schlinder, L. (1988). Therapist and patient factors in the behavioural treatment of phobic patients. *British Journal of Clinical Psychology*, **27**, 145–150.

Benson, H., Shapiro, D., Tursky, B. & Schwartz, G. E. (1971). Decreased systolic blood pressure through operant conditioning techniques in patients with essential hypertension. *Science*, **173**, 740–742.

Berger, E. M. (1952). The relation between expressed acceptance of self and expressed acceptance of others. *Journal of Abnormal and Social Psychology*, **47**, 778–782.

Berman, J. S., Miller, R. C. & Massman, P. J. (1985). Cognitive therapy versus systematic desensitization: Is one treatment superior? *Psychological Bulletin*, **97**, 451–461.

Bernstein, D. A. & Nietzel, M. T. (1974). Behavioral avoidance tests: The effects of demand characteristics and repeated measures on two types of subjects. *Behavior Therapy*, **5**, 183–192.

Bieber, I. (1980). *Cognitive Psychoanalysis*. New York: Jason Aronson.

Bieri, J. (1955). Cognitive complexity–simplicity and predictive behaviour. *Journal of Abnormal and Social Behavior*, **51**, 263–268.

Bills, R. E., Vance, E. I. & McLean, O. S. (1951). An index of adjustment and values. *Journal of Consulting Psychology*, **15**, 257–261.

Black, A. H. (1959). Heart rate changes during avoidance learning in dogs. *Canadian Journal of Psychology*, **13**, 229–242.

Blackburn, I. M. & Bishop, S. (1983). Changes in cognition with pharmacotherapy and cognitive therapy. *British Journal of Psychiatry*, **143**, 609–617.

Blackburn, I. M., Bishop, S., Glen, A. I. M. *et al.* (1981). The efficacy of cognitive therapy in depression: A treatment trial using cognitive therapy and pharmacotherapy, each alone and in combination. *British Journal of Psychiatry*, **139**, 181–189.

Blackburn, I. M., Jones, S. & Lewin, R. J. P. (1986). Cognitive style in depression. *British Journal of Clinical Psychology*, **25**, 241–251.

Blanchard, E. B. (1970). Relative contributions of modeling, informational influences, and physical contact in extinction of phobic behavior. *Journal of Abnormal Behavior*, **76**, 55–61.

164 Personality and psychotherapy

Blanchard, E. B. & Epstein, L. H. (1977). The clinical usefulness of biofeedback. In M. Hersen, R. M. Eisler & P. M. Miller (eds.), *Progress in Behavior Modification*, **4**, 163–249. New York: Academic Press.

Boersma, K., Den Hengst, S., Dekker, J. *et al.* (1976). Exposure and response prevention in the natural environment: A comparison with obsessive–compulsive patients. *Behaviour Research and Therapy*, **14**, 19–24.

Bolton, B. (1977). Evidence for the 16PF primary and secondary factors. *Multivariate Experimental Clinical Research*, **3**, 1–15.

Bond, M. (1986). Defense Style Questionnaire. In G. E. Vaillant (ed.), *Empirical Studies of Ego Mechanisms of Defense*, pp. 146–152. Washington, DC: American Psychiatric Press.

Bond, M., Gardner, S. T., Christian, J. & Sigal, J. J. (1983). Empirical study of self-rated defense styles. *Archives of General Psychiatry*, **40**, 333–338.

Borkovec, T. D. (1973). The role of expectancy and physiological feedback in fear research: A review with special reference to subject characteristics. *Behavior Therapy*, **4**, 491–505.

Boudewyns, P. A. & Wilson, A. E. (1972). Implosive therapy and desensitization therapy using free association in the treatment of inpatients. *Journal of Abnormal Psychology*, **79**, 259–268.

Boulougouris, J. C., Marks, I. & Marset, P. (1971). Superiority of flooding (implosion) to desensitization for reducing pathological fear. *Behaviour Research and Therapy*, **9**, 7–16.

Bourdon, K. H., Boyd, J. H., Rae, D. S. *et al.* (1988). Gender differences in phobias: Results of the ECA community survey. *Journal of Anxiety Disorders*, **2**, 227–241.

Bowers, T. G. & Clum, G. A. (1988). Relative contribution of specific and non-specific treatment effects: Meta-analysis of placebo-controlled behavior therapy research. *Psychological Bulletin*, **103**, 315–323.

Bozarth, J. D. & Grace, D. P. (1970). Objective ratings and client perceptions of therapeutic conditions with university counseling clients. *Journal of Clinical Psychology*, **26**, 117–118.

Breland, K. & Breland, M. (1966). *Animal Behavior*. New York: Macmillan.

Breuer, J. & Freud, S. (1955). Studies on hysteria. In J. Strachey (ed. and trans.), *The Standard Edition of the Complete Psychological Works of Sigmund Freud*, Vol. 2. London: Hogarth Press. (Original work published 1893–1895)

Brewer, W. F. (1974). There is no convincing evidence for operant or classical conditioning in adult humans. In W. B. Weimer & D. S. Palermo (eds.), *Cognition and the Symbolic Processes*, pp. 1–42. Hillsdale, NJ: Lawrence Erlbaum.

Bridger, W. H. & Mandel, I. J. (1965). Abolition of the PRE by instructions in GSR conditioning. *Journal of Experimental Psychology*, **69**, 476–482.

Brill, N. Q., Koegler, R. R., Epstein, L. J. & Forgy, E. W. (1964). Controlled study of psychiatric outpatient treatment. *Archives of General Psychiatry*, **10**, 581–595.

Bruneau, W., Roux, S., Perse, J. & Lelord, G. (1984). Frontal evoked responses, stimulus intensity control, and the extraversion dimension. *Annals of the New York Academy of Sciences*, **425**, 546–550.

Brush, F. R. (1957). The effects of shock intensity on the acquisition and extinction of an avoidance response in dogs. *Journal of Comparative and Physiological Psychology*, **50**, 547–552.

Bryant, B. M., Trower, P. E., Yardley, K. *et al.* (1976). A survey of social inadequacy among psychiatric outpatients. *Psychological Medicine*, **6**, 101–112.

Bryer, J. B., Nelson, B. A., Miller, J. B. & Krol, P. A. (1987). Childhood sexual and physical abuse as factors in adult psychiatric illness. *American Journal of Psychiatry*, **144**, 1426–1430.

Bryman, A. & Cramer, D. (1990). *Quantitative Data Analysis for Social Scientists*. London: Routledge.

Burbach, D. J., Kashani, J. H. & Rosenberg, T. K. (1989). Parental bonding and depressive disorders in adolescents. *Journal of Child Psychology and Psychiatry*, **30**, 417–429.

Burchinal, L. G., Hawkes, G. R. & Gardner, B. (1957). Personality characteristics and marital satisfaction. *Social Forces*, **35**, 218–222.

Burke, K. C., Burke, Jr., J. D., Regier, D. A. & Rae, D. S. (1990). Age at onset of selected mental disorders in five community populations. *Archives of General Psychiatry*, **47**, 511–518.

Burstein, J. W. & Carkhuff, R. R. (1968). Objective, therapist and client ratings of therapist-offered facilitative conditions of moderate to low functioning therapists. *Journal of Clinical Psychology*, **24**, 240–241.

Butler, J. M. (1968). Self-ideal congruence in psychotherapy. *Psychotherapy: Theory, Research and Practice*, **5**, 13–17.

Butler, J. M. & Haigh, G. V. (1954). Changes in the relation between self-concepts and ideal concepts consequent upon client-centered counseling. In C. R. Rogers & R. F. Dymond (eds.), *Psychotherapy and Personality Change: Co-ordinated Research Studies in the Client-Centered Approach*, pp. 55–75. Chicago: University of Chicago Press.

Campbell, D. T. & Stanley, J. C. (1963). *Experimental and Quasi-Experimental Designs for Research*. Chicago: Rand McNally.

Cattell, R. B. (1946). *Description and Measurement of Personality*. London: Harrap.

Cattell, R. B. (1973). *Personality by Mood and Questionnaire*. New York: Jossey-Bass.

Cattell, R. B. & Nichols, K. E. (1972). An improved definition, from 10 researchers, of second order personality factors in Q data (with cross-cultural checks). *Journal of Social Psychology*, **86**, 187–203.

Cattell, R. B. & Sells, S. (1974). *The Clinical Analysis Questionnaire*. Champaign, IL: Institute for Personality and Ability Testing.

Cattell, R. B., Eber, H. W. & Tatsuoka, M. M. (1970). *Handbook for the Sixteen Personality Factor Questionnaire (16PF)*. Champaign, IL: Institute for Personality and Ability Testing.

Cautela, J. R. (1966). Treatment of compulsive behavior by covert sensitization. *Psychological Records*, **16**, 33–41.

Cederlof, R., Friberg, L., Jonnson, E. & Kaij, L. (1961). Studies on similarity diagnosis in twins with the aid of mailed questionnaires. *Acta Genetica et Statistica Medica*, **11**, 338–362.

Chaney, E. F., O'Leary, M. R. & Marlatt, G. A. (1978). Skill training with alcoholics. *Journal of Consulting and Clinical Psychology*, **46**, 1092–1104.

Church, R. M. & Black, A. H. (1958). Latency of the conditioned heart rate as a function of the CS–UCS interval. *Journal of Comparative and Physiological Psychology*, **51**, 478–482.

Clancy, J., Vanderhoof, E. & Campbell, P. (1966). Evaluation of an aversive technique as a treatment for alcoholism; controlled with succinylcholine-induced apnea. *Quarterly Journal of Studies on Alcohol*, **27**, 739.

Clark, J. V. & Culbert, S. A. (1965). Mutually therapeutic perception and self-awareness in a T group. *Journal of Applied Behavioral Science*, **1**, 180–194.

Clark, D. A., Beck, A. T. & Brown, G. (1989). Cognitive mediation in general psychiatric outpatients: A test of the content-specificity hypothesis. *Journal of Personality and Social Psychology*, **56**, 958–964.

Clarkin, J. F., Hurt, S. W. & Crilly, J. L. (1987). Therapeutic alliance and hospital treatment outcome. *Hospital and Community Psychiatry*, **38**, 871–875.

Coles, M. G. H., Gale, A. & Kline, P. (1971). Personality and habituation of the orienting reaction: Tonic and response measures of electrodermal activity. *Psychophysiology*, **8**, 54–63.

Comrey, A. L. & Duffy, K. E. (1968). Cattell and Eysenck factor scores related to Comrey personality factors. *Multivariate Behavioral Research*, **3**, 379–392.

Conley, J. J. (1984). The hierarchy of consistency: A review and model of longitudinal findings on adult individual differences in intelligence, personality and self-opinion. *Personality and Individual Differences*, **5**, 11–25.

Connors, M. E., Johnson, C. L. & Stuckey, M. K. (1984). Treatment of bulimia with brief psychoeducational group therapy. *American Journal of Psychiatry*, **141**, 1512–1516.

Cook, E. W., III, Hodes, R. L. & Lang, P. J. (1986). Preparedness and phobia: Effect of stimulus content on human visceral conditioning. *Journal of Abnormal Psychology*, **95**, 195–207.

Coppen, A. & Metcalfe, M. (1965). Effect of a depressive illness on M.P.I. scores. *British Journal of Psychiatry*, **111**, 236–240.

Costa, P. T., Jr. & McCrae, R. R. (1977). Age differences in personality structure revisited: Studies in validity, stability, and change. *Aging and Human Development*, **8**, 261–275.

Costa, P. T., Jr. & McCrae, R. R. (1985). *The NEO Personality Inventory Manual*. Odessa, FL: Psychological Assessment Resources.

Costa, P. T., Jr., McCrae, R. R. & Arenberg, D. (1980). Enduring dispositions in adult males. *Journal of Personality and Social Psychology*, **38**, 793–800.

Cox, D. J., Freundlich, A. & Meyer, R. G. (1975). Differential effectiveness of electromyograph feedback, verbal relaxation instructions, and medication placebo with tension headaches. *Journal of Consulting and Clinical Psychology*, **43**, 892–898.

Cox, B. D., Blaxter, M., Buckle, A. L. J. *et al.* (1987). *The Health and Lifestyle Survey*. London: Health Promotion Research Trust.

Coyne, J. C. (1976). Depression and the response of others. *Journal of Abnormal Psychology*, **85**, 186–193.

Crafts, L. W., Schneirla, T. C., Robinson, E. E. & Gilbert, R. W. (1938). *Recent Experiments in Psychology*. New York: McGraw-Hill.

Craig, K. D., Best, H. & Ward, L. W. (1975). Social modeling influences on psychophysical judgments of electrical stimulation. *Journal of Abnormal Psychology*, **84**, 366–373.

Craig, K. D. & Neidermayer, H. (1974). Autonomic correlates of pain thresholds influenced by social modeling. *Journal of Personality and Social Psychology*, **29**, 246–252.

Craighead, L. W. (1979). Self-instructional training for assertive–refusal behavior. *Behavior Therapy*, **10**, 529–542.

Cramer, D. (1985a). An item factor analysis of the Irrational Beliefs Test. *British Journal of Cognitive Psychotherapy*, **3**, 70–76.

Cramer, D. (1985b). Psychological adjustment and the facilitative nature of close personal relationships. *British Journal of Medical Psychology*, **58**, 165–168.

Cramer, D. (1986a). An item factor analysis of the original Relationship Inventory. *Journal of Personal and Social Relationships*, **3**, 121–127.

Cramer, D. (1986b). An item factor analysis of the revised Barrett–Lennard Relationship Inventory. *British Journal of Guidance and Counselling*, **14**, 314–325.

Cramer, D. (1987). Self-esteem, advice-giving, and the facilitative nature of close personal relationships. *Person-Centered Review*, **2**, 99–110.

Cramer, D. (1988). Self-esteem and facilitative close relationships: A cross-lagged panel correlation analysis. *British Journal of Social Psychology*, **27**, 115–126.

Cramer, D. (1989). Self-esteem and the facilitativeness of parents and close friends. *Person-Centered Review*, **4**, 61–76.

Cramer, D. (1990a). The necessary conditions for evaluating client-centered therapy. In G. Lietaer, J. Rombauts & R. van Balen (eds.), *Client-Centered and Experiential Psychotherapy in the Nineties*, pp. 415–428. Leuven: Leuven University Press.

Cramer, D. (1990b). Towards assessing the therapeutic value of Rogers's core conditions. *Counselling Psychology Quarterly*, **3**, 57–66.

Cramer, D. (1990c). Disclosure of personal problems, self-esteem, and the facilitativeness of friends and lovers. *British Journal of Guidance and Counselling*, **18**, 186–196.

Cramer, D. (1990d). Psychological adjustment, close relationships and personality: A comment on McLennan & Omodei. *British Journal of Medical Psychology*, **63**, 341–343.

Cramer, D. (1990e). Self-esteem and close relationships: A statistical refinement. *British Journal of Social Psychology*, **29**, 189–191.

Cramer, D. (1990f). Helpful actions of close friends to personal problems and distress. *British Journal of Guidance and Counselling*, **18**, 281–293.

Cramer, D. (1991a). Type A behaviour pattern, extraversion, neuroticism and psychological distress. *British Journal of Medical Psychology*, **64**, 73–83.

Cramer, D. (1991b). Patients' experience of the therapist relationship: A universal factor of therapeutic change? *The 1990 Principles Congress Proceedings*. Lisse: Swets & Zeitlinger. In press.

Cramer, D. (1991c). Social support and psychological distress in women and men. *British Journal of Medical Psychology*, **64**, 147–58.

Cramer, D. (1991d). Neuroticism, psychological distress and conjugal bereavement. *Personality and Individual Differences*. In press.

Cramer, D. & Ellis, A. (1988). Irrational beliefs and strength versus inappropriateness of feelings: A debate. In W. Dryden & P. Trower (eds.), *Developments in Rational–Emotive Therapy*, pp.56–64. Milton Keynes: Open University Press.

Cramer, D. & Fong, J. (1991). Effects of rational and irrational beliefs on intensity and 'inappropriateness' of feelings: A test of rational–emotive theory. *Cognitive Therapy and Research*, **15**, pp. 319–329.

Cramer, D. & Kupshik, G. (1991). *Effect of Rational and Irrational Statements on Intensity and 'Inappropriateness' of Emotional Distress in Patients.* Manuscript submitted for publication.

Crisp, A. H. (1966). Transference, symptom emergence and social repercussion in behaviour therapy. *British Journal of Medical Psychology*, **39**, 179–196.

Crisp, A. H., Hsu, L. K. G. & Stonehill, E. (1979). Personality, body weight and ultimate outcome in anorexia nervosa. *Journal of Clinical Psychiatry*, **40**, 332–335.

Crits-Cristoph, P., Cooper, A. & Luborsky, L. (1988). The accuracy of therapists' interpretations and the outcome of dynamic psychotherapy. *Journal of Consulting and Clinical Psychology*, **56**, 490–495.

Cross, D. G., Sheehan, P. W. & Khan, J. A. (1982). Short- and long-term follow-up of clients receiving insight-oriented therapy and behavior therapy. *Journal of Consulting and Clinical Psychology*, **50**, 103–112.

Crowe, M. J., Marks, I. M., Agras, W. S. & Leitenberg, H. (1972). Time-limited desensitization, implosion and shaping for phobic patients: A crossover study. *Behaviour Research and Therapy*, **10**, 319–328.

Crowne, D. P., Stephens, M. W. & Kelly, R. (1961). The validity and equivalence of tests of self-acceptance. *Journal of Psychology*, **51**, 101–112.

Culbert, S. A. (1968). Trainer self-disclosure and member growth in two T groups. *Journal of Applied Behavioral Science*, **4**, 47–73.

Daly, M. J. & Burton, R. L. (1983). Self-esteem and irrational beliefs: An exploratory investigation with implications for counseling. *Journal of Counseling Psychology*, **30**, 361–366.

Davis, C. & Cowles, M. (1988). A laboratory study of temperament and arousal: A test of Gale's hypothesis. *Journal of Research in Personality*, **22**, 101–116.

Davis, H. (1974). What does the P scale measure? *British Journal of Psychiatry*, **125**, 161–167.

Dean, C., Surtees, P. G. & Sashidharian, S. P. (1983). Comparison of research diagnostic systems in an Edinburgh community sample. *British Journal of Psychiatry*, **142**, 247–256.

de Boeck, P. (1981). An interpretation of loose construing in schizophrenic thought disorder. In H. Bonarius, R. Holland & S. Rosenberg (eds.), *Recent Advances in the Theory and Practice of Personal Construct Psychology*. London: Macmillan.

Derogatis, L. R. (1977). *SCL-90 Administration, Scoring and Procedures Manual*. Baltimore, MD: Johns Hopkins University Press.

Derogatis, L. R. (1983). *SCL-90-R Administration, Scoring and Procedures Manual, II*. Towson, MD: Clinical Psychometric Research.

Derogatis, L. R. & Cleary, P. A. (1977). Confirmation of the dimensional structure of the SCL-90: A study in construct validation. *Journal of Clinical Psychology*, **33**, 981–989.

DeSilva, P., Rachman, S. & Seligman, M. E. P. (1977). Prepared phobias and obsessions: Therapeutic outcome. *Behaviour Research and Therapy*, **15**, 65–77.

DiClemente, C. C. & Prochaska, J. O. (1982). Self-change and therapy change of smoking behavior: A comparison of processes of change in cessation and maintenance. *Addictive Behaviors*, **7**, 133–142.

Digman, J. M. & Inouye, J. (1986). Further specification of the five robust factors of personality. *Journal of Personality and Social Psychology*, **50**, 116–123.

DiLoreto, A. O. (1971). *Comparative Psychotherapy: An Experimental Analysis*. Chicago: Aldine-Atherton.

Dobson, K. S. & Shaw, B. F. (1986). Cognitive assessment with major depressive disorders. *Cognitive Therapy and Research*, **10**, 13–29.

Dohrenwend, B. S., Krasnoff, L., Askenasy, A. R. & Dohrenwend, B. P. (1978). Exemplification of a method for scaling life events: The PERI Life Events Scale. *Journal of Health and Social Behavior*, **19**, 205–229.

Doleys, D. M. (1977). Behavioral treatments for nocturnal enuresis in children: A review of the recent literature. *Psychological Bulletin*, **84**, 30–54.

Dollard, J. & Miller, N. E. (1950). *Personality and Psychotherapy: An Analysis in Terms of Learning, Thinking, and Culture.* New York: McGraw-Hill.

Eastman, C. & Marzillier, J. S. (1984). Theoretical and methodological difficulties in Bandura's self-efficacy theory. *Cognitive Therapy and Research,* **8**, 213–229.

Eaves, G. & Rush, A. J. (1984). Cognitive patterns in symptomatic and remitted unipolar major depression. *Journal of Abnormal Psychology,* **93**, 31–40.

Eaves, L. J., Eysenck, H. J. & Martin, N. G. (1989). *Genes, Culture and Personality: An Empirical Approach.* London: Academic Press.

Eckert, E. D., Goldberg, S. C., Halmi, K. A., Casper, R. C. & Davis, J. M. (1979). Behaviour therapy in anorexia nervosa. *British Journal of Psychiatry,* **134**, 55–59.

Eidelson, R. J. & Epstein, N. (1982). Cognition and relationship maladjustment: Development of a measure of dysfunctional relationship beliefs. *Journal of Consulting and Clinical Psychology,* **50**, 715–720.

Eisler, R. M., Blanchard, E. B., Fitts, H. & Williams, J. G. (1978). Social skill training with and without modeling for schizophrenic and non-psychotic hospitalized psychiatric patients. *Behavior Modification,* **2**, 147–172.

Elliott, R. (1985). Helpful and nonhelpful events in brief counseling interviews: An empirical taxonomy. *Journal of Counseling Psychology,* **32**, 307–322.

Elliott, R. & Shapiro, D. A. (1988). Brief Structured Recall: A more efficient method for studying significant therapy events. *British Journal of Medical Psychology,* **61**, 141–153.

Elliott, R., James. E., Reimschuessel, C., Cislo, D. & Sack, N. (1985). Significant events and the analysis of immediate therapeutic impacts. *Psychotherapy,* **22**, 620–630.

Ellis, A. (1957a). *How to Live with a Neurotic.* New York: Crown.

Ellis, A. (1957b). Rational psychotherapy and individual psychology. *Journal of Individual Psychology,* **13**, 38–44.

Ellis, A. (1957c). Outcome of employing three techniques of psychotherapy. *Journal of Clinical Psychotherapy,* **13**, 344–350.

Ellis, A. (1959). Requisite conditions for basic personality change. *Journal of Consulting Psychology,* **23**, 538–540.

Ellis, A. (1962). *Reason and Emotion in Psychotherapy.* Secaucus, NJ: Lyle Stuart.

Ellis, A. (1971). *Growth Through Reason: Verbatim Cases in Rational–Emotive Therapy.* Hollywood, CA: Wilshire.

Ellis, A. & Harper, R. A. (1961). *A Guide to Rational Living.* Englewood Cliffs, NJ: Prentice-Hall.

Ellis, A. & Harper, R. A. (1975). *A New Guide to Rational Living.* North Hollywood, CA: Wilshire.

Ellis, T. E. & Ratliff, K. G. (1986). Cognitive characteristics of suicidal and nonsuicidal psychiatric patients. *Cognitive Therapy and Research,* **10**, 625–634.

Emmelkamp, P. M. G. (1974). Self-observation versus flooding in the treatment of agoraphobia. *Behaviour Research and Therapy,* **12**, 229–237.

Emmelkamp, P. M. G. & Ultee, K. A. (1974). A comparison of 'successive approximation' and 'self-observation' in the treatment of agoraphobia. *Behavior Therapy,* **5**, 606–613.

Emmelkamp, P. M. G. & Wessels, H. (1975). Flooding *in imagination* vs flooding *in vivo*: A comparison with agoraphobics. *Behaviour Research and Therapy,* **13**, 7–15.

Emmelkamp, P. M. G. & Kwee, K. G. (1977). Obsessional ruminations: A comparison between thought-stopping and prolonged exposure in imagination. *Behaviour Research and Therapy*, **15**, 441–444.

Emmelkamp, P. M. G. & Kuipers, A. C. M. (1979). Agoraphobia: A follow-up study four years after treatment. *British Journal of Psychiatry*, **134**, 352–355.

Emmelkamp, P. M. G. & Mersch, P. P. A. (1982). Cognition and exposure *in vivo* in the treatment of agoraphobia: Short-term and delayed effects. *Cognitive Therapy and Research*, **6**, 77–90.

Emmelkamp, P. M. G., Kuipers, A. C. M. & Eggeraat, J. B. (1978). Cognitive modification versus prolonged exposure *in vivo*: A comparison with agoraphobics as subjects. *Behaviour Research and Therapy*, **16**, 33–41.

Emmelkamp, P. M. G., Mersch, P. P., Vissia, E. & van der Helm, M. (1985). Social phobia: A comparative evaluation of cognitive and behavioral interventions. *Behaviour Research and Therapy*, **23**, 365–369.

Ends, E. J. & Page, C. W. (1957). A study of three types of group psychotherapy with hospitalized male inebriates. *Quarterly Journal of Studies on Alcohol*, **18**, 263–277.

Evenson, R. C., Holland, R. A., Metha, S. & Yasif, F. (1980). Factor analysis of the Symptom Checklist-90. *Psychological Reports*, **46**, 695–699.

Everaerd, W. T. A. M., Rijken, H. M. & Emmelkamp, P. M. G. (1973). A comparison of 'flooding' and 'successive approximation' in the treatment of agoraphobia. *Behaviour Research and Therapy*, **11**, 105–117.

Eysenck, H. J. (1957). *The Dynamics of Anxiety and Hysteria*. London: Routledge & Kegan Paul.

Eysenck, H. J. (1959a). Learning theory and behaviour therapy. *Journal of Mental Science*, **105**, 61–75.

Eysenck, H. J. (1959b). Personality and verbal conditioning. *Psychological Reports*, **5**, 570.

Eysenck, H. J. (ed.) (1960). *Behaviour Therapy and the Neuroses*. Oxford: Pergamon Press.

Eysenck, H. J. (1965). Extraversion and the acquisition of eyeblink and GSR conditioned responses. *Psychological Bulletin*, **63**, 258–270.

Eysenck, H. J. (1967). *The Biological Basis of Personality*. Springfield, IL: C. C. Thomas.

Eysenck, H. J. (1970a). *The Structure of Human Personality*, 3rd edn. London: Methuen.

Eysenck, H. J. (1970b). A dimensional system of psychodiagnostics. In A. R. Mahrer (ed.), *New Approaches to Personality Classification*, pp. 169–207. New York: Columbia University Press.

Eysenck, H. J. (1976a). Behaviour therapy–dogma or applied science? In M. P. Feldman & A. Broadhurst (eds.), *Theoretical and Experimental Bases of the Behaviour Therapies*, pp. 333–363. London: Wiley.

Eysenck, H. J. (1976b). The learning theory model of neurosis—A new approach. *Behaviour Research and Therapy*, **14**, 251–267.

Eysenck, H. J. (1979). The conditioning model of neurosis. *Behavior and Brain Sciences*, **2**, 155–199.

Eysenck, H. J. & Eysenck, S. B. G. (1965). *Manual of the Eysenck Personality Inventory*. London: Hodder & Stoughton (San Diego: Edits).

Eysenck, H. J. & Eysenck, S. B. G. (1969a). *Personality Structure and Measurement*. London: Routledge & Kegan Paul.

Eysenck, H. J. & Levey, A. (1972). Conditioning, introversion–extraversion and the strength of the nervous system. In V. D. Nebylitsyn & J. A. Gray (eds.), *Biological Bases of Individual Behaviour*, pp. 206–220. London: Academic Press.

Eysenck, H. J. & Wilson, G. (eds.). (1973). *The Experimental Study of Freudian Theories*. London: Methuen.

Eysenck, H. J. & Eysenck, S. B. G. (1975). *Manual of the Eysenck Personality Questionnaire*. London: Hodder & Stoughton (San Diego: Edits).

Eysenck, H. J. & Eysenck, S. B. G. (1976). *Psychoticism as a Dimension of Personality*. London: Hodder & Stoughton.

Eysenck, H. J. & Wakefield, J. R., Jr. (1981). Psychological factors as predictors of marital satisfaction. *Advances in Behaviour Research and Therapy*, **3**, 151–192.

Eysenck, H. J. & Eysenck, M. W. (1985). *Personality and Individual Differences: A Natural Science Approach*. New York & London: Plenum Press.

Eysenck, S. B. G. & Eysenck, H. J. (1969b). Scores on three personality variables as a function of age, sex and social class. *British Journal of Social and Clinical Psychology*, **8**, 69–76.

Eysenck, S. B. G., White, O. & Eysenck, H. J. (1976). Personality and mental illness. *Psychological Reports*, **39**, 1011–1022.

Fairburn, C. G., Kirk, J., O'Connor, M. & Cooper, P. J. (1986). A comparison of two psychological treatments for bulimia nervosa. *Behaviour Research and Therapy*, **24**, 629–643.

Falloon, I. R. H., Lindley, P., McDonald, R. & Marks, I. M. (1977). Social skills training of out-patient groups: A controlled study of rehearsal and homework. *British Journal of Psychiatry*, **131**, 599–609.

Feather, B. W. & Rhoads, J. M. (1972a). Psychodynamic behavior therapy: I. Theory and rationale. *Archives of General Psychiatry*, **26**, 495–502.

Feather, B. W. & Rhoads, J. M. (1972b). Psychodynamic behavior therapy: II. Clinical aspects. *Archives of General Psychiatry*, **26**, 503–511.

Feldman, M. P. & MacCulloch, M. J. (1965). The application of anticipatory avoidance learning to the treatment of homosexuality: I. Theory, technique and preliminary results. *Behaviour Research and Therapy*, **3**, 165–183.

Feldman, M. P. & MacCulloch, M. J. (1971). *Homosexual Behaviour: Therapy and Assessment*. Oxford: Pergamon Press.

Fennell, M. J. V. & Campbell, E. A. (1984). The Cognitions Questionnaire: Specific thinking errors in depression. *British Journal of Clinical Psychology*, **23**, 81–92.

Ferster, C. B. (1973). A functional analysis of depression. *American Psychologist*, **28**, 857–870.

Ferster, C. B. & Skinner, B. F. (1957). *Schedules of Reinforcement*. New York: Appleton–Century–Crofts.

Finch, B. E. & Wallace, C. J. (1977). Successful interpersonal skills training with schizophrenic patients. *Journal of Consulting and Clinical Psychology*, **45**, 885–890.

Finkelhor, D. (1979). *Sexually Victimized Children*. New York: Free Press.

Finkelhor, D., Araji, S., Baron, L. *et al.* (1986). *A Sourcebook on Child Sexual Abuse*. Beverly Hills, CA: Sage.

Finkelhor, D., Hotaling, G., Lewis, I. A. & Smith, C. (1990). Sexual abuse in a national survey of adult men and women: Prevalence, characteristics, and risk factors. *Child Abuse and Neglect*, **14**, 19–28.

Fisher, S. & Greenberg, R. (1977). *The Scientific Credibility of Freud's Theories and Therapy*. Brighton: Harvester Press.

Floderus-Myrhed, B., Pedersen, N. & Rasmussen, I. (1980). Assessment of heritability for personality based on a short form of the Eysenck Personality Inventory. *Behavior Genetics*, **10**, 153–162.

Ford, J. D. (1978). Therapeutic relationship in behavior therapy: An empirical analysis. *Journal of Consulting and Clinical Psychology*, **46**, 1302–1314.

Foulds, G. A. (1976). *The Hierarchical Nature of Personal Illness*. London: Academic Press.

Fox, E. E. & Davies, R. L. (1971). Test your rationality. *Rational Living*, **5**, 23–25.

Frank, A. F. & Gunderson, J. G. (1990). The role of the therapeutic alliance in the treatment of schizophrenia: Relationship to course and outcome. *Archives of General Psychiatry*, **47**, 228–236.

Frank, J. D. (1973). *Persuasion and Healing: A Comparative Study of Psychotherapy* (rev. edn.). Baltimore, MD: Johns Hopkins University Press.

Fransella, F. (1972). *Personal Change and Reconstruction*. London: Academic Press.

Freeman, C. P. L., Barry, F., Dunkeld-Turnbull, J. & Henderson, A. (1988). Controlled trial of psychotherapy for bulimia nervosa. *British Medical Journal*, **296**, 521–525.

French, T. M. (1933). Interrelations between psychoanalysis and the experimental work of Pavlov. *American Journal of Psychiatry*, **89**, 1165–1203.

Freud, A. (1937). *The Ego and the Mechanisms of Defence*. London: Hogarth Press.

Freud, S. (1910). The origin and development of psychoanalysis. *American Journal of Psychology*, **12**, 181–218.

Freud, S. (1955). Lines of advance in psycho-analytic therapy. In J. Strachey (ed. and trans.), *The Standard Edition of the Complete Psychological Works of Sigmund Freud*, Vol. 17, pp. 157–168. London: Hogarth Press. (Original work published 1919)

Freud, S. (1958a). Papers on technique. In J. Strachey (ed. and trans.), *The Standard Edition of the Complete Psychological Works of Sigmund Freud*, Vol. 12, pp. 83–173. London: Hogarth Press. (Original work published 1911–1915)

Freud, S. (1958b). Types of onset of neurosis. In J. Strachey (ed. and trans.), *The Standard Edition of the Complete Psychological Works of Sigmund Freud*, Vol. 12, pp. 229–238. London: Hogarth Press. (Original work published 1912)

Freud, S. (1959). Inhibitions, symptoms and anxiety. In J. Strachey (ed. and trans.), *The Standard Edition of the Complete Psychological Works of Sigmund Freud*, Vol. 20, pp. 77–175. London: Hogarth Press. (Original work published 1926)

Freud, S. (1961). Introductory lectures on psychoanalysis. In J. Strachey (ed. and trans.), *The Standard Edition of the Complete Psychological Works of Sigmund Freud*, Vol. 15–16. London: Hogarth Press. (Original work published 1916–1917)

Freud, S. (1964a). New introductory lectures on psychoanalysis. In J. Strachey (ed. and trans.), *The Standard Edition of the Complete Psychological Works of Sigmund Freud*, Vol. 22, pp. 3–182. London: Hogarth Press. (Original work published 1933)

Freud, S. (1964b). An outline of psychoanalysis. In J. Strachey (ed. and trans.), *The Standard Edition of the Complete Psychological Works of Sigmund Freud*, Vol. 23, pp. 141–207. London: Hogarth Press. (Original work published 1940)

Freund, K. (1960). Some problems in the treatment of homosexuality. In H. J. Eysenck (ed.), *Behaviour Therapy and the Neuroses*, pp. 312–326. London: Pergamon Press.

Friedman, I. (1955). Phenomenal, ideal, and projected conceptions of self. *Journal of Abnormal and Social Psychology*, **51**, 611–615.

Friedman, P. (1959). The phobias. In S. Arieti (ed.), *American Handbook of Psychiatry*, Vol. 1, pp. 293–306. New York: Basic Books.

Frith, C. D. & Lillie, F. J. (1972). Why does the Repertory Grid Test indicate thought disorder? *British Journal of Social and Clinical Psychology*, **11**, 73–78.

Gale, A. (1973). The psychophysiology of individual differences: Studies of extraversion and the EEG. In P. Kline (ed.), *New Approaches in Psychological Measurement*, pp. 211–256. New York: Wiley.

Gale, A. (1983). Electroencephalographic studies of extraversion–introversion: A case study in the psychophysiology of individual differences. *Personality and Individual Differences*, **4**, 371–380.

Galton, F. (1883). *Inquiries into Human Faculty*. London: Macmillan.

Garfield, S. L. & Kurtz, R. (1976). Clinical psychologists in the 1970s. *American Psychologist*, **31**, 1–9.

Garfield, S. L. & Kurtz, R. (1977). A study of eclectic views. *Journal of Consulting and Clinical Psychology*, **45**, 78–83.

Gelder, M. G., Bancroft, J. H. J., Gath, D. H. *et al.* (1973). Specific and non-specific factors in behaviour therapy. *British Journal of Psychiatry*, **123**, 445–462.

Gellhorn, E. (1967). *Principles of Autonomic-Somatic Integrations*. Minneapolis, MN: University of Minnesota Press.

Gerstley, L., McLellan, A. T., Alterman, A. I. *et al.* (1989). Ability to form an alliance with the therapist: A possible marker of prognosis for patients with antisocial personality disorder. *American Journal of Psychiatry*, **146**, 508–512.

Gibson, H. B. (1971). The validity of the Eysenck Personality Inventory studied by a technique of peer-rating item by item, and by sociometric comparisons. *British Journal of Social and Clinical Psychology*, **10**, 213–220.

Gillan, P. & Rachman, S. (1974). An experimental investigation of desensitization in phobic patients. *British Journal of Psychiatry*, **124**, 392–401.

Gold, H. (1946). The use of placebos in therapy. *New York State Journal of Medicine*, **46**, 1723.

Goldberg, D. P. (1972). *The Detection of Psychiatric Illness by Questionnaire*. Oxford: Oxford University Press.

Goldfried, M. R. & Sobocinski, D. (1975). Effect of irrational beliefs on emotional arousal. *Journal of Consulting and Clinical Psychology*, **43**, 504–510.

Goldfried, M. R. & Goldfried, A. P. (1977). Importance of hierarchy content in the self-control of anxiety. *Journal of Consulting and Clinical Psychology*, **45**, 124–134.

Goldfried, M. R., Decenteceo, E. T. & Weinberg, L. (1974). Systematic rational restructuring as a self-control technique. *Behavior Therapy*, **5**, 247–254.

Goldsmith, J. B. & McFall, R. M. (1975). Development and evaluation of an interpersonal skill-training program for psychiatric inpatients. *Journal of Abnormal Psychology*, **84**, 51–58.

Gorsuch, R. L. & Cattell, R. B. (1967). Second stratum personality factors defined in the questionnaire realm by the 16 P.F. *Multivariate Behavioral Research*, **2**, 211–223.

Gotlib, I. H. (1982). Self-reinforcement and depression in interpersonal interaction: The role of performance level. *Journal of Abnormal Psychology*, **91**, 3–13.

Gray, J. A. (1970). The psychophysiological basis of introversion-extraversion. *Behaviour Research and Therapy*, **8**, 249–266.

Greenson, R. R. (1965). The working alliance and the transference neurosis. *The Psychoanalytic Quarterly*, **34**, 155–181.

Grossberg, J. M. & Wilson, H. K. (1968). Physiological changes accompanying the visualization of fearful and neutral situations. *Journal of Personality and Social Psychology*, **10**, 124–133.

Guilford, J. P. (1975). Factors and factors of personality. *Psychological Bulletin*, **82**, 802–814.

Guilford, J. P. & Zimmerman, W. S. (1949). *The Guilford–Zimmerman Temperament Survey: Manual*. Beverly Hills, CA: Sheridan Supply.

Gunderson, J. G., Frank, A. F., Katz, H. M. *et al.* (1984). Effects of psychotherapy in schizophrenia: II. Comparative outcome of two forms of treatment. *Schizophrenia Bulletin*, **10**, 564–598.

Gupta, B. S. (1976). Extraversion and reinforcement in verbal operant conditioning. *British Journal of Psychology*, **67**, 47–52.

Gurman, A. S. (1977). The patient's perception of the therapeutic relationship. In A. S. Gurman & A. M. Razin (eds.), *Effective Psychotherapy: A Handbook of Research*, pp. 503–543. New York: Pergamon.

Hackmann, A. & McLean, C. (1975). A comparison of flooding and thought stopping in the treatment of obsessional neurosis. *Behaviour Research and Therapy*, **13**, 263–269.

Hafner, J. & Marks, I. (1976). Exposure *in vivo* of agoraphobics: Contributions of diazepam, group exposure, and anxiety evocation. *Psychological Medicine*, **6**, 71–88.

Hall, R. & Goldberg, D. (1977). The role of social anxiety in social interaction difficulties. *British Journal of Psychiatry*, **131**, 610–615.

Hallam, R. S. (1976). The Eysenck personality scales: Stability and change after therapy. *Behaviour Research and Therapy*, **14**, 369–372.

Hallam, R., Rachman, S. & Falkowski, W. (1972). Subjective, attitudinal and physiological effects of electrical aversion therapy. *Behaviour Research and Therapy*, **10**, 1–13.

Hamburg, D. A., Bibring, G. L., Fisher, C. *et al.* (1967). Report of Ad Hoc Committee on Central Fact-Gathering Data of the American Psychoanalytic Association. *Journal of American Psychoanalytic Association*, **15**, 841–861.

Hamilton, E. W. & Abramson, L. Y. (1983). Cognitive patterns and major depressive disorder: A longitudinal study in a hospital setting. *Journal of Abnormal Psychology*, **92**, 173–184.

Hansen, J. C., Moore, G. D. & Carkhuff, R. R. (1968). The differential relationships of objective and client perceptions of counseling. *Journal of Clinical Psychology*, **24**, 244–246.

Harris, A. (1954). A comparative study of results in neurotic patients treated by two different methods. *Journal of Mental Science*, **100**, 718–721.

Harrison, A. & Phillips, J. P. N. (1979). The specificity of schizophrenic thought disorder. *British Journal of Medical Psychology*, **52**, 105–117.

Hartley, D. E. & Strupp, H. H. (1983). The therapeutic alliance: Its relationship to outcome in brief psychotherapy. In J. Masling (ed.), *Empirical Studies of Psychoanalytical Theories*, Vol. 1, pp. 1–37. Hillsdale, NJ: Analytic Press.

Hartman, G. J. (1968). Sixty revealing questions for 20 minutes. *Rational Living*, **6**, 7–8.

Haynes, E. T. & Phillips, J. P. N. (1973). Inconsistency, loose construing and schizophrenic thought disorder. *British Journal of Psychiatry*, **123**, 209–217.

Haynes, S. G., Levine, S., Scotch, N. *et al.* (1978). The relationship of psychosocial factors to coronary heart disease in the Framingham Study: I. Methods and risk factors. *American Journal of Epidemiology*, **107**, 362–383.

Heather, N. (1976). The specificity of schizophrenic thought disorder: A replication and extension of previous findings. *British Journal of Social and Clinical Psychology*, **15**, 131–137.

Hedberg, A. G. & Campbell, L., III. (1974). A comparison of four behavioral treatments of alcoholism. *Journal of Behavior Therapy and Experimental Psychiatry*, **5**, 251–256.

Heilbrunn, G. (1966). Results with psychoanalytic therapy and professional commitment. *American Journal of Psychotherapy*, **20**, 89–99.

Heine, R. W. (1953). A comparison of patients' reports on psychotherapeutic experience with psychoanalytic, nondirective and Adlerian therapists. *American Journal of Psychotherapy*, **7**, 16–23.

Hekmat, H. (1971). Extraversion, neuroticism and verbal conditioning of affective self-disclosures. *Journal of Counseling Psychology*, **18**, 64–69.

Henderson, S., Byrne, D. G. & Duncan-Jones, P. (1981). *Neurosis and the Social Environment*. Sydney: Academic Press.

Herman, J., Russell, D. & Trocki, K. (1986). Long-term effects of incestuous abuse in childhood. *American Journal of Psychiatry*, **143**, 1293–1296.

Hersen, M., Bellack, A. S., Himmelhoch, J. M. & Thase, M. E. (1984). Effects of social skill training, amitriptyline, and psychotherapy in unipolar depressed women. *Behavior Therapy*, **15**, 21–40.

Hersen, M., Eisler, R. M., Miller, P. M. *et al.* (1973). Effects of practice, instructions, and modeling on components of assertive behavior. *Behavior Research and Therapy*, **11**, 443–451.

Hewstone, M., Hooper, D. & Miller, K. (1981). Psychological change in neurotic depression: A repertory grid and personal construct theory approach. *British Journal of Psychiatry*, **139**, 47–51.

Hilgard, E. R. & Bower, G. H. (1981). *Theories of Learning* (5th edn.). Englewood Cliffs, NJ: Prentice-Hall.

Hillson, J. S. & Worchel, P. (1957). Self concept and defensive behavior in the maladjusted. *Journal of Consulting Psychology*, **21**, 83–88.

Himle, D. P., Thyer, B. A. & Papsdorf, J. D. (1982). Relationships between rational beliefs and anxiety. *Cognitive Therapy and Research*, **6**, 219–223.

Hoffmann, N. G. & Overall, P. G. (1978). Factor structure of the SCL-90 in a psychiatric population. *Journal of Consulting and Clinical Psychology*, **46**, 1187–1191.

Holcomb, W. R., Adams, N. A. & Ponder, H. M. (1983). Factor structure of the Symptom Checklist-90 with acute psychiatric inpatients. *Journal of Consulting and Clinical Psychology*, **51**, 535–538.

Hollenbeck, G. P. (1965). Conditions and outcomes in the student–parent relationship. *Journal of Consulting Psychology*, **29**, 237–241.

Hollon, S. D. & Kendall, P. C. (1980). Cognitive self-statements in depression: Development of an automatic thoughts questionnaire. *Cognitive Therapy and Research*, **4**, 383–395.

Hollon, S. D., Kendall, P. C. & Lumry, A. (1986). Specificity of depressotypic cognitions in clinical depression. *Journal of Abnormal Psychology*, **95**, 52–59.

Holroyd, K. A., Penzien, D. B., Hursey, K. G. *et al.* (1984). Change mechanisms in EMG biofeedback training: Cognitive changes underlying improvements

176 Personality and psychotherapy

in tension headache. *Journal of Consulting and Clinical Psychology*, **52**, 1039–1053.

Hoogduin, C. A. L., de Haan, E. & Schaap, C. (1989). The significance of the patient–therapist relationship in the treatment of obsessive–compulsive neurosis. *British Journal of Clinical Psychology*, **28**, 185–186.

Horvath, A. O. & Greenberg, L. S. (1986). The development of the Working Alliance Inventory. In L. S. Greenberg & W. M. Pinsoff (eds.), *The Psychotherapeutic Process: A Research Handbook*, pp. 529–556. New York: Guilford Press.

Horwood, L. J. & Fergusson, D. M. (1986). Neuroticism, depression and life events: A structural equation model. *Social Psychiatry*, **21**, 63–71.

Humm, D. G. & Wadsworth, G. W. (1935). The Humm–Wadsworth Temperament Scale. *American Journal of Psychiatry*, **92**, 163–200.

Hussain, M. Z. (1971). Desensitization and flooding (implosion) in treatment of phobias. *American Journal of Psychiatry*, **127**, 1509–1514.

Ilfeld, F. W. (1978). Psychologic status of community residents along major demographic dimensions. *Archives of General Psychiatry*, **35**, 716–724.

Ingham, J. G. (1966). Changes in M.P.I. scores in neurotic patients: A three year follow-up. *British Journal of Psychiatry*, **112**, 931–939.

Ingham, J. G., Kreitman, N. B., McC. Miller, P. *et al.* (1986). Self-esteem, vulnerability and psychiatric disorder in the community. *British Journal of Psychiatry*, **148**, 375–385.

Jacobson, E. (1938). *Progressive Relaxation*. Chicago: Chicago University Press.

Jaffe, P. G. & Carlson, P. M. (1976). Relative efficacy of modeling and instructions in eliciting social behavior from chronic psychiatric patients. *Journal of Consulting and Clinical Psychology*, **44**, 200–207.

Jones, E. (1953). *Sigmund Freud: Life and Work*, Vol. 1. London: Hogarth Press.

Jones, J., Eysenck, H. J., Martin, I. & Levey, A. B. (1981). Personality and the topography of the conditioned eyelid response. *Personality and Individual Differences*, **2**, 61–84.

Jones, M. C. (1924). The elimination of children's fears. *Journal of Experimental Psychology*, **7**, 382–390.

Jones, R. G. (1969). A Factored Measure of Ellis' Irrational Belief System with Personality and Maladjustment Correlates. Doctoral dissertation, Texas Technical College, 1968. *Dissertation Abstracts International*, **29**(11-B), 4379–4380. (University Microfilms No. 69-6443)

Kadushin, C. (1969). *Why People go to Psychiatrists*. New York: Atherton.

Kanter, N. J. & Goldfried, M. R. (1979). Relative effectiveness of rational restructuring and self-control desensitization in the reduction of interpersonal anxiety. *Behavior Therapy*, **10**, 472–490.

Kaplan, H. B. & Pokorny, A. D. (1969). Self-derogation and psychosocial adjustment. *Journal of Nervous and Mental Disease*, **149**, 421–434.

Karst, T. O. & Trexler, L. D. (1970). Initial study using fixed-role and rational–emotive therapy in treating public-speaking anxiety. *Journal of Consulting and Clinical Psychology*, **34**, 360–366.

Keilson, M. V., Dworkin, F. H. & Gelso, C. J. (1979). The effectiveness of time-limited psychotherapy in a university counseling center. *Journal of Clinical Psychology*, **35**, 631–636.

Kelly, E. L. (1961). Clinical psychology—1960. Report of survey findings. *Newsletter: Division of Clinical Psychology of the American Psychological Association*, **14**, 1–11.

Kelly, E. L. & Conley, J. J. (1987). Personality and compatibility: A prospective analysis of marital stability and marital satisfaction. *Journal of Personality and Social Psychology*, **52**, 27–40.

Kelly, G. A. (1955a). *The Psychology of Personal Constructs*. Volume 1: *A Theory of Personality*. New York: Norton.

Kelly, G. A. (1955b). *The Psychology of Personal Constructs*. Volume 2: *Clinical Diagnosis and Psychotherapy*. New York: Norton.

Kendell, R. E. & DiScipio, W. J. (1968). Eysenck Personality Inventory scores of patients with depressive illnesses. *British Journal of Psychiatry*, **114**, 767–770.

Kerr, T. A., Schapira, K., Roth, M. & Garside, R. F. (1970). The relationship between the Maudsley Personality Inventory and the course of affective disorders. *British Journal of Psychiatry*, **116**, 11–19.

Kiesler, D. J., Klein, M. H. & Mathieu, P. L. (1976a). Therapist conditions and patient process. In C. R. Rogers, E. T. Gendlin, D. J. Kiesler & C. B. Truax (eds.), *The Therapeutic Relationship and its Impact: A study of Psychotherapy with Schizophrenics*, pp. 187–219. Westport, CT: Greenwood. (Original work published 1967)

Kiesler, D. J., Klein, M. H., Mathieu, P. L. & Schoeninger, D. (1976b). Constructive personality change for therapy and control patients. In C. R. Rogers, E. T. Gendlin, D. J. Kiesler & C. B. Truax (eds.), *The Therapeutic Relationship and its Impact: A study of Psychotherapy with Schizophrenics*, pp. 251–294. Westport, CT: Greenwood. (Original work published 1967)

Kiesler, D. J., Mathieu, P. L. & Klein, M. H. (1976c). Measurement of conditions and process variables. In C. R. Rogers, E. T. Gendlin, D. J. Kiesler & C. B. Truax (eds.), *The Therapeutic Relationship and its Impact: A Study of Psychotherapy with Schizophrenics*, pp. 135–185. Westport, CT: Greenwood. (Original work published 1967)

King, D. A. & Heller, K. (1984). Depression and the response of others. *Journal of Abnormal Psychology*, **93**, 477–480.

Kirkley, B. G., Schneider, J. A., Agras, W. S. & Bachman, J. A. (1985). Comparison of two group treatments for bulimia. *Journal of Consulting and Clinical Psychology*, **53**, 43–48.

Kline, P. (1981). *Fact and Fantasy in Freudian Theory* (2nd edn.). London: Methuen.

Klion, R. E. (1988). Construct system organization and schizophrenia: The role of construct integration. *Journal of Social and Clinical Psychology*, **6**, 439–447.

Knight, R. P. (1941). Evaluation of the results of psychoanalytic therapy. *American Journal of Psychiatry*, **98**, 434–446.

Kockott, G., Dittmar, F. & Nusselt, L. (1975). Systematic desensitization of erectile impotence: A controlled study. *Archives of Sexual Behavior*, **4**, 493–500.

Korner, I. N., Allison, R. B., Donoviel, S. J. & Boswell, J. D. (1963). Some measures of self-acceptance. *Journal of Clinical Psychology*, **19**, 131–132.

Kovacs, M., Rush, A. J., Beck, A. T. & Hollon, S. D. (1981). Depressed outpatients treated with cognitive therapy or pharmacotherapy: A one-year follow-up. *Archives of General Psychiatry*, **38**, 33–39.

Krantz, S. & Hammen, C. L. (1979). Assessment of cognitive bias in depression. *Journal of Abnormal Psychology*, **88**, 611–619.

Krasner, L. (1962). The therapist as a social reinforcement machine. In H. H. Strupp & L. Luborsky (eds.), *Research in Psychotherapy*, Volume II, pp. 61–94. Washington, DC: American Psychological Association.

Krug, S. E. & Laughlin, J. E. (1977). Second-order factors among normal and pathological primary personality traits. *Journal of Consulting and Clinical Psychology*, **45**, 575–582.

Kubie, L. S. (1934). Relation of the conditioned reflex to psychoanalytic technic. *Archives of Neurology and Psychiatry*, **32**, 1137–1142.

Kurtz, R. R. & Grummon, D. (1972). Different approaches to the measurement of therapist empathy and their relationship to therapy outcomes. *Journal of Consulting and Clinical Psychology*, **39**, 106–115.

Lacey, J. H. (1983). Bulimia nervosa, binge eating, and psychogenic vomiting: A controlled treatment study and long-term outcome. *British Medical Journal*, **286**, 1609–1613.

Lake, A., Rainey, J. & Papsdorf, J. D. (1979). Biofeedback and rational–emotive therapy in the management of migraine headache. *Journal of Applied Behavior Analysis*, **12**, 127–140.

Lamb, D. H. (1973). The effect of two stressors on state anxiety for students who differ in trait anxiety. *Journal of Research in Personality*, **7**, 116–126.

Landfield, A. W. & Schmittdiel, C. J. (1983). The interpersonal transaction group: Evolving measurements in the pursuit of theory. In J. Adams-Webber & J. C. Mancuso (eds.), *Applications of Personal Construct Theory*, pp. 207–218. Don Mills, Ontario: Academic Press.

Lang, P. J. & Melamed, B. G. (1969). Avoidance conditioning therapy of an infant with chronic ruminative vomiting. *Journal of Abnormal Psychology*, **74**, 1–8.

Laughridge, S. (1971). *A Test of Irrational Thinking as it Relates to Psychological Maladjustment*. Master's thesis, University of Oregon, WA.

Laughridge, S. (1975). Differential diagnosis with a Test of Irrational Ideation. *Rational Living*, **10**, 21–23.

Lautch, H. (1971). Dental phobia. *British Journal of Psychiatry*, **119**, 151–158.

Laxer, R. M. (1964). Self-concept changes of depressive patients in general hospital treatment. *Journal of Consulting Psychology*, **28**, 214–219.

Lazarus, A. A. (1973). Multimodal behavior therapy: Treating the 'basic id'. *Journal of Nervous and Mental Disease*, **156**, 404–411.

Lazarus, A. A. (1976). *Multimodal Behavior Therapy*. New York: Springer.

Lazarus, A. A. (1989). *The Practice of Multimodal Therapy: Systematic, Comprehensive, and Effective Psychotherapy*. Baltimore, MD: Johns Hopkins University Press.

Lazarus, A. A., Davison, G. C. & Polefka, D. A. (1965). Classical and operant factors in the treatment of a school phobia. *Journal of Abnormal Psychology*, **70**, 225–229.

Lee, N. L. & Rush, A. J. (1986). Cognitive–behavioral group therapy for bulimia. *International Journal of Eating Disorders*, **5**, 599–615.

Leeuw, P. (1971). On the development of the concept of defense. *International Journal of Psycho-Analysis*, **52**, 51–58.

Leitenberg, H. & Rosen, J. (1989). Cognitive–behavioral therapy with and without exposure plus response prevention in treatment of bulimia nervosa: Comment on Agras, Schneider, Arnow, Raeburn, and Telch. *Journal of Consulting and Clinical Psychology*, **57**, 776–777.

Leitenberg, H., Agras, W. S. & Thomson, L. E. (1968). A sequential analysis of the effect of selective positive reinforcement in modifying anorexia nervosa. *Behaviour Research and Therapy*, **6**, 211–218.

Leitenberg, H., Agras, S., Butz, R. & Wincze, J. (1971). Relationship between heart rate and behavioral change during the treatment of phobias. *Journal of Abnormal Psychology*, **78**, 59–68.

Lemere, F. & Voegtlin, W. L. (1950). An evaluation of the aversion treatment of alcoholism. *Quarterly Journal of Studies on Alcohol*, **11**, 199–204.

Lemere, F., Voegtlin, W. L., Broz, W. R. *et al.* (1942). Conditioned reflex treatment of chronic alcoholism. VII. Technic. *Diseases of the Nervous System*, **3**, 243–247.

Leon, G. R., Gillum, B., Gillum, R. & Gouze, M. (1979). Personality stability and change over a 30-year period—Middle to old age. *Journal of Consulting and Clinical Psychology*, **47**, 517–524.

Lepper, M. R., Sagotsky, G. & Mailer, J. (1975). Generalization and persistence of effects of exposure to self-reinforcement models. *Child Development*, **46**, 618–630.

Levey, A. B. & Martin, I. (1975). Classical conditioning of human evaluative response. *Behaviour Research and Therapy*, **13**, 221–226.

Lewis, D. (1875). *Chastity: Or our Secret Sins*. Philadelphia: Maclean.

Lick, J. (1975). Expectancy, false galvanic skin response feedback, and systematic desensitization in the modification of phobic behavior. *Journal of Consulting and Clinical Psychology*, **43**, 557–567.

Lietaer, G. (1976). Nederlandstalige revisie van Barrett–Lennard's Relationship Inventory voor individueel-terapeutische relaties [Dutch revision of the Barrett–Lennard Relationship Inventory for individual therapeutic relationships]. *Psychologica Belgica*, **16**, 73–94.

Lietaer, G. & Neirinck, M. (1986). Client and therapist perceptions of helping processes in client-centered/experiential psychotherapy. *Person-Centered Review*, **1**, 436–455.

Likierman, H. & Rachman, S. (1982). Obsessions: An experimental investigation of thought-stopping and habituation training. *Behavioural Psychotherapy*, **10**, 324–338.

Lindsley, O. R., Skinner, B. F. & Solomon, H. C. (1953). *Studies in Behavior Therapy*. Waltham, MA: Metropolitan State Hospital.

Lipsky, M. J., Kassinove, H. & Miller, N. J. (1980). Effects of rational–emotive therapy, rational role reversal, and rational–emotive imagery on the emotional adjustment of community mental health center patients. *Journal of Consulting and Clinical Psychology*, **48**, 366–374.

Little, L. M., Curran, J. P. & Gilbert, F. S. (1977). The importance of subject recruitment procedures in therapy analogue studies on heterosexual–social anxiety. *Behavior Therapy*, **8**, 24–29.

Llewelyn, S. P., Elliott, R., Shapiro, D. A., Firth-Cozens, J. & Hardy, G. (1988). Client perceptions of significant events in prescriptive and exploratory periods of individual therapy. *British Journal of Clinical Psychology*, **27**, 105–114.

Loehlin, J. C. & Nichols, R. C. (1976). *Heredity, Environment, and Personality: A Study of 850 Sets of Twins*. Austin: University of Texas Press.

Lohr, J. M. & Bonge, D. (1982a). The factorial validity of the Irrational Beliefs Test: A psychometric investigation. *Cognitive Therapy and Research*, **6**, 225–230.

Lohr, J. M. & Bonge, D. (1982b). Relationship between assertiveness and factorially validated measures of irrational beliefs. *Cognitive Therapy and Research*, **6**, 353–356.

Luborsky, L. (1976). Helping alliances in psychotherapy: The groundwork for a study of their relationship to its outcome. In J. L. Claghorn (ed.), *Successful Psychotherapy*, pp. 92–116. New York: Brunner/Mazel.

Luborsky, L., Chandler, M., Auerbach, A. H. *et al.* (1971). Factors influencing the outcome of psychotherapy: A review of quantitative research. *Psychological Bulletin*, **75**, 145–185.

Luborsky, L., Singer, B. & Luborsky, L. (1975). Comparative studies of psychotherapies: Is it true that 'Everyone has won and all must have prizes'? *Archives of General Psychiatry*, **32**, 995–1008.

Luborsky, L., Mintz, J., Auerbach, A. *et al.* (1980). Predicting the outcome of psychotherapy: Findings of the Penn Psychotherapy Project. *Archives of General Psychiatry*, **37**, 471–481.

Luborsky, L., Crits-Christoph, P., Alexander, L. *et al.* (1983). Two helping alliance methods for predicting outcomes of psychotherapy: A counting signs vs. a global rating method. *Journal of Nervous and Mental Disease*, **171**, 480–491.

Luborsky, L., McLellan, T., Woody, G. E., O'Brien, C. P. & Auerbach, A. (1985). Therapist success and its determinants. *Archives of General Psychiatry*, **42**, 602–611.

Lukianowicz, N. (1972). Incest. I: Paternal incest. *British Journal of Psychiatry*, **120**, 301–313.

MacCulloch, M. J., Feldman, M. P., Orford, J. F. & MacCulloch, M. L. (1966). Anticipatory avoidance learning in the treatment of alcoholism: A record of therapeutic failure. *Behaviour Research and Therapy*, **4**, 187–196.

Madill, M-F., Campbell, D., Laverty, S. G. *et al.* (1966). Aversion treatment of alcoholics by succinylcholine-induced apneic paralysis: An analysis of early changes in drinking behavior. *Quarterly Journal of Studies on Alcohol*, **27**, 483–509.

Magnus, P., Berg, K. & Nance, W. E. (1983). Predicting zygosity in Norwegian twin pairs born 1915–1960. *Clinical Genetics*, **24**, 103–112.

Makhlouf Norris, F., Jones, H. W. & Norris, H. (1970). Articulation of the conceptual structure in obsessional neurosis. *British Journal of Social and Clinical Psychology*, **9**, 264–274.

Malleson, N. (1959). Panic and phobia: A possible method of treatment. *Lancet*, **1**, 225–227.

Malouff, J. M. & Schutte, N. S. (1986). Development and validation of a measure of irrational belief. *Journal of Consulting and Clinical Psychology*, **54**, 860–862.

Mannuzza, S., Fyer, A. J., Martin, L. Y. *et al.* (1989). Reliability of anxiety assessment: I. Diagnostic agreement. *Archives of General Psychiatry*, **46**, 1093–1101.

Marks, I. (1971). Phobic disorders four years after treatment: A prospective follow-up. *British Journal of Psychiatry*, **118**, 683–688.

Marks, I., Boulougouris, J. & Marset, P. (1971). Flooding versus desensitization in the treatment of phobic patients: A crossover study. *British Journal of Psychiatry*, **119**, 353–375.

Marks, I. M. & Gelder, M. G. (1966). Common ground between behaviour therapy and psychodynamic methods. *British Journal of Medical Psychology*, **39**, 11–23.

Marks, I. M. & Gelder, M. G. (1967). Transvestism and fetishism: Clinical and psychological changes during faradic aversion. *British Journal of Psychiatry*, **113**, 711–729.

Marks, I. M., Gelder, M. G. & Edwards, G. (1968). Hypnosis and desensitization for phobias: A controlled prospective trial. *British Journal of Psychiatry*, **114**, 1263–1274.

Marks, I. M., Hodgson, R. & Rachman, S. (1975). Treatment of chronic obsessive–compulsive neurosis by *in-vivo* exposure: A two-year follow-up and issues in treatment. *British Journal of Psychiatry*, **127**, 349–364.

Marmar, C. R., Horowitz, M. J., Weiss, D. S. & Marziali, E. (1986). The development of the Therapeutic Alliance Rating System. In L. S. Greenberg & W. M. Pinsoff (eds.), *The Psychotherapeutic Process: A Research Handbook*, pp. 367–390. New York: Guilford Press.

Marshall, D. & Cattell, R. B. (1973). *The Seven Scale Supplement to the 16PF*. Champaign, IL: Institute for Personality and Ability Testing.

Martin, L. M., Dolliver, R. H. & Irvin, J. A. (1977). A construct validity study of five measures of irrational beliefs. *Rational Living*, **12**, 20–24.

Martin, N. G. & Jardine, R. (1986). Eysenck's contribution to behaviour genetics. In S. Modgil & C. Modgil (eds.), *Hans Eysenck: Consensus and Controversy*, pp. 13–62. Lewes, Sussex: Falmar Press.

Martorano, R. D. & Nathan, P. E. (1972). Syndromes of psychosis and neurosis: Factor analysis of a systems analysis. *Journal of Abnormal Psychology*, **80**, 1–10.

Marziali, E. A. (1984). Prediction of outcome of brief psychotherapy from therapist interpretive interventions. *Archives of General Psychiatry*, **41**, 301–304.

Marziali, E., Marmar, C. & Krupnick, J. (1981). Therapeutic alliance scales: Development and relationship to psychotherapy outcome. *American Journal of Psychiatry*, **138**, 361–364.

Marzillier, J. S., Lambert, C. & Kellett, J. (1976). A controlled evaluation of systematic desensitization and social skills training for socially inadequate psychiatric patients. *Behaviour Research and Therapy*, **14**, 225–238.

Masling, J. (ed.) (1983). *Empirical Studies of Psychoanalytic Theories*, Vol. 1. Hillsdale, NJ: Analytic Press.

Masserman, J. H. (1943). *Behavior and Neurosis: An Experimental Psychoanalytic Approach to Psychobiologic Principles*. Chicago: Chicago University Press.

Masson, J. M. (1984). *Freud: The Assault on Truth, Freud's Suppression of the Seduction Theory*. London: Faber & Faber.

Mathews, A. M. & Gelder, M. G. (1969). Psychophysiological investigations of brief relaxation training. *Journal of Psychosomatic Research*, **13**, 1–12.

Mathews, A. M., Johnston, D. W., Shaw, P. M. & Gelder, M. G. (1974). Process variables and the prediction of outcome in behaviour therapy. *British Journal of Psychiatry*, **125**, 256–264.

Mathews, A. M., Johnston, D. W., Lancashire, M. *et al.* (1976). Imaginal flooding and exposure to real phobic situations: Treatment outcome with agoraphobic patients. *British Journal of Psychiatry*, **129**, 362–371.

Mavreas, V. G., Beis, A., Mouyias, A., Rigoni, F. & Lyketsos, G. C. (1986). Prevalence of psychiatric disorders in Athens: A community study. *Social Psychiatry*, **21**, 172–181.

Max, L. W. (1935). Breaking up a homosexual fixation by the conditioned reaction technique: A case study. *Psychological Bulletin*, **32**, 734.

McConaghy, N. & Barr, R. F. (1973). Classical, avoidance and backward conditioning treatments of homosexuality. *British Journal of Psychiatry*, **122**, 151–162.

McConnaughy, E. A., Prochaska, J. O. & Velicer, W. F. (1983). Stages of change in psychotherapy: Measurement and sample profiles. *Psychotherapy: Theory, Research and Practice*, **20**, 368–375.

McCrae, R. M. & Costa, P. T., Jr. (1987). Validation of the five-factor model of personality across instruments and observers. *Journal of Personality and Social Psychology*, **52**, 81–90.

McDaniel, S. H., Stiles, W. B. & McGaughey, K. J. (1981). Correlations of male college students' verbal response mode use in psychotherapy with measures of psychological disturbance and psychotherapy outcome. *Journal of Consulting and Clinical Psychology*, **49**, 571–582.

McIntyre, C. J. (1952). Acceptance by others and its relation to acceptance of self and others. *Journal of Abnormal and Social Psychology*, **47**, 624–625.

McLean, P. D. & Hakstian, A. R. (1979). Clinical depression: Comparative efficacy of outpatient treatments. *Journal of Consulting and Clinical Psychology*, **47**, 818–836.

McPherson, F. M., Antram, M. C., Bagshaw, V. E. & Carmichael, S. K. (1977). A test of the hierarchical model of personal illness. *British Journal of Psychiatry*, **131**, 56–58.

McPherson, F. M. & Buckley, F. (1970). Thought-process disorder and personal construct subsystems. *British Journal of Social and Clinical Psychology*, **9**, 380–381.

McPherson, F. M., Blackburn, I. M., Draffan, J. W. & McFadyen, M. (1973). A further study of the Grid Test of Thought Disorder. *British Journal of Social and Clinical Psychology*, **12**, 420–427.

McPherson, F. M., Presley, A. S., Armstrong, J. & Curtis, R. H. (1974). 'Psychoticism' and psychotic illness. *British Journal of Psychiatry*, **125**, 152–160.

McPherson, F. M., Armstrong, J. & Heather, B. B. (1975). Psychological construing, 'difficulty' and thought disorder. *British Journal of Medical Psychology*, **48**, 303–315.

McPherson, F. M., Armstrong, J. & Heather, B. B. (1978). Psychological construing and thought disorder: Another test of the 'difficulty' hypothesis. *British Journal of Medical Psychology*, **50**, 319–324.

McPherson, F. M., Brougham, L. & McLaren, S. (1980). Maintenance of improvement in agoraphobic patients treated by behavioural methods—a four-year follow-up. *Behaviour Therapy and Research*, **18**, 150–152.

McWhirter, J. J. (1973). Two measures of the facilitative conditions: A correlation study. *Journal of Counseling Psychology*, **20**, 317–320.

Meador, B. D. & Rogers, C. R. (1979). Person-centered therapy. In R. J. Corsini (ed.), *Current Psychotherapies* (2nd edn.), pp. 131–184. Itasca, IL: Peacock.

Medinnus, G. R. & Curtis, F. J. (1963). The relation between maternal self-acceptance and child acceptance. *Journal of Consulting Psychology*, **27**, 542–544.

Meichenbaum, D. (1977). *Cognitive-Behavior Modification: An Integrative Approach*. New York: Plenum.

Messer, S. B. (1989). Integration and eclecticism in counselling and psychotherapy: Cautionary notes. *British Journal of Guidance and Counselling*, **17**, 274–285.

Metzner, R. (1963). Some experimental analogues of obsession. *Behaviour Research and Therapy*, **1**, 231–236.

Meyer, A.-E. (ed.) (1981). The Hamburg short psychotherapy comparison experiment. *Psychotherapy and Psychosomatics*, **35**, 81–207.

Michaelis, W. & Eysenck, H. J. (1971). The determination of personality inventory factor patterns and intercorrelations by changes in real-life motivation. *Journal of Genetic Psychology*, **118**, 223–234.

Miller, I. W., Norman, W. H. & Keitner, G. I. (1989a). Cognitive-behavioral treatment of depressed inpatients: Six- and twelve-month follow-up. *American Journal of Psychiatry*, **146**, 1274–1279.

Miller, I. W., Norman, W. H., Keitner, G. I., Bishop, S. B. & Dow, M. G. (1989b). Cognitive–behavioral treatment of depressed inpatients. *Behavior Therapy*, **20**, 25–47.

Miller, L. C., Barrett, C. L., Hampe, E. & Noble, H. (1972). Comparison of reciprocal inhibition, psychotherapy, and waiting list control for phobic children. *Journal of Abnormal Psychology*, **79**, 269–279.

Miller, N. E. (1948). Theory and experiment relating psychoanalytic displacement to stimulus–response generalization. *Journal of Abnormal and Social Psychology*, **43**, 155–178.

Miller, N. E. (1978). Biofeedback and visceral learning. *Annual Review of Psychology*, **29**, 373–404.

Mills, D. H. & Zytowski, D. G. (1967). Helping relationship: A structural analysis. *Journal of Counseling Psychology*, **14**, 193–197.

Mitchell, K. M., Truax, C. B., Bozarth, J. D. & Krauft, C. C. (1973). *Antecedents to Psychotherapeutic Outcome*. (Final Report, NIMH MH 12306). Fayetteville, AR: University of Arkansas, Arkansas Rehabilitation Research and Training Center.

Mitchell, K. M., Bozarth, J. D. & Krauft, C. C. (1977). A reappraisal of the therapeutic effectiveness of accurate empathy, nonpossessive warmth, and genuineness. In A. S. Gurman & A. M. Razin (eds.), *Effective Psychotherapy: A Handbook of Research*, pp. 482–502. New York: Pergamon.

Monti, P. M., Fink, E., Norman, W. *et al.* (1979). Effect of social skills training groups and social skills bibliotherapy with psychiatric patients. *Journal of Consulting and Clinical Psychology*, **47**, 189–191.

Monti, P. M., Curran, J. P., Corriveau, D. P., DeLancey, A. L. & Hagerman, S. M. (1980). Effects of social skills training groups and sensitivity groups with psychiatric patients. *Journal of Consulting and Clinical Psychology*, **48**, 241–248.

Moreno, J. L. (1946). *Psychodrama*. Volume 1. New York: Beacon House.

Morgan, R., Luborsky, L., Crits-Cristoph, P. *et al.* (1982). Predicting the outcomes of psychotherapy by the Penn helping alliance rating method. *Archives of General Psychiatry*, **39**, 397–402.

Morgenstern, F. S., Pearce, J. F. & Linford Rees, W. (1965). Predicting the outcome of behaviour therapy by psychological tests. *Behaviour Research and Therapy*, **2**, 191–200.

Morris, R. J. & Suckerman, K. R. (1974a). Therapist warmth as a factor in automated systematic desensitization. *Journal of Consulting and Clinical Psychology*, **42**, 244–250.

Morris, R. J. & Suckerman, K. R. (1974b). The importance of the therapeutic relationship in systematic desensitization. *Journal of Consulting and Clinical Psychology*, **42**, 148.

Morris, R. J. & Magrath, K. H. (1979). Contribution of therapist warmth to the contact desensitization treatment of acrophobia. *Journal of Consulting and Clinical Psychology*, **47**, 786–788.

Mowrer, O. H. (1947). On the dual nature of learning—A re-interpretation of 'conditioning' and 'problem-solving'. *Harvard Educational Review*, **17**, 102–148.

Mowrer, O. H. & Mowrer, W. M. (1938). Enuresis: A method for its study and treatment. *American Journal of Orthopsychiatry*, **8**, 436–459.

184 Personality and psychotherapy

Mowrer, O. H. & Lamoreaux, R. R. (1942). Avoidance conditioning and signal duration—a study of secondary motivation and reward. *Psychological Monograph*, **54** (5, Whole No. 247).

Mullen, P. E., Romans-Clarkson, S. E., Walton, V. A. & Herbison, G. P. (1988). Impact of sexual and physical abuse on women's mental health. *Lancet*, **1**, 841–845.

Munby, M. & Johnston, D. W. (1980). Agoraphobia: The long-term follow-up of behavioural treatment. *British Journal of Psychiatry*, **137**, 418–427.

Murphy, G. E., Simons, A. D., Wetzel, R. D. & Lustman, P. J. (1984a). Cognitive therapy and pharmacotherapy: Singly and together in the treatment of depression. *Archives of General Psychiatry*, **41**, 33–41.

Murphy, P. M., Cramer, D. & Lillie, F. J. (1984b). The relationship between curative factors perceived by patients in their psychotherapy and treatment outcome: An exploratory study. *British Journal of Medical Psychology*, **57**, 187–192.

Nagpal, M. & Gupta, R. S. (1979). Personality, reinforcement and verbal operant conditioning. *British Journal of Psychology*, **70**, 471–476.

Nash, C. L. & West, D. J. (1985). Sexual molestation of young girls: A retrospective survey. In D. J. West (ed.), *Sexual Victimisation: Two Recent Researches into Sex Problems and Their Social Effects*, pp. 1–92. Aldershot: Gower.

Nelson, R. E. (1977). Irrational beliefs in depression. *Journal of Consulting and Clinical Psychology*, **45**, 1190–1191.

Nelson, R. E. & Craighead, W. E. (1977). Selective recall of positive and negative feedback, self-control behaviors, and depression. *Journal of Abnormal Psychology*, **86**, 379–388.

Neuringer, C. (1961). Dichotomous evaluations in suicidal individuals. *Journal of Consulting Psychology*, **25**, 445–449.

Newmark, C. S. & Whitt, J. K. (1983). Endorsements of Ellis' irrational beliefs as a function of DSM-III psychotic diagnoses. *Journal of Clinical Psychology*, **39**, 820–830.

Newmark, C. S., Frerking, R. A., Cook, L. & Newmark, L. (1973). Endorsement of Ellis' irrational beliefs as a function of psychopathology. *Journal of Clinical Psychology*, **29**, 300–302.

Nias, D. K. B. (1972). A note on the effects of administration conditions upon personality scores in children. *Journal of Child Psychology and Psychiatry*, **13**, 115–119.

Norcross, J. C. & Prochaska, J. O. (1982). A national survey of clinical psychologists: Affiliations and orientations. *The Clinical Psychologist*, **35**, 1–6.

Norcross, J. C., Prochaska, J. O. & Gallagher, K. M. (1989). Clinical psychologists in the 1980s: II. Theory, research, and practice. *The Clinical Psychologist*, **42**, 45–53.

Norman, W. T. (1963). Toward an adequate taxonomy of personality attributes: Replicated factor structure in peer nomination personality ratings. *Journal of Abnormal and Social Psychology*, **66**, 574–583.

O'Connor, R. D. (1972). Relative efficacy of modeling, shaping, and the combined procedures for modication of social withdrawal. *Journal of Abnormal Psychology*, **79**, 327–334.

O'Leary, K. D. & Borkovec, T. D. (1978). Conceptual, methodological, and ethical problems in placebo groups in psychotherapy research. *American Psychologist*, **33**, 821–830.

Omwake, K. T. (1954). The relation between acceptance of self and acceptance of others shown by three personality inventories. *Journal of Consulting Psychology*, **18**, 443–446.

Orley, J. & Wing, J. K. (1979). Psychiatric disorders in two African villages. *Archives of General Psychiatry*, **36**, 513–520.

Orlinsky, D. E. & Howard, K. I. (1986). Process and outcome in psychotherapy. In S. L. Garfield & A. E. Bergin (eds.), *Handbook of Psychotherapy and Behavior Change* (3rd edn.), pp. 311–381. New York: Wiley.

Ost, L.-G. (1985). Ways of acquiring phobias and outcome of behavioral treatments. *Behaviour Research and Therapy*, **23**, 683–689.

Ost, L.-G. & Hugdahl, K. (1981). Acquisition of phobias and anxiety response patterns in clinical patients. *Behaviour Research and Therapy*, **19**, 439–447.

Page, H. A. & Hall, J. F. (1953). Experimental extinction as a function of the prevention of a response. *Journal of Comparative and Physiological Psychology*, **46**, 33–34.

Parloff, M. B. (1986). Placebo controls in psychotherapy research: A *sine qua non* or a placebo for research problems? *Journal of Consulting and Clinical Psychology*, **54**, 79–87.

Patterson, V., Levene, H. & Breger, L. (1971). Treatment and training outcomes with two time-limited therapies. *Archives of General Psychiatry*, **25**, 161–167.

Pavlov, I. P. (1927). *Conditioned Reflexes: An Investigation of the Physiological Activity of the Cerebral Cortex* (G. V. Anrep, trans.). London: Oxford University Press.

Pavlov, I. P. (1962). *Psychopathology and Psychiatry: Selected Works* (Y. Popov & L. Rokhlin, eds.). Moscow: Foreign Languages Publishing House.

Paykel, E. S., McGuiness, B. & Gomez, J. (1976). An Anglo-American comparison of the scaling of life events. *British Journal of Medical Psychology*, **49**, 237–247.

Pedersen, N. L., Plomin, R., McLearn, G. E. & Friberg, L. (1988). Neuroticism, extraversion, and related traits in adult twins reared apart and reared together. *Journal of Personality and Social Psychology*, **55**, 950–957.

Percell, L. P., Berwick, P. T. & Beigel, A. (1974). The effects of assertive training on self-concept and anxiety. *Archives of General Psychiatry*, **31**, 502–504.

Peselow, E. D., Robins, C., Block, P., Barouche, F. & Fieve, R. R. (1990). Dysfunctional attitudes in depressed patients before and after clinical treatment and in normal control subjects. *American Journal of Psychiatry*, **147**, 439–444.

Phillips, E. L. (1951). Attitudes toward self and others: A brief questionnaire report. *Journal of Consulting Psychology*, **15**, 79–81.

Phillips, E. L., Raiford, A. & El-Batrawi, S. (1965). The Q sort reevaluated. *Journal of Consulting Psychology*, **29**, 422–425.

Phillips, L. & Zigler, E. (1961). Social competence: The action–thought parameter and vicariousness in normal and pathological behaviors. *Journal of Abnormal and Social Psychology*, **63**, 137–146.

Piers, E. V. & Kirchner, E. P. (1969). Eyelid conditioning and personality: Positive results from nonpartisans. *Journal of Abnormal Psychology*, **74**, 336–339.

Piper, W., Debanne, E., Bienvenu, J., de Carufel, F. & Garant, J. (1986). Relationships between the object focus of therapist interpretations and outcome in short term individual psychotherapy. *British Journal of Medical Psychology*, **59**, 1–11.

Polin, A. T. (1959). The effect of flooding and physical suppression as extinction techniques on an anxiety-motivated avoidance locomotor response. *Journal of Psychology*, **47**, 253–255.

Popper, K. R. (1963). *Conjectures and Refutations*. London: Routledge & Kegan Paul.

Prigatano, G. P. & Johnson, H. J. (1974). Autonomic nervous system changes associated with a spider phobic reaction. *Journal of Abnormal Psychology*, **83**, 169–177.

Prochaska, J. O. (1979). *Systems of Psychotherapy: A Transtheoretical Analysis*. Homewood, IL: Dorsey Press.

Prochaska, J. O. & DiClemente, C. C. (1982). Transtheoretical therapy: Toward a more integrative model of change. *Psychotherapy: Theory, Research and Practice*, **19**, 276–288.

Prochaska, J. O. & DiClemente, C. C. (1984). *The Transtheoretical Approach: Crossing the Traditional Boundaries of Therapy*. Homewood, IL: Dow Jones-Irwin.

Prochaska, J. O. & Norcross, J. C. (1983a). Contemporary psychotherapists: A national survey of characteristics, practices, orientations, and attitudes. *Psychotherapy: Theory, Research and Practice*, **20**, 161–173.

Prochaska, J. O. & Norcross, J. C. (1983b). Psychotherapists' perspectives on treating themselves and their clients for psychic distress. *Professional Psychology: Research and Practice*, **14**, 642–655.

Prochaska, J. O., Velicer, W. F., DiClemente, C. C. & Fava, J. (1988). Measuring processes of change: Applications to the cessation of smoking. *Journal of Consulting and Clinical Psychology*, **56**, 520–528.

Protinsky, H. & Popp, R. (1978). Irrational philosophies in popular music. *Cognitive Therapy and Research*, **2**, 71–74.

Quick, E. & Jacob, T. (1973). Marital disturbance in relation to role theory and relationship theory. *Journal of Abnormal Psychology*, **82**, 309–316.

Rachman, S. (1966). Studies in desensitization: I. Flooding. *Behaviour Research and Therapy*, **4**, 1–16.

Rachman, S. (1971). *The Effects of Psychotherapy*. Oxford: Pergamon Press.

Rachman, S. (1977). The conditioning theory of fear-acquisition: A critical examination. *Behaviour Research and Therapy*, **15**, 375–387.

Rachman, S. J. & Wilson, G. T. (1980). *The Effects of Psychological Therapy* (2nd edn.). Oxford: Pergamon Press.

Rachman, S., Hodgson, R. & Marks, I. (1971). The treatment of chronic obsessional neurosis. *Behaviour Research and Therapy*, **9**, 237–247.

Rachman, S., Marks, I. & Hodgson, R. (1973). The treatment of chronic obsessive-compulsive neurosis by modelling and flooding *in vivo*. *Behaviour Research and Therapy*, **11**, 463–471.

Radley, A. R. (1974). Schizophrenic thought disorder and the nature of personal constructs. *British Journal of Social and Clinical Psychology*, **13**, 315–327.

Rapaport, D. (1967). The theory of ego autonomy: A generalization. In M. M. Gill (ed.), *The Collected Papers of David Rapoport*, pp. 722–744. New York: Basic Books.

Regier, D. A., Boyd, J. H., Burke, J. D., Jr. *et al.* (1988). One-month prevalence of mental disorders in the United States: Based on five Epidemiologic Catchment Area sites. *Archives of General Psychiatry*, **45**, 977–986.

Rhoads, J. M. & Feather, B. W. (1972). Transference and resistance observed in behaviour therapy. *British Journal of Medical Psychology*, **45**, 99–103.

Ritter, B. (1969). The use of contact desensitization, demonstration-plus-participation, and demonstration alone in the treatment of acrophobia. *Behaviour Research and Therapy*, **7**, 157–164.

Rivers, W. H. R. (1908). *The Influence of Alcohol and Other Drugs on Fatigue*. London: Arnold.

Roback, H. B. & Strassberg, D. S. (1975). Relationship between perceived therapist-offered conditions and therapeutic movement in group psychotherapy. *Small Group Behavior*, **6**, 345–352.

Roehling, P. V. & Robin, A. L. (1986). Development and validation of the Family Beliefs Inventory: A measure of unrealistic beliefs among parents and adolescents. *Journal of Consulting and Clinical Psychology*, **54**, 693–697.

Rogers, C. R. (1946). Significant aspects of client-centered therapy. *American Psychologist*, **1**, 415–422.

Rogers, C. R. (1951). *Client-Centred Therapy: Its Current Practice, Implications and Theory*. Boston: Houghton Mifflin.

Rogers, C. R. (1957). The necessary and sufficient conditions of therapeutic personality change. *Journal of Consulting Psychology*, **21**, 95–103.

Rogers, C. R. (1959). A theory of therapy, personality, and interpersonal relationships, as developed in the client-centered framework. In S. Koch (ed.), *Psychology: A study of a science*. Volume 3: *Formulations of the Person and the Social Context*, pp. 184–256. New York: McGraw-Hill.

Rogers, C. R. (1961a). *On Becoming a Person: A Therapist's View of Psychotherapy*. Boston: Houghton Mifflin.

Rogers, C. R. (1961b). The process equation of psychotherapy. *American Journal of Psychotherapy*, **15**, 27–45.

Rogers, C. R. & Truax, C. B. (1976). The therapeutic conditions antecedent to change: A theoretical view. In C. R. Rogers, E. T. Gendlin, D. J. Kiesler & C. B. Truax (eds.), *The Therapeutic Relationship and its Impact: A Study of Psychotherapy with Schizophrenics*, pp. 97–108. Westport, CT: Greenwood. (Original work published 1967)

Roper, G., Rachman, S. & Marks, I. M. (1975). Passive and participant modelling in exposure treatment of obsessive–compulsive neurotics. *Behaviour Research and Therapy*, **13**, 271–279.

Rorsman, B., Grasbeck, A., Hagnell, O. *et al.* (1990). A prospective study of first-incidence depression: The Lundby Study, 1957–72. *British Journal of Psychiatry*, **156**, 336–342.

Rose, R. J., Koskenvuo, M., Kaprio, J., Sarna, S. & Langinvaino, H. (1988). Shared genes, shared experiences, and similarity of personality: Data from 14 288 adult Finnish co-twins. *Journal of Personality and Social Psychology*, **54**, 161–171.

Rosen, G. M., Glasgow, R. E. & Barrera, M., Jr. (1976). A controlled study to assess the clinical efficacy of totally self-administered systematic desensitization. *Journal of Consulting and Clinical Psychology*, **44**, 208–217.

Rosenberg, M. (1965). *Society and the Adolescent Self-Image*. Princeton, NJ: Princeton University Press.

Rosenfeld, A. A. (1979). Incidence of a history of incest among 18 female psychiatric patients. *American Journal of Psychiatry*, **136**, 791–795.

Rosenthal, D. & Frank, J. D. (1956). Psychotherapy and the placebo effect. *Psychological Bulletin*, **53**, 294–302.

Rosenthal, T. L. & Bandura, A. (1978). Psychological modeling: Theory and practice. In S. L. Garfield & A. E. Bergin (eds.), *Handbook of Psychotherapy and Behavior Change: An Empirical Analysis* (2nd edn.), pp. 621–658. New York: Wiley.

Rosenzweig, S. (1936). Some implicit common factors in diverse methods of psychotherapy. *American Journal of Orthopsychiatry*, **6**, 412–415.

Rosin, L. & Nelson, W. M., III (1983). The effects of rational and irrational self-verbalizations on performance efficiency and levels of anxiety. *Journal of Clinical Psychology*, **39**, 208–213.

Rozensky, R. H., Rehm, L. P., Pry, G. & Ruth, D. (1977). Depression and self-reinforcement behavior in hospitalized patients. *Journal of Behavior Therapy and Experimental Psychiatry*, **8**, 35–38.

Rush, A. J., Beck, A. T., Kovacs, M. & Hollon, S. (1977). Comparative efficacy of cognitive therapy and pharmacotherapy in the treatment of depressed outpatients. *Cognitive Therapy and Research*, **1**, 17–37.

Rush, A. J., Beck, A. T., Kovacs, M. *et al.* (1982). Comparison of the effects of cognitive therapy and pharmacotherapy on hopelessness and self-concept. *American Journal of Psychiatry*, **139**, 862–866.

Rushton, J. P. & Chrisjohn, R. D. (1981). Extraversion, neuroticism, psychoticism and self-reported delinquency: Evidence from eight separate samples. *Personality and Individual Differences*, **2**, 11–20.

Russell, D. E. H. (1983). The incidence and prevalence of intrafamilial sexual abuse of female children. *Child Abuse and Neglect*, **7**, 133–146.

Ryle, A. (1984). How can we compare different psychotherapies? Why are they all effective? *British Journal of Medical Psychology*, **57**, 261–264.

Salter, A. (1949). *Conditioned Reflex Therapy: The Direct Approach to the Reconstruction of Personality*. New York: Creative Age.

Saltzman, C., Luetgert, M. J., Roth, C. H., Creaser, J. & Howard, L. (1976). Formation of a therapeutic relationship: Experiences during the initial phase of psychotherapy as predictors of treatment duration and outcome. *Journal of Consulting and Clinical Psychology*, **44**, 546–555.

Sartorius, N., Jablensky, A., Korten, A. *et al.* (1986). Early manifestations and first-contact incidence of schizophrenia in different cultures. *Psychological Medicine*, **16**, 909–928.

Sartorius, N., Jablensky, A., Cooper, J. E. & Burke, J. D. (1988) (eds.). Psychiatric classification in an international perspective with special reference to Chapter V (F) of the 10th revision of the International Classification of Diseases 'Mental, Behavioural and Developmental Disorders'. *British Journal of Psychiatry*, **152** (Supplement 1).

Saville, P. & Blinkhorn, S. (1976). *Undergraduate Personality by Factored Scales: A Large Scale Study on Cattell's 16PF and the Eysenck Personality Inventory*. Windsor: NFER.

Scarr, S. (1968). Environmental bias in twin studies. *Eugenics Quarterly*, **15**, 34–40.

Schuerger, J. M., Tait, E. & Tavernelli, M. (1982). Temporal stability of personality by questionnaire. *Journal of Personality and Social Psychology*, **43**, 176–182.

Sedney, M. A. & Brooks, B. (1984). Factors associated with a history of childhood sexual experience in a nonclinical female population. *Journal of the American Academy of Child Psychiatry*, **23**, 215–218.

Seligman, M. E. P. (1971). Phobias and preparedness. *Behavior Therapy*, **2**, 307–320.

Selmi, P. M., Klein, M. H., Greist, J. H. *et al.* (1990). Computer-administered cognitive–behavioral therapy for depression. *American Journal of Psychiatry*, **147**, 51–56.

Shapiro, A. K. (1960). A contribution to a history of the placebo effect. *Behavioral Science*, **5**, 109–135.

Shapiro, D., Crider, A. B. & Tursky, B. (1964). Differentiation of an autonomic response through operant conditioning. *Psychonomic Science*, **1**, 147–148.

Shapiro, D. & Surwit, R. S. (1976). Learned control of physiological function and disease. In H. Leitenberg (ed.), *Handbook of Behavior Modification and Behavior Therapy*, pp. 74–123. Englewood Cliffs, NJ: Prentice-Hall.

Shapiro, D. A. & Shapiro, D. (1982). Meta-analysis of comparative therapy outcome studies: A replication and refinement. *Psychological Bulletin*, **92**, 581–604.

Shapiro, S., Skinner, E. A., Kessler, L. G. *et al.* (1984). Utilization of health and mental health services: Three Epidemiologic Catchment Area sites. *Archives of General Psychiatry*, **41**, 971–978.

Shaw, B. F. (1977). Comparison of cognitive therapy and behavior therapy in the treatment of depression. *Journal of Consulting and Clinical Psychology*, **45**, 543–551.

Shaw, D. W. & Thoresen, C. E. (1974). Effects of modeling and desensitization in reducing dentist phobia. *Journal of Counseling Psychology*, **21**, 415–420.

Shaw, P. (1979). A comparison of three behaviour therapies in the treatment of social phobia. *British Journal of Psychiatry*, **134**, 620–623.

Sheehan, M. J. (1985). A personal construct study of depression. *British Journal of Medical Psychology*, **58**, 119–128.

Sheerer, E. T. (1949). An analysis of the relationship between acceptance of and respect for self and acceptance of and respect for others in ten counseling cases. *Journal of Consulting Psychology*, **13**, 169–175.

Sherrington, C. S. (1906). *Integrative Action of the Nervous System*. New York: Scribner.

Shields, J. (1962). *Monozygotic Twins: Brought Up Apart and Brought Up Together*. London: Oxford University Press.

Shlien, J. M. (1962). Toward what level of abstraction in criteria? In H. H. Strupp & L. Luborsky (eds.), *Research in Psychotherapy*. Volume II, pp. 142–154. Washington, DC: American Psychological Association.

Shlien, J. M., Mosak, H. H. & Dreikurs, R. (1962). Effect of time limits: A comparison of two psychotherapies. *Journal of Counseling Psychology*, **9**, 31–34.

Shoben, E. J. (1949). Psychotherapy as a problem in learning theory. *Psychological Bulletin*, **46**, 366–392.

Shorkey, C. T. & Whiteman, V. L. (1977). Development of the Rational Behavior Inventory: Initial validity and reliability. *Educational and Psychological Measurement*, **37**, 527–534.

Shorkey, C. T. & Sutton-Simon, K. (1983). Reliability and validity of the Rational Behavior Inventory with a clinical population. *Journal of Clinical Psychology*, **39**, 34–38.

Shrout, P. E., Spitzer, R. L. & Fleiss, J. L. (1987). Quantification of agreement in psychiatric diagnosis revisited. *Archives of General Psychiatry*, **44**, 172–177.

Shutty, M. S., Jr., DeGood, D. E. & Schwartz, D. P. (1986). Psychological dimensions of distress in chronic pain patients: A factor analytic study of Symptom Checklist-90 responses. *Journal of Consulting and Clinical Psychology*, **54**, 836–842.

Silber, E. & Tippett, J. S. (1965). Self-esteem: Clinical assessment and measurement validation. *Psychological Reports*, **16**, 1017–1071.

Silverman, J. S., Silverman, J. A. & Eardley, D. A. (1984). Do maladaptive attitudes cause depression? *Archives of General Psychiatry*, **41**, 28–30.

Simon, A. & Thomas, A. (1983). Means, standard deviations and stability coefficients on the EPI for Further Education and College of Education Students. *Personality and Individual Differences*, **4**, 95–96.

Simons, A. D., Garfield, S. L. & Murphy, G. E. (1984). The process of change in cognitive therapy and pharmacotherapy for depression: Changes in mood and cognition. *Archives of General Psychiatry*, **41**, 45–51.

Simons, A. D., Murphy, G. E., Levine, G. L. & Wetzel, R. D. (1986). Cognitive therapy and pharmacotherapy for depression: Sustained improvement over one year. *Archives of General Psychiatry*, **43**, 43–48.

Skinner, B. F. (1938). *The Behavior of Organisms*. New York: Appleton–Century–Crofts.

Skinner, B. F. (1953). *Science and Human Behavior*. New York: Macmillan.

Slater, P. (ed.) (1977). *The Measurement of Intrapersonal Space by Grid Technique*. Volume 2: *Dimensions of Intrapersonal Space*. London: Wiley.

Sloane, R. D., Staples, F. R., Cristol, A. H., Yorkston, N. J. & Whipple, K. (1975). *Psychotherapy versus Behavior Therapy*. Cambridge, MA: Harvard University Press.

Smith, D. (1982). Trends in counseling and psychotherapy. *American Psychologist*, **37**, 802–809.

Smith, J. K. (1982). Irrational beliefs in a college population. *Rational Living*, **17**, 35–36.

Smith, M. L. & Glass, G. V. (1977). Meta-analysis of psychotherapy outcome studies. *American Psychologist*, **32**; 752–760.

Smith, M. L., Glass, G. V. & Miller, T. I. (1980). *The Benefits of Psychotherapy*. Baltimore, MD: Johns Hopkins University Press.

Smith, T. W. & Zurawski, R. M. (1983). Assessment of irrational beliefs: The question of discriminant validity. *Journal of Clinical Psychology*, **39**, 976–979.

Smith, T. W. & Allred, K. D. (1986). Rationality revisited: A reassessment of the empirical support for the rational–emotive model. In P. C. Kendall (ed.), *Advances in Cognitive–Behavioral Research and Therapy*, Vol. 5, pp. 63–87. New York: Academic Press.

Solomon, R. L. & Wynne, L. C. (1954). Traumatic avoidance learning: The principles of anxiety conservation and partial irreversibility. *Psychological Review*, **61**, 353–385.

Solomon, R. L., Kamin, L. J. & Wynne, L. C. (1953). Traumatic avoidance learning: The outcomes of several extinction procedures with dogs. *Journal of Abnormal and Social Psychology*, **48**, 291–302.

Spitzer, R. L., Forman, J. B. W. & Nee, J. (1979). DSM-III field trials: I. Initial inter-rater diagnostic reliability. *American Journal of Psychiatry*, **136**, 815–817.

Spitzer, S. P., Stratton, J. R., Fitzgerald, J. D. & Mach, B. K. (1966). The self-concept: Test equivalence and perceived validity. *Sociological Quarterly*, **7**, 265–280.

Stampfl, T. G. & Levis, D. J. (1967). Essentials of implosive therapy: A learning-theory-based psychodynamic behavioral therapy. *Journal of Abnormal Psychology*, **72**, 496–503.

Stampfl, T. G. & Levis, D. J. (1973). Implosive therapy. In R. M. Jurjevich (ed.), *Direct Psychotherapy*: Volume I, pp. 83–105. Chapel Hill: University of North Carolina Press.

Stelmack, R. M., Achorn, E. & Michaud, A. (1977). Extraversion and individual differences in auditory evoked response. *Psychophysiology*, **14**, 368–374.

Stephenson, W. (1953). *The Study of Behavior: Q-Technique and its Methodology.* Chicago: University of Chicago Press.

Stern, R. & Marks, I. (1973). Brief and prolonged flooding: A comparison in agoraphobic patients. *Archives of General Psychiatry,* **28**, 270–276.

Stiles, W. B., Shapiro, D. A. & Elliott, R. (1986). 'Are all psychotherapies equivalent?' *American Psychologist,* **41**, 165–180.

Stock, D. (1949). An investigation into the interrelations between the self concept and feelings directed toward other persons and groups. *Journal of Consulting Psychology,* **13**, 176–180.

Strassberg, D. S., Roback, H. B., Anchor, K. N. & Abramowitz, S. I. (1975). Self-disclosure in group therapy with schizophrenics. *Archives of General Psychiatry,* **32**, 1259–1261.

Stravynski, A., Marks, I. & Yule, W. (1982). Social skills problems in neurotic outpatients: Social skills training with and without cognitive modification. *Archives of General Psychiatry,* **39**, 1378–1385.

Stroebe, W. & Stroebe, M. S. (1987). *Bereavement and Health: The Psychological and Physical Consequences of Partner Loss.* Cambridge: Cambridge University Press.

Strupp, H. H., Wallach, M. S. & Wogan, M. (1964). Psychotherapy experience in retrospect: Questionnaire survey of former patients and their therapists. *Psychological Monographs: General and Applied,* **78** (Whole No. 588).

Suinn, R. M. (1961). The relationship between self-acceptance and acceptance of others: A learning theory analysis. *Journal of Abnormal and Social Psychology,* **63**, 37–42.

Sullivan, H. S. (1953). *The Interpersonal Theory of Psychiatry.* New York: Norton.

Surtees, P. G. & Kendell, R. E. (1979). The hierarchical model of psychiatric symptomatology: An investigation based on Present State Examination ratings. *British Journal of Psychiatry,* **135**, 438–443.

Swett, C., Jr., Surrey, J. & Cohen, C. (1990). Sexual and physical abuse histories and psychiatric symptoms among male psychiatric outpatients. *American Journal of Psychiatry,* **147**, 632–636.

Taylor, J. G. (1963). A behavioural interpretation of obsessive–compulsive neurosis. *Behaviour Research and Therapy,* **1**, 237–244.

Teasdale, J. D., Fennell, M. J. V., Hibbert, G. A. & Amies, P. L. (1984). Cognitive therapy for major depressive disorder in primary care. *British Journal of Psychiatry,* **144**, 400–406.

Thorndike, E. L. (1898). Animal intelligence: An experimental study of the associative processes in animals. *Psychological Review, Monograph Supplements,* **2**, 1–109.

Tosi, D. J. & Eshbaugh, D. M. (1976). The Personal Beliefs Inventory: A factor analytic study. *Journal of Clinical Psychology,* **32**, 322–327.

Tosi, D. J., Forman, M. A., Rudy, D. R. & Murphy, M. A. (1986). Factor analysis of the Common Beliefs Survey. III: A replication study. *Journal of Consulting and Clinical Psychology,* **54**, 404–405.

Tracey, T. J. & Kokotovic, A. M. (1989). Factor structure of the Working Alliance Inventory. *Psychological Assessment: A Journal of Consulting and Clinical Psychology,* **1**, 207–210.

Trower, P. (1980). Situational analysis of the components and processes of behavior of socially skilled and unskilled patients. *Journal of Consulting and Clinical Psychology,* **48**, 327–339.

Trower, P., Yardley, K., Bryant, B. M. & Shaw, P. (1978). The treatment of social failure: A comparison of anxiety-reduction and skills-acquisition procedures on two social problems. *Behavior Modification*, **2**, 41–46.

Truax, C. B. (1966a). Reinforcement and nonreinforcement in Rogerian psychotherapy. *Journal of Abnormal Psychology*, **71**, 1–9.

Truax, C. B. (1966b). Therapist empathy, warmth, and genuineness and patient personality change in group psychotherapy: A comparison between interaction unit measures, time sample measures, patient perception measures. *Journal of Clinical Psychology*, **22**, 225–229.

Truax, C. B. (1970). Effects of client-centered psychotherapy with schizophrenic patients: Nine years pretherapy and nine years posttherapy hospitalization. *Journal of Consulting and Clinical Psychology*, **35**, 417–422.

Truax, C. B. & Carkhuff, R. R. (1967). *Toward Effective Counseling and Psychotherapy: Training and Practice*. Chicago: Aldine.

Truax, C. B., Schuldt, W. J. & Wargo, D. G. (1968). Self-ideal concept congruence and improvement in group psychotherapy. *Journal of Consulting and Clinical Psychology*, **32**, 47–53.

Ullmann, L. P. & Krasner, L. (eds.) (1965). *Case Studies in Behavior Modification*. New York: Holt, Rinehart & Winston.

Vachon, M. L. S., Rogers, J., Lyall, W. A. *et al.* (1982). Predictors and correlates of adaptation to conjugal bereavement. *American Journal of Psychiatry*, **139**, 998–1002.

Vaillant, G. E. (1971). Theoretical hierarchy of adaptive ego mechanisms: A 30–year follow-up of 30 men selected for psychological health. *Archives of General Psychiatry*, **24**, 107–118.

Vaillant, G. E. (1976). Natural history of male psychological health. V. The relation of choice of ego mechanisms of defense to adult adjustment. *Archives of General Psychiatry*, **33**, 535–545.

Vaillant, G. E. & Vaillant, C. O. (1990). Natural history of male psychological health. XII: A 45–year study of predictors of successful aging at age 65. *American Journal of Psychiatry*, **147**, 31–37.

Vaillant, G. E., Bond, M. & Vaillant, C. O. (1986). An empirically validated hierarchy of defense mechanisms. *Archives of General Psychiatry*, **43**, 786–794.

van den Bergh, O., de Boeck, P. & Claeys, W. (1981). Research findings on the nature of constructs in schizophrenics. *British Journal of Clinical Psychology*, **20**, 123–130.

van den Bergh, O., de Boeck, P. & Claeys, W. (1985). Schizophrenia: What is loose in schizophrenic construing? In E. Button (ed.), *Personal Construct and Mental Health: Theory, Research and Practice*, pp. 59–81. Beckenham: Croom Helm.

van der Veen, F. (1967). Basic elements in the process of psychotherapy: A research study. *Journal of Consulting Psychology*, **31**, 295–303.

van der Veen, F. & Novak, A. L. (1971). Perceived parental attitudes and family concepts of disturbed adolescents, normal siblings and normal controls. *Family Process*, **10**, 327–343.

Vanfossen, B. E. (1981). Sex differences in the mental health effects of spouse support and equity. *Journal of Health and Social Behavior*, **22**, 130–143.

Vasta, R. & Brockner, J. (1979). Self-esteem and self-evaluative covert statements. *Journal of Consulting and Clinical Psychology*, **47**, 776–777.

Verma, R. M. & Eysenck, H. J. (1973). Severity and type of psychotic illness as a function of personality. *British Journal of Psychiatry*, **122**, 573–585.

Viney, L. L. (1966). Congruence of measures of self-regard. *Psychological Record*, **16**, 487–493.

Viney, L. L., Benjamin, Y. N. & Preston, C. A. (1989). An evaluation of personal construct therapy for the elderly. *British Journal of Medical Psychology*, **62**, 35–41.

Vogler, R. E., Lunde, S. E., Johnson, G. R. & Martin, P. L. (1970). Electrical aversion conditioning with chronic alcoholics. *Journal of Consulting and Clinical Psychology*, **34**, 302–307.

Wachtel, P. L. (1977). *Psychoanalysis and Behavior: Toward an Integration*. New York: Basic Books.

Wachtel, P. L. (1987). *Action and Insight*. New York: Guilford Press.

Walton, D. & Mather, M. D. (1963). The application of learning principles to the treatment of obsessive–compulsive states in the acute and chronic phases of illness. *Behaviour Research and Therapy*, **1**, 163–174.

Watkins, C. E., Jr., Lopez, F. G., Campbell, V. L. & Himmell, C. D. (1986). Contemporary counseling psychology: Results of a national survey. *Journal of Counseling Psychology*, **33**, 301–309.

Watkins, J. T. & Rush, A. J. (1983). Cognitive Response Test. *Cognitive Therapy and Research*, **7**, 425–436.

Watson, J. B. (1913). Psychology as the behaviorist views it. *Psychological Review*, **20**, 158–177.

Watson, J. B. & Rayner, R. (1920). Conditioned emotional reactions. *Journal of Experimental Psychology*, **3**, 1–14.

Watson, J. P. & Marks, I. M. (1971). Relevant and irrelevant fear in flooding—A crossover study of phobic patients. *Behavior Therapy*, **2**, 275–293.

Watson, J. P., Mullett, G. E. & Pillay, H. (1973). The effects of prolonged exposure to phobic situations upon agoraphobic patients treated in groups. *Behaviour Research and Therapy*, **11**, 531–545.

Watson, N. (1984). The empirical status of Rogers's hypotheses of the necessary and sufficient conditions for effective psychotherapy change. In R. F. Levant & J. M. Shlien (eds.), *Client-Centered and the Person-Centered Approach: New Directions in Theory, Research and Practice*, pp. 17–40. New York: Praeger.

Weinberg, N. H. & Zaslove, M. (1963). Resistance to systematic desensitization of phobias. *Journal of Clinical Psychology*, **19**, 179–181.

Weissman, A. N. (1979). The Dysfunctional Attitude Scale: A validation study. Dissertation, University of Pennsylvania. *Dissertation Abstracts International*, **40**, 1389–1390B. (University Microfilm No. 79-19533)

Weitzman, B. (1967). Behavior therapy and psychotherapy. *Psychological Review*, **74**, 300–317.

Whiteman, V. L. & Shorkey, C. T. (1978). Validation testing of the Rational Behavior Inventory. *Educational and Psychological Measurement*, **38**, 1143–1149.

Wilkins, W. (1984). Psychotherapy: The powerful placebo. *Journal of Consulting and Clinical Psychology*, **52**, 570–573.

Wilkinson, I. M. & Blackburn, I. M. (1981). Cognitive style in depressed and recovered patients. *British Journal of Clinical Psychology*, **20**, 283–297.

Williams, E. (1971). The effect of varying the elements in the Bannister–Fransella Grid Test of Thought Disorder. *British Journal of Psychiatry*, **119**, 207–212.

194 Personality and psychotherapy

Williams, R. I. & Blanton, R. L. (1968). Verbal conditioning in a psychotherapeutic situation. *Behaviour Research and Therapy*, **6**, 97–103.

Williams, S. L., Dooseman, G. & Kleifield, E. (1984). Comparative effectiveness of guided mastery and exposure treatments for intractable phobias. *Journal of Consulting and Clinical Psychology*, **52**, 505–518.

Wilson, G. D. (1968). Reversal of differential GSR conditioning by instructions. *Journal of Experimental Psychology*, **76**, 491–493.

Wilson, G. T., Rossiter, E., Kleifeld, E. I. & Lindholm, L. (1986). Cognitive-behavioral treatment of bulimia nervosa: A controlled evaluation. *Behaviour Research and Therapy*, **24**, 277–288.

Wincze, J. P. & Caird, W. K. (1976). The effects of systematic desensitization and video desensitization in the treatment of essential sexual dysfunction in women. *Behavior Therapy*, **7**, 335–342.

Wing, J. H., Cooper, J. E. & Sartorius, N. (1974). *Description and Classification of Psychiatric Symptoms*. Cambridge: Cambridge University Press.

Wing, J. H., Nixon, J., Mann, S. A. & Leff, J. P. (1977). Reliability of the PSE (ninth edition) used in a population survey. *Psychological Medicine*, **7**, 505–516.

Wing, J. H., Mann, S. A., Leff, J. P. & Nixon, J. M. (1978). The concept of a 'case' in psychiatric population surveys. *Psychological Medicine*, **8**, 203–217.

Winkler, R. C. & Meyers, R. A. (1963). Some concomitants of self-deal discrepancy measures of self-acceptance. *Journal of Counseling Psychology*, **10**, 83–86.

Wolchik, S. A., Weiss, L. & Katzman, M. A. (1986). An empirically validated, short-term psychoeducational group treatment program for bulimia. *International Journal of Eating Disorders*, **5**, 21–34.

Wolpe, J. (1952). Experimental neuroses as learned behaviour. *British Journal of Psychology*, **43**, 243–268.

Wolpe, J. (1954). Reciprocal inhibition as the main basis of psychotherapeutic effects. *Archives of Neurology and Psychiatry*, **72**, 205–226.

Wolpe, J. (1958). *Psychotherapy by Reciprocal Inhibition*. Stanford, CA: Stanford University Press.

Wolpe, J. (1982). *The Practice of Behavior Therapy* (3rd edn.). New York: Pergamon Press.

Woody, G. E., Luborsky, L., McLellan, A. T. *et al.* (1983). Psychotherapy for opiate addicts: Does it help? *Archives of General Psychiatry*, **40**, 639–645.

Woody, G. E., McLellan, A. T., Luborsky, L. & O'Brien, C. P. (1987). Twelve-month follow-up of psychotherapy for opiate dependence. *American Journal of Psychiatry*, **144**, 590–596.

Woolfolk, R. L. (1974). The multimodal model as a framework for decision-making in psychotherapy. *Psychological Reports*, **34**, 831–834.

World Health Organization (1978). *Mental Disorders: Glossary and Guide to their Classification in Accordance with the Ninth Revision of the International Classification of Diseases*. Geneva: WHO.

Yates, A. J. (1983). Behaviour therapy and psychodynamic psychotherapy: Basic conflict or reconciliation and integration? *British Journal of Clinical Psychology*, **22**, 107–125.

Zeiss, A. M., Lewinsohn, P. M. & Munoz, R. F. (1979). Nonspecific improvement effects in depression using interpersonal skills training, pleasant activity schedules, or cognitive training. *Journal of Consulting and Clinical Psychology*, **47**, 427–439.

Zetzel, E. R. (1956). Current concepts of transference. *International Journal of Psychoanalysis*, **37**, 369–378.

Zigler, E. & Phillips, L. (1960). Social effectiveness and symptomatic behaviors. *Journal of Abnormal and Social Psychology*, **61**, 231–238.

Zimmerman, M., Coryell, W., Corenthal, C. & Wilson, S. (1986). Dysfunctional attitudes and attribution style in healthy controls and patients with schizophrenia, psychotic depression, and nonpsychotic depression. *Journal of Abnormal Psychology*, **95**, 403–405.

Zinbarg, R. & Revelle, W. (1989). Personality and conditioning: A test of four models. *Journal of Personality and Social Psychology*, **57**, 301–314.

Author index

Subject index